The Management
Mythbuster

The Management Mythbuster

David A. J. Axson

WILEY

John Wiley & Sons, Inc.

For general information on our other products and services or for technical support, please contact our Customer Care Department within the United States at (800) 762-2974, outside the United States at (317) 572-3993 or fax (317) 572-4002.

Wiley also publishes its books in a variety of electronic formats. Some content that appears in print may not be available in electronic books. For more information about Wiley products, visit our web site at www.wiley.com.

Library of Congress Cataloging-in-Publication Data

Axson, David A. J.
  The management mythbuster / David A. J. Axson.
      p. cm.
  Includes bibliographical references and index.
      ISBN 978-0-470-46362-8 (cloth)
  1. Industrial management. 2. Strategic planning. 3. Employee motivation. 4. Success in business. I. Title.
HD31.A97 2010
658—dc22

                                                                    2009031698

Printed in the United States of America

10 9 8 7 6 5 4 3 2 1

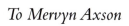
To Mervyn Axson

Contents

Acknowledgments

T he origins of this book emerged in the late 1970s at a time
when I had matured enough to have sensible conversations
with my Dad. As I sought to peer through the fog of cigar
smoke that was ever-present in his study, we would endlessly debate the
truth behind so many commonly accepted "home truths" that were in
reality absolute rubbish. My Dad was a curmudgeon and a cynic and
never once apologized for it. I guess the apple doesn't fall far from
the tree.

The material for this book has come from many sources and for
that I thank all my former colleagues at Lloyds Bank; Deloitte, Haskins
& Sells; A.T. Kearney; The Hackett Group; Bank of America; and the
more than 200 organizations that I have had the privilege of calling
clients over the last 25 years. I also thank those fellow cynics, cur-
mudgeons, and anti-management communists who have allowed me to
debate the myths of management with them. Thank you—you know
who you are. Thanks to the team at John Wiley for guiding me through
the publishing process yet again.

Most important of all is family. My wife Donna puts up with my
angst, fake writer's block, and inexhaustible caffeine addiction; Eleanor

and James occasionally remember that when Daddy is in his office he is not just playing on the Internet; and finally, Monty and Baxter who are my constant companions and serve to prove that a dog and cat can be inspirational aids to the creative process!

About the Author

D avid Axson is an author and consultant specializing in strategy, finance, and management. His previous books include *Best Practices in Planning and Performance Management* (John Wiley & Sons, 2007) and *Half the World Away* (Countinghouse Press, 2009).

David was a cofounder of The Hackett Group, a leading benchmarking and business advisory firm, and during his eleven years with the firm, he was responsible for developing a number of the firm's market-leading benchmarks. He has also served as Head of Corporate Planning at Bank of America on a one-year assignment during 2003. Prior to moving to the United States in 1991, David was affiliated with A.T. Kearney; Deloitte, Haskins & Sells; and Lloyds Bank in London, England. He has degrees in accounting and computer science from the University of Leeds in England and is a Member of the British Computer Society. David lives with his wife and two children in Bath, Ohio.

Further information can be found at www.davidaxson.com.

Preface

My son James is a big fan of the Discovery Channel series *Mythbusters* during which various common myths, rumors, and accepted "truths" are tested for validity. It makes for good entertainment. In almost thirty years of observing managers in action I have encountered more than my share of commonly accepted wisdom that gets passed down from generation to generation without question. From "the customer is always right" to "we pay for performance," the list of management philosophies that are more honored in the breach is long. So as the world was rocked by the near collapse of global financial system in 2008, it seemed like a good time to take a look at many of the practices and processes that govern much of modern management behavior yet have been found wanting. So here is *The Management Mythbuster*, a serious but irreverent (i.e., seriously irreverent!) look at some of the myths that drive mediocrity in modern management.

DAVID A. J. AXSON
December 2009

About This Book

When I started to write the first draft of this book, it looked like so many others: a series of chapters that tried to make a few useful points using real-world examples for illustration. In short, it had the potential to be really boring. I didn't want that—there are enough earnest tomes out there already. So I did two things. First, I tried to make this book entertaining. Could I really make people smile when considering the merits of budgeting? Would people laugh at the absurdity of modern financial statements? I don't know, but it's worth a try—so forgive my irreverence, and if my attempts at humor fail, at least admire the effort.

The second change I made from that first draft was to blend fact and fiction. I always love stories that illustrate a point. In my speeches I liberally sprinkle in metaphors to help my audience understand the points I am making. So I decided to take a risk. Why not tell a story as well as offer a guidebook to some of the absurd management practices that are obsolete in today's turbulent, but very exciting, world? To that end, you will follow the trials and tribulations of the management team of Cruciant Inc. throughout this book.

Cruciant is a fast-growing, $3 billion, global company specializing in delivering highly innovative services for both the corporate and consumer markets. Note that I don't actually tell you what Cruciant does, but as you will see, that is part of the point. The saga of Cruciant will help illustrate the destructive power of many of the management myths that continue to govern decision making in today's uncertain world.

After each episode in the Cruciant story, I will look at the real-world lessons to be learned and end each chapter with a section entitled "So What?" that seeks to capture the sound bites you should remember.

As we embark upon our journey through the maze of management myths, you will quickly see that in today's turbulent world, fact really is stranger than fiction.

Introduction

There are only two problems with the theory and practice of management today. We take the topic far too seriously, as the rows of earnest tomes in the bookshop testify, and we are too trusting. The body of commonly accepted wisdom is huge, and most of it is junk. Homilies such as pay for performance or using technology for competitive advantage are convenient and politically correct but rarely true. My aim with *The Management Mythbuster* is to take a seriously irreverent look at some of the more popular myths.

The genesis of this book can be traced back to September 5, 1983. On that day a somewhat arrogant, egotistical, but, in truth, incredibly naïve 21-year-old began work for a bank in the City of London. Sometime during that first day I asked myself a question that has been repeated thousands of times since. The question was, "Why do we do it that way? It doesn't make sense." At first, I thought it was just ignorance on my part and that over time the mysteries of management practice would be revealed in all their glory. But that time never came. Today I have little to be arrogant or egotistical about—marriage, children, thinning hair, and a thickening waist made sure of that, but I still find myself asking the same question many times a day. For a long time my questioning (or is it cynicism?) simply served to help me in my chosen career as a management consultant

1

where asking obvious questions that others deem beneath them is actually a valued skill—and then came 2008. Within the space of a few months much of the framework of modern management practice came crashing down. Corporate titans were humbled, strategies were abandoned, budgets became obsolete on a daily basis, and the only certainty about any forecast was that it would be wrong. Add in the failure of long-established compensation practices, the inability of markets to set prices for assets, and the almost complete absence of credit for months at a time, and the world was irrevocably changed.

To make matters all the more interesting, it all happened against a background of a volatile and fast-changing global order: terrorist attacks in Mumbai, China becoming the world's second largest economy, oil rocketing to $147 a barrel and then falling just as fast to $35, a small flu outbreak in Mexico becoming a global pandemic in less than seven days, a changing of the political order in the world's largest economy, and the emergence of environmental consciousness as the defining issue of the new millennium.

When historians look back on the first decade of the twenty-first century, they will almost certainly mark it down as a period of transformational change in the world of commerce.

I also suspect that the year of 2008 will be remembered as the date when the management practices that governed the world of commerce for over a half century were found to have failed hopelessly. Perhaps the one good thing to emerge from these tumultuous times is that questioning the effectiveness of long-established management practices has gone from being interesting to imperative. Managers everywhere are finding that the traditional rules and processes that have governed planning, forecasting, budgeting, reporting, accounting, and risk management are obsolete.

The world has been transformed from a series of loosely connected economies with reasonably predictable flows between them to a complex web of relationships where the global impact of local events is felt almost instantaneously. While the crash of 2008 may have started in the financial sector, exposing yet again the flaws in that industry's sophisticated but ultimately flawed risk management model, the impact hit all sectors of the economy and all corners of the globe within weeks. As Russian Prime Minister Vladimir Putin observed during his speech at the World Economic Forum in Davos, Switzerland, in January 2009:

"The world is now facing the first truly global economic crisis, which is continuing to develop at an unprecedented pace."

In quieter, gentler times the impact of events in one part of the world on another would have been limited to an item on the news. In today's instantaneous, globally connected world the ripples have become a tsunami.

This raises some interesting questions. In this turbulent world where have all the re-engineered processes, balanced scorecards, six sigma processes, self-directed work teams, and core competencies got us? Are managers in a better position to manage risk and uncertainty? Based on recent evidence, the answer must be no.

Over the next few years there will be numerous postmortems seeking to explain how all this happened. The usual suspects of greed, stupidity, overregulation, underregulation, all things American, and probably even global warming will be earnestly analyzed for their culpability. We should add the basics of management practice to the list. Corporations are saddled with a rigid set of discrete management tools that are incapable of working effectively in times of uncertainty and rapid change (i.e., now and the foreseeable future). The bedrock of the management process is built upon multi-year strategic plans, annual budgets, quarterly forecasts, monthly reports, and most dangerous of all, a compensation philosophy that is as likely to reward failure as it is success. The implications are significant. These relatively static processes upon which organizations have relied for decades will no longer get the job done. The litany of business failures and shareholder value destruction driven by unprecedented volatility and historic shifts in economic behavior should confirm to managers that their management processes are irretrievably broken. Actually, it's worse than that: Many of the long-established practices that managers rely upon are downright dangerous since they provide a false sense of security that masks the realities of doing business in today's volatile and uncertain world. Tried and trusted techniques of planning, budgeting, forecasting, reporting, and analysis have simply failed to cope with the speed, volatility, and complexity of today's markets. We are managing twenty-first-century businesses with twentieth-century processes.

The first cracks appeared in the 1990s as the potent combination of globalization and technology drove the redefinition of markets (who

It Really Is a Different World!

I sat listening to Putin's speech back in January 2009 and was struck by two things. First, he was dead right. Second, as someone who grew up during the Cold War, it was certainly different to hear economic insight coming from a Russian! I well remember visiting Soviet Russia in 1977 as a 15-year-old high school student. In order to make the trip somewhat educational (although bartering ballpoint pens for bottles of vodka outside the Kremlin taught me a lot about economics), we attended a lecture on the Soviet economic miracle. One chart showed the rate of inflation in the USSR since the end of World War II—it was a horizontal line at the zero percent level on the y-axis. At the time, inflation in the UK was running rampant, so this was an impressive statistic. Not long after the lecture we visited Moscow's premier department store, Gum, which is on Red Square opposite the Kremlin. It was easy to see why inflation was nonexistent—there was nothing to buy! With that as a backdrop, I found it hard to believe that a Russian (and a former Communist and KGB official) could offer accurate economic insights on the subject of managing in a world of turbulence? But Putin's words made perfect sense. First, he nailed the economic downturn of 2008, and he went on to liken the events to a perfect storm and offered sage advice to managers trying to cope in such an environment: "Responsible and knowledgeable people must prepare for it." He went on to outline some of the failings that resulted in a singular lack of preparation: weak regulation, greed, and a failure to acknowledge risk. However, to a Cold War baby like me, his most startling statement of all was "Excessive intervention in economic activity and blind faith in the state's omnipotence is another possible mistake." Wow! We've certainly come a long way in the last twenty years when a Russian warns America against excessive government intervention.

As a postscript I returned to Moscow 32 years after that first visit in 1977 and returned to Gum; it is now stocked to the rafters with designer goods—inflation is higher, but at least you can now find a good Gucci purse.

needs a bookstore to buy a book?) and supply chains (why own a factory in Ohio? Let's just contract it out to someone in India, China, or Vietnam). Technology coupled with a relatively loose regulatory environment also spurred exponential growth in the variety and complexity of financing and securitization options that could be continuously traded on a global basis. The accountants struggled to keep up, never mind the managers tasked with making decisions.

Traditional management processes were neither designed nor suited to operate in a diverse and fast-moving environment. The pain increased as organizations struggled to adapt to a series of events that rocked the status quo: the Internet bubble, 9/11, the aftermath of Enron and Sarbanes-Oxley, Hurricanes Katrina and Rita, the Asian tsunami, and then the housing market/subprime meltdown/credit crisis of 2007–2008. Volatility became the norm and predictability flew out of the window, yet companies still slaved over detailed budgets and forecasts that described in mind-numbing detail exactly what they would do long into a, by now, very uncertain future. Of course, the only thing all this wonderful detail achieved was to create even more variances. The problems are systemic but thankfully there are only six of them!

Strategic Plans Are of Little Use in Times of Great Uncertainty and Volatility

At many companies, strategy has become mechanical and inflexible, witness General Motors' stubborn focus on trucks and sport utility vehicles as the source of profitable growth or Kodak's reluctance to acknowledge the rise of digital photography.

All too often strategic planning has been reduced to a multi-year financial planning or budgeting exercise that produces some arbitrary financial results rather than a roadmap for the achievement of a tangible objective that clearly defines success. The result is that any material variation from the expected course results in a loss of confidence and creates tremendous uncertainty that can paralyze decision making. We need to revisit the original military origins of strategy to regain some perspective. B.H. Liddell Hart in his classic book *Strategy*[1] described eight axioms of strategy, five of which provide a valuable test of the quality of any business strategies:

1. *Adjust your end to your means.* Match your desire with your capabilities.
2. *Keep your object in mind while adapting your plan to circumstances.* The recession of 2007–2009 has clearly changed the pace and tactics that companies can follow, but it does not have to change the end game. Some have seen it as an opportunity: Disney, Johnson & Johnson, Pfizer, Oracle, and IBM all took advantage of the opportunity to acquire assets at attractive prices.
3. *Take a line of operation that offers alternative objectives.* Both General Electric and IBM have successfully transformed themselves from primarily product companies to add in a portfolio of service-related offerings that complement their historic core at higher margins and with more attractive growth prospects.
4. *Ensure both plan and dispositions are flexible.* The inability of U.S. automotive makers to rapidly adjust their product portfolios to changing consumer and economic conditions, reduce labor costs, (particularly healthcare and retirement costs), or rationalize bloated dealer networks drove two of the big three into bankruptcy.
5. *Do not renew an attack along the same line (or in the same form) after it has once failed.* How many times has someone tried to compete with Southwest Airlines? We have had Continental Lite, United's Ted, and Delta's Song. Kmart spent thirty years trying to compete with Wal-Mart before succumbing to a merger with another fallen giant, Sears. Meanwhile, Target was able to succeed by offering a differentiated approach that allowed it to thrive in a Wal-Mart world.

Operating Plans and Budgets Provide a False Sense of Security

"It's O.K., it's in the budget" is a comforting response to any question; however, what if the budget was based upon a flawed set of assumptions about the future? How many budgets developed in the waning months of 2007 projected oil prices rising to $147 a barrel and falling to less than $35 just a few months later, or anticipated a 20 percent decline in car sales or an 8 percent decline in consumer spending over the 2008 holiday season?

The traditional approach to planning and budgeting assumes a "business as usual" view. Past performance is seen as an accurate predictor of the future and for half a century that worked—most of the time. Rarely do plans contemplate seismic economic, political, or social events, nor do they spend much time discussing the impact of changes in customer and competitor behavior on the business. Operating plans and budgets provide an almost completely internal view of how the business is expected to perform in the future. You can find out precisely how much a company plans to spend on travel but try finding out how much it plans to invest in keeping its best customers. Plans and budgets describe the accountant's view of a business, not the manager's view of the business. In today's world, that's a joke.

Management Reporting Is Driven by an Obsolete View of the World

Management reporting follows the same format as the budget and it is about as useful. How many companies can tell you how much they spend on air travel and can also tell you how much of the total travel spending generates incremental revenue? Very few. We have an accounting and reporting model that is driven by what we spend money on, not why we are spending the money. Despite investing billions in data warehouses, data marts and management information systems, few managers have access to just the right data they need to make effective decisions.

Incentive Compensation Rewards Poor Performance and Penalizes Outstanding Performance

Most organizations base their bonus and reward systems on meeting the plan or budget. In light of the difficulty in creating a credible budget (see above), how smart is it to base rewards on a meaningless set of numbers? Actually, it is much worse than that. Managers are often richly rewarded for sub-par performance and penalized for truly heroic performance simply because the budget comes nowhere close to predicting what actually happens.

Investments in Staff Education Have Been Inadequate and Misdirected

CEOs are always going on about how people are their organization's most valuable resource, yet at the first sign of trouble the cuts in training are swift and deep, revealing the true value most organizations place on staff development. Beyond the volatile level of investment, the focus of much of the investment is flawed. Training and education has not adapted to the skills that determine success in today's world—managing uncertainty and ambiguity, leveraging new technologies to gain competitive insights, adapting to a global business environment, and working collaboratively across borders are rarely part of the curriculum. We continue to train people to use Microsoft Excel but spend little time helping them understand the story behind the numbers they are playing with.

Technology Has Failed to Improve and in Many Cases Has Reduced the Effectiveness of Management

Organizations have invested billions of dollars, pounds, euros, and yen in technology over the last half-century. The impact has been significant, and yet in terms of the management process, all too often the result of automation has simply been more data, not better information. Organizations are also locked into a calendar-driven cycle of reporting. Information is reported on a weekly, monthly, or quarterly cycle regardless of what is happening in the real world. All too often reports cannot be made available until the accountants have closed the books, which can take 5–10 days.

If we are to adapt to a turbulent but very exciting world, we cannot keep managing real-time businesses with batch processes. We need a new set of practical tools that are tuned to a world where:

- Volatility will remain high due to the ever-increasing interdependence of customers, suppliers, regulators, and markets.
- Events formerly viewed as extraordinary are now part of the normal course of business. All companies need to be able to understand

how they will respond to unexpected material events, both positive and negative.

- Opportunities for competitive advantage and differentiation will increasingly depend upon an organization's ability to lead markets (e.g., Apple's purposeful obsolescence of its own products to maintain market leadership) or exploit opportunities (McDonald's and Wal-Mart's ability to capitalize on consumer's renewed focus on low cost).

We need a new generation of informed, skeptical, risk-aware, and decisive managers. As Alfred P. Sloan commented half a century ago: "The rapidity of modern technological change makes the search for facts a permanently necessary feature . . ."[2]

What I Really Think!

Enough of polite and reasoned argument, here is what I really think:

We've finally lost it! All sense of perspective has disappeared from the practice of management, buried under the overwhelming weight of methodologies, theories, best practices, models, tools, systems, processes, benchmarks, scorecards, competencies, mission statements, and value propositions. Today's increasingly competitive, volatile, and uncertain world should be causing every executive to challenge conventional management wisdom. How can something as simple as delivering a product or service that someone wants, at a price they are willing to pay, while providing a reasonable return to investors have become so complicated? Common sense has been subjugated by nonsense. It's all "BS" and its time to fight back.

The Berlin Wall fell more than twenty years ago, but communism is alive and well in the corporate world. Companies have spent billions on standardizing almost every aspect of their operations. Repeatable processes and global standards are the name of the game. We increasingly live in a one-size-fits-all corporate world where conformity and uniformity are prized. Over the past few decades, corporations have charged herd-like after each new management fad. It is a long list: strategic business units, zero-based budgeting, activity-based costing, core competencies, total quality management, six sigma, lean manufacturing, balanced scorecards, shareholder value added (SVA), rolling forecasts, re-engineering, best practices, outsourcing, off-shoring, enterprise resource planning (ERP), web-enablement and virtualization, to name but a few. Each promised to revolutionize corporate operations and turbocharge the bottom line; yet while substantial gains have been made in productivity, quality, cost, and other key measures, are today's companies better able to navigate today's turbulent world? Up until 2008, many thought the answer was yes, but not now.

It is interesting to note that the companies that stand out from the crowd do so for one very simple reason—they do something a little different. Think Apple, Google, Southwest Airlines, Toyota, Nintendo, Disney, or Wal-Mart. Sure they standardize where it makes sense, but they also understand that differentiation equals innovation. You know what these companies stand for, and they provoke a reaction from you. Now when was the last time you walked down High Street or through the mall and thought—that's a really distinctive shoe shop; or name a real estate agent that sets your heart aflutter by the uniqueness of the service he or she provides? How about a network news show? A gas station? An accountant?

The war on management communism starts now and here is the manifesto. "Root out pomposity and egotism, isolate management stupidity, ask the dumb questions, sacrifice all the sacred cows, and above all, keep it real."

It is time to introduce some common sense. It doesn't have to be that complicated. Unfortunately, many academics, gurus, consultants, and technology vendors profit from complexity, but I know that in the back of your mind, you are just a teeny-weeny bit skeptical. You know most of it is absurd, but how do you break out of the straitjacket? After all, it is almost heretical to question the wisdom of so many people—many of them your teachers, professors, and bosses. Are you brave enough?

Notes

1. B.H. Liddell Hart, *Strategy* (London: Faber and Faber, 1967).
2. Alfred P. Sloan, Jr., *My Years at General Motors* (New York: Doubleday, 1963), p. xxi.

Chapter 1

Missions, Visions, and Other Expensive Pastimes

Mission and vision statements are now organizational imperatives—which in plain English means that no self-respecting organization would be seen dead without them. No business dares venture into the marketplace without a pithy statement of its mission and vision. Any study of high-performing organizations will identify the pervasive presence of these "softer" strategic elements. Southwest Airlines, General Electric, Microsoft, Johnson & Johnson, Nordstrom, and Toyota all have distinctive styles, cultures, and values that are at the heart of much of what they do. Unfortunately, any list of failed entities will also contain a high proportion with crisp mission and vision statements. As Johnson & Johnson's CEO, William Weldon, commented, "Some of the best business principles ever written were Enron's. It's just an extraordinary document."[1]

So what's the difference between success and failure? It is pretty simple really—you must walk the talk. Missions and visions must guide behavior and decision making; otherwise, they are just empty words. Mission and vision statements that exist only on paper are a great leading indicator of an organization that will struggle in times of great opportunity never mind times of stress. Of course, there is no chance that Cruciant's mission and vision statements will be empty promises.

Fiction: Meeting Room at an Exclusive Country Club, Northern New Jersey—February 2007

Three consultants from Innovisions, a firm specializing in the "innovative articulation of corporate missions and visions" are leading the Cruciant executive team through a facilitated workshop to craft new mission and vision statements that "clearly represent everything Cruciant stands for to all stakeholders." After an opening presentation that describes the role of mission and vision statements in inspiring customers, associates (the politically correct term for employees), and other stakeholders, the management team is divided into three groups to brainstorm possible elements of Cruciant's mission and vision. An Innovisions consultant leads each group through a discussion of the "words or phrases that capture the essence of Cruciant." After 45 minutes the teams reconvene and share their ideas. A sampling of the words and phrases resulting from the exercise includes innovative, responsible corporate citizen, inspiring, ethical, insanely great, global, technologically advanced, respectful, respected, people-centric, empathic, authentic, growth-oriented, a great place to work, talented, exciting, customer-focused, and trusted.

For the next two hours there is considerable, sometimes heated, debate about many of the attributes during which a number of the executives reveal a previously hidden passion for lexicography. This is highlighted by a rather distracting argument about whether the correct word to use is empathic or empathetic, during which an online dictionary and thesaurus are consulted. (Author's note: At a nonprofit on whose board I sit, we had this precise debate; it consumed the best part of three months over two board meetings and numerous email exchanges.)

Eventually, the consultants manage to bring some order to the proceedings and lead the management team through a prioritization and ranking exercise to come up with a short list of mission and vision attributes. As the meeting draws to a close, Innovisions undertakes to take the "great output" from the session and develop a few "drafts, or straw-man mission and vision statements" for the management team to consider.

As the meeting breaks up, four members of the management team duck into the locker rooms and emerge a few minutes later on the first tee, while the others head back to the office.

Over the next few weeks there are a couple more sessions during which the wordsmithing debate reaches new heights. The empathic/empathetic debate continues, and one of the team members even consults his former English college professor to seek an opinion. Unable to reach consensus, the group finally decides that being empathic or empathetic isn't really that important after all (the same conclusion we reached at our nonprofit). Finally, they agree on the following mission statement:

"Cruciant creates insanely great products that inspire our customers to become our strongest advocates. We measure our success by the value we deliver to our customers and shareholders and the loyalty of our hugely talented associates. We will always adhere to the highest ethical standards in everything we do and will be acknowledged as an outstanding corporate citizen."

The accompanying vision statement reads:

"Cruciant will be one of the most respected companies in the world, recognized as a great place to work, a source of breakthrough innovations and a leader in environmental sustainability."

CEO Steve Borden is happy the process is complete and he is anxious to get on with growing the company; however, at the next management meeting he cautions his team that "Now the hard work starts. We have to live and breathe the mission and vision in everything we do. It is your job as leaders to ensure that all our associates buy into what we are trying to accomplish." Everyone nods his or her head.

A few weeks after signing off on the mission and vision statements, large posters start to appear in every company facility and all employees—sorry, associates—are given a handy laminated card with the mission and vision statements printed on one side. On the other side is a list of actions that every associate can take to "Walk the talk at Cruciant." It includes such penetrating advice as "be respectful to all your fellow associates" and "always ask yourself, is this in the best interests of Cruciant?"

A comprehensive series of mission and vision briefings are held across the company at which teams of associates discuss what the statements mean to them and how they can "live the mission" on a daily basis. A new catchphrase pops up on bulletin boards, t-shirts, and coffee mugs, "Is it insanely great enough?"

A few weeks later, Henry, Cruciant's CFO, scrawls his initials on Innovisions invoice for $375,000 to signify its approval for payment.

Facts: "We Are on a Mission from God"[2]

Scott Adams, through his comic strip creation "Dilbert," defined a mission statement as "a long awkward sentence that demonstrates management's inability to think clearly."[3] Like most humor, it is painfully close to the truth.

The first problem with mission and vision statements is trying to understand the difference between them. While researching an earlier book of mine, *Best Practices in Planning and Performance Management* (John Wiley & Sons, 2007), which has achieved some renown as a cure for insomnia, I spent quite a bit of time seeking a clear definition of the difference. At the time, I failed. The best I could come up with was the following from William Drohan:

> "A vision statement pushes the association toward some future goal or achievement, while a mission statement guides current, critical, strategic decision making."[4]

I am not sure this helps much, so here is my own humble attempt to differentiate between them:

- Vision: Describes a dream or goal.
- Mission: Describes a way in which you would like to fulfill the vision.

Despite the tremendous investments of both time and money that organizations make, most mission or vision statements are worthless.

The supposed objective is to create a short, pithy statement that, in the words of one nameless commentator, "motivates the type of individual behavior that maximizes the probability of achieving strategic objectives." My own unscientific research indicates that maybe one in twenty associates can accurately recite his or her employer's vision and mission.

Despite my cynicism, there are mission and vision statements that work well. I hate to be yet another Google sycophant—after all, it is well on the way to becoming the Microsoft of the twenty-first century—but I love its mission statement. No one is left in any doubt as to the company's modest aspirations!

"Google's mission is to organize the world's information and make it universally accessible and useful."[5]

This is what a mission statement should be. It is ambitious, unambiguous, and to geeks like me, exciting.

Mission and Visions Twenty-First-Century Style
In recent years, mission and vision statements have become as much about marketing and strategy as they are about motivating employees. A great example is Lululemon—where do they get these names? Lululemon is a fashionable retailer focused on the yoga lifestyle. Founded in 1998 with a single store in Vancouver, British Columbia, it has grown to over 100 outlets around the world. Lululemon is the latest in a long line of health and fitness brands that probably started with Nike's waffle-iron-soled running shoes in the 1960s. Being cool also means that the company is rather full of itself, as its website demonstrates.

On the day I first looked at the site, it was touting that one of the key advantages of shopping online was being able to do so in the nude. The mental image this created confirmed that I was not their target demographic. The site went on to explain Lululemon's growth strategy: "Although the initial goal was to only have one store, it was soon obvious that to provide a fulfilling life of growth, family, salary, and mortgage for our amazing staff, we would have to provide more opportunities. It was really a matter of grow or die because active minds need a challenge." In a strange way, it is very honest—Lululemon is saying that it is in business to make money and have fun—customers and products are merely means to that end.

Lululemon's mission is described as "creating components for people to live a longer, healthier, more fun life," and one of their core values is described this way: "Fun—When I die, I want to die like my grandmother who died peacefully in her sleep. Not screaming like all the passengers in her car."[6] Are we supposed to take this seriously? I don't know, but it certainty grabs your attention.

The site also offers up *The Lululemon Manifesto,* offering such pithy homilies as, "Friends are more important than money" and "Dance, sing, floss, and travel." This is not a lifestyle brand but a cult. But at its heart, Lululemon is all about marketing. In a March 2009 interview, CEO Christine Day invoked the first commandment of modern marketing when she described the company's secret for success as, "If you want to be successful in this industry, it's about being authentic."[7]

Being authentic appears to be the most important attribute for anyone seeking a place in today's branded lifestyle world; although being customer-centric and environmentally responsible follows close behind. At Lululemon everyone takes authenticity very seriously; the company's community director emphasizes the importance: "Your job is pretty easy when you are authentic with people." I guess authenticity is very important when selecting your $54 Basic Yoga Tote; after all, no authentic Indian yogi would be seen dead without one.

Lululemon has successfully wrapped its relatively humble products, workout tops, bras, and hoodies, in a lifestyle of calm and vitality. While I may make fun of them, Lululemon's performance is no joke. During 2008, not exactly a banner year for retailers, the company increased its sales by 30 percent to more than $350 million and its earnings by 10 percent to $56 million. So beneath all that authenticity is a well-run business.

Even boring businesses can seem more attractive with a pithy mission or vision statement. Federal Express makes package delivery sound sexy with its vision: "By accelerating global connections, we provide access to new opportunities and empower people and businesses with more choices and greater confidence."[8]

Other companies are less direct, opting for vision statements that give little hint of what the company actually does. For example, BMW promises, "The uncompromising pursuit of the superlative,"[9] and Alcoa modestly strives "to be the best company in the world—in the eyes of our customers, shareholders, communities and people." Tesco, the UK supermarket leader, seeks "to create value for customers to earn their lifetime loyalty."

Such statements do not limit a company strategically; as long as BMW is both uncompromising and superlative, it can fulfill its vision. Similarly, Tesco can pursue many diverse lines of business and still fulfill its core purpose of creating value for customers. However, such statements offer little insight and, frankly, appear vacuous. No doubt we can expect BMW to launch an uncompromisingly, superlative line of toasters, while Tesco will no doubt expand into a range of highly effective erectile dysfunction treatments that will put a smile on the face of all its customers, thereby securing a lifetime of gratitude and hence loyalty.

Mission statements can be boring and yet still effective. Cemex, the Mexican building materials company, is clearly not as sexy a company as Google, and its mission is consequently more mundane:

"Our goal is to serve the global building needs of our customers and create value for our stakeholders by becoming the world's most efficient and innovative building materials company."[10]

Despite its lack of glitz it works. It is simple and focuses on the basics of business—efficiency and innovation.

I suspect that deep in the bowels of a consulting firm somewhere a couple of nerdy programmers are developing a neat little computer program that takes all the politically correct words that can be used in a mission and vision statement and automatically generates a random set of three possible statements based upon a few simple inputs in an effort to corner the market. Unfortunately, their effort will be wasted. A company called Kinectic Wisdom already offers a product called Mission Expert, which promises to help you in "creating effective organizational mission statements" all for less than $25.

At this rate, the whole exercise will be reduced to checking a box on some form that simply confirms that your organization conforms to the world's first globally applicable mission statement, which will be something along the lines of:

> "We will be authentically innovative while being insanely focused on our customers and operating in a socially and environmentally responsible manner in pursuit of superior stakeholder returns."

As you will no doubt have discerned, my cynicism knows no bounds and I'm only just getting started. Despite this, I am a believer in the value of mission and vision statements (I am also a hypocrite). Used correctly, mission and vision statements can serve as an effective communication vehicle both internally and externally, but it is important to keep things in proportion—a great mission statement does not make a great company, nor is the absence of one an indicator of impending demise.

Some companies have spectacularly failed to live up to the aspirations contained in their mission or vision statements. AIG in its 2006 annual report assured readers that "Financial strength is the bedrock of AIG. By putting strategies into action that enhance our strong capital position, we create value for our shareholders and investors." Enron promised to "work with customers and prospects openly, honestly and sincerely."

UK mortgage lender Northern Rock described the secret of its success in terms of a virtuous circle that embraced cost control, enhanced earnings per share growth, improved returns, enhanced capital efficiency, high-quality asset growth, competitive products, innovation, and transparency. Clearly, the virtuous circle collapsed during 2007, leading to the company's eventual bailout by the British government.

> **Mythbuster Wisdom: The Best Mission Statements of All Time**
>
> In second place, but only by a whisker, is John F. Kennedy's challenge to America made in a special address to Congress in 1961: "I believe this nation should commit itself to achieving the goal, before this decade is out, of landing a man on the moon and returning him safely to earth."[11] It has all the attributes: It's short, just 29 words; heroic; unambiguous; and above all, inspiring. It probably should be number one, but I have a soft spot for a mission statement that has echoed across four decades. It first appeared in a not-very-successful, two-season television show in the late 1960s. Today, forty years later, it still resonates. In the immortal words of the organization's CEO, Captain James T. Kirk: "Space, the final frontier. These are the voyages of the Starship Enterprise, its five-year mission to explore strange new worlds, to seek out new life and new civilizations, to boldly go where no man has gone before." Now isn't that an organization you want to work for?

So What?

- Keep it simple: If a fifth grader gets it, you are probably okay.
- You have to walk the talk and that starts at the top.
- Results prove words: If you say you will be innovative, you'd better deliver.
- Avoid clichés: Everyone wants to be authentic, innovative, and socially responsible—we get it.
- An enemy helps: For years Pepsi's mission was succinct—Beat Coke; in the 1970s Honda set its sights on Yamaha in the motorcycle market and rallied behind the cry of "Yamaha wo tsubusu," which apparently means we will crush, squash, slaughter Yamaha—not much ambiguity there.

Notes

1. Geoff Colvin and Jessica Shambora, "J&J: Secrets of Success," *Fortune*, May 4, 2009.

2. Elwood Blues, *The Blues Brothers*, 1981.

3. Scott Adams, *The Dilbert Principle* (New York: HarperCollins, 1996).

4. William Drohan, "Writing a Mission Statement." *Association Management*, vol. 51, 1999, p. 117.

5. Google.com, September 2009.

6. Lululemon.com, April 2009.

7. Danielle Sacks, "Lululemon's Cult of Selling," *Fast Company*, March 18, 2009.

8. Fedex.com, April 6, 2009.

9. BMWGroup.com, April 2009.

10. Cemex.com

11. John F. Kennedy, Special Address to Congress, May 25, 1961.

Chapter 2

Strategy and Other Confusing Stuff

C onfuse or clarify? Complicate or simplify? Strategic planning has been one of the biggest growth areas in management over the last fifty years. Today everything has to be strategic. No project would ever dare to describe itself as not being strategic. Managers pride themselves on their ability as strategic thinkers who can see the big picture by taking a holistic view of the business. It has become one of those essential attributes along with being a team player and a good communicator with exceptional interpersonal skills. Yet for many, strategy has ceased to be an effective tool. As early as 1990, *Fortune* magazine commented:

> "At too many companies, strategic planning has become overly bureaucratic, absurdly quantitative, and largely irrelevant. In executive suites across America, countless five-year plans, updated annually, solemnly clad in three-ring binders are gathering

dust—their impossibly specific prognostications about costs, process, and market share long forgotten."

For Cruciant, strategy is seen as incredibly valuable while also providing the perfect excuse for an executive offsite meeting.

Fiction: The Four Seasons Hotel, Nevis—Early May 2007

Steve Borden strides into the meeting room just after 8 AM. He is dressed in typical executive retreat–style clothes: logoed golf shirt, from Pine Valley no less; khaki chinos; tasseled loafers worn without socks, and a Hart Schaffner and Marx blazer. His management team is already seated around the table along with a couple of consultants from the White Hot Strategy Group. Steve takes off his jacket and hangs it over the back of his chair and sits down. He opens the meeting: "Good morning, it's great to have you all here today. First, let's switch all Blackberries and cells off; I want one hundred percent attention throughout our sessions.

"Last night I met with The Board over dinner and they love the strategy we put together. With continued rapid growth in Asia and sustained strong growth in North America and Europe, the next three years will be the time for Cruciant to emerge as a true leader with growth in revenues and earnings that far outstrips the competition. I am looking for the stock price to hit $75 a share by the end of 2008, up from the current $32. The Board loved the focus on innovation and emerging markets. They particularly liked the opportunity to steal share from Global Local and Transoceanic as customers increasingly buy into our value proposition and the global economy moves in the direction of our value-priced, high-touch offerings.

"The only concerns they expressed were over the size of the capital investments required and the pace at which those investments start to generate meaningful earnings in today's markets. The bottom line—it is all about cash flow. Over the next two days we need to revisit the financial model and translate the five-year view into one-year planning targets that can be used to kick off the annual planning process. Remember, 6 percent revenue growth and 11 percent earnings growth are non-negotiable targets for the next two years if we are to hit the long-term incentive payout threshold. I'm sure you agree that's one target none of us can afford to miss!"

Steve turns to the two consultants: "I've asked Tom and Mitch from White Hot to join us for the next two days. As you know, they led all the work that went into the strategy and have already worked up a couple of scenarios for me around targets for the next fiscal year that can get us started."

Turning back to the group, Steve continues, "So let's get on with it. We will break at 3 PM today for the spa sessions; cocktails are at 6 PM followed by dinner at 7 PM. Tomorrow we start early at 7:30 AM so we can be on the first tee by 1 PM."

The meeting starts with the consultants spending a couple of hours taking the management team through the strategy, discussing the implications for next year's plan and reviewing the detailed market research that White Hot has completed. Not surprisingly, the research strongly supports the argument for aggressively investing in developing innovative new products specifically targeted at emerging markets. The 110-page PowerPoint presentation is well organized, in full color, and sits in front of each member of the management team in a nice leather binder embossed with each executive's name and the White Hot logo. At the end of their presentation, Tom and Mitch suggest a break before the team splits into two sub-groups to review the two financial scenarios that they prepared for Steve.

By lunchtime the team has reconvened, and discussion centers on which scenario works best for the company. Debate is fierce. Rich (Marketing and Product Development) and Sarah (Sales) argue forcefully that scenario A is the best answer. Sarah sums up their point of view: "Scenario A is the only one that makes sense. It lays out a steady ramp up in marketing and sales efforts tied directly to the development and launch of new products. By making the proposed cuts in operations and the back office, we can hit the long-term incentive targets without too much risk of missing product launch dates. It will also allow me to make sure we hire and train the very best sales teams for each new market. As you know, when you enter a new market with new products, it is imperative to take enough time to ensure the sales force can make the case to the prospective customers. I know scenario A means we do not hit the full run rate until year three, but the overall risk is much lower."

As Sarah finishes, Martin (Operations) starts to make the argument for scenario B: "I understand Sarah's concerns about ramping up too fast and the risks of missing launch dates, but if we really want to own the market we must move fast. I know for a fact that Transoceanic is already gearing up production in the region, and their advance marketing team is ahead of ours in creating awareness among the target demographic. As for relying on cost cuts to make the numbers, that strikes me as a very negative approach. If we really believe the numbers in White Hot's report, this market is enormous. We must go for it aggressively—now."

For the rest of the day the team debates the merits of each scenario but struggles to come to closure. Steve moves in and out of the meeting—he is the only one allowed to make phone calls or check his Blackberry. During the afternoon, he does a quick interview with the *Wall Street Journal* where he talks enthusiastically about the company's strong performance and exciting growth prospects. As the meeting breaks up, debate is still raging. In an attempt to bring some closure to the day's events, Tom and Mitch offer to "take a cut" at a third scenario that seeks to balance the need to aggressively capture the new market opportunities with the risks of moving too fast. The group quickly agrees and heads off to the spa.

As they leave, Steve takes Tom and Mitch aside and says: "OK, so you are going to introduce scenario C in the morning. That's the one we worked up last night after the board dinner?" Mitch replies, "That's right. It should make everyone happy."

Next morning, the group reconvenes around 8 AM, a little later than planned as the post-dinner nightcaps and cigars ran well past midnight. As soon as everyone is suitably caffeinated, Tom and Mitch bring up the slides of the spreadsheet showing scenario C. As they walk through the details, each member of management team begins to nod. There is little debate about the overall scenario; the questions now focus on detailed elements such as Rich's: "Do you think the phasing of the marketing budget over the second and third quarters accurately reflects the ramp up in advertising?" Steve sits back in his chair with a slight smile on his face. By 11 AM the group has reached a general agreement on scenario C. As CFO, Henry Pritchett says, "This scenario provides a sound baseline for budget development and gives plenty to work with in terms of detailed tactical planning."

After Steve outlines the next steps, it is off to the first tee before heading out to the airport to catch the company jet back to headquarters. All agree that it has been a very productive couple of days and that the downtime has been good for bonding and team building. On the way out of the meeting, Mitch, from White Hot, hands Henry an envelope; inside is the latest invoice for White Hot's monthly retainer—it is for $275,000 plus expenses.

Facts: Yes, We Are Very Strategic

The whole subject of strategy has become too confusing. It seems that everything is strategic; otherwise, it is not really that important. Even one of the most renowned strategy gurus, Michael Porter of Harvard Business School, confessed to the dangers: "Strategy is a word that gets used in so many ways with so many meanings that it can end up being meaningless."[1] He is right.

> **Mythbuster Wisdom**
> One academic paper began, "We investigated whether the memorability-based strategy, a process supporting the rejection of non-experienced event occurrence, could be promoted through training."[2] Got that?

We are overwhelmed with strategic plans, strategic thinking, strategic insight, strategic management, strategic information, strategic marketing, strategic branding, strategic positioning, and even strategic bombing. Appending strategy or strategic to anything elevates its significance and that of anyone associated with it. "Oh, I'm working on a strategic project," marks you as a very important person who is going places. But what exactly is strategy? Unfortunately, no one seems to know. It appears that you can define strategy just about any way you like, and that is a large part of the problem. Here are just a few definitions ranging from the confusing to the merely stupid:

- Strategy bridges the gap between policy and tactics.
- Strategy is the means by which policy is implemented.
- Strategy is the art of distributing and applying resources to fulfill the ends of policy.
- Strategy answers the question: What should the organization be doing?
- Strategy is a plan, a "how," a means of getting from here to there.
- Strategy is a pattern in actions over time.
- Strategy is position; strategy is perspective.
- Strategy emerges over time as intentions collide with and accommodate a changing reality.

However, none of these make my top three listing of the most absurd definitions of strategy. In best beauty pageant form, here they are in reverse order, with my comments in italics:

3. "Strategy has no existence apart from the ends sought." *I love this one as it reminds me of late-night, alcohol-infused philosophical discussions while in college on the meaning of life or the real message behind Led Zeppelin's "Stairway to Heaven."*

2. "Strategy is a broad, ambiguous topic. We must all come to our own understanding, definition, and meaning." *Well, that clears things up doesn't it?*

1. "Strategy is what top management does that is of great importance to the organization." *Ah, so that is what they do!*

Clearly, there is no clarity. Yet strategic planning should be both important and valuable provided it is kept in perspective—strategies are not five-year budgets, obscure aspirational statements that have little grounding in reality, or excuses for each new management team to put its own stamp on an organization. Strategy lays out a direction and focus that guides an organization's actions and provides a foundation for tactical and financial planning. Personally, I like Michael Porter's description of strategy as answering two questions: What markets are we going to participate (compete) in? How are we going to compete in those markets?

For example, both McDonalds and Morton's participate in the same broad market—food service—but they clearly have very different participation strategies that in turn frame much of their respective business models.

Keeping strategy simple makes it very easy to ask basic questions as ideas, opportunities, or events arise that impact an organization such as: Does this help us in reaching our goals and is it consistent with our participation and positioning? At U.S. retailer Target, the question is always, "How does this decision reinforce the brand?"

Despite all the hype surrounding strategy, the truth is that very few organizations or managers are truly strategic. When push comes to shove, strategic thinking flies out of the window as the pressure to make budget or hit the quarterly numbers takes over and anything that does not directly contribute to making near-term goals gets ignored. During 2008, billions of dollars worth of strategic plans were tossed out the window.

Companies love applauding themselves on their strategies. In its 2006 annual report GM trumpeted the progress: "At GM, we made a lot of progress last year. Our performance was validation that we have the right strategy, and it's working."[3] At the time, General Motors' strategy was based upon selling lots of large SUV's and trucks as the engines of profit growth. As gasoline soared to over $4 a gallon in mid-2008 and vehicle sales declined from an annual rate of more than 16 million to less than 9 million, the logic of betting on gas-guzzling vehicles seemed less compelling. By December 2008, CEO Richard Wagoner had forsaken the corporate jet for a Chevy Malibu hybrid to drive to Washington, DC, to beg for government loans to save the company as vehicle sales plummeted by more than 20 percent in twelve months. By March 2009 he was out of a job and GM was headed for bankruptcy; so much for having the right strategy.

Mortgage company Countrywide built its strategy on dominating the mortgage market. Even as the housing market was already beginning its sharp decline, Countrywide described the company's strategy in its 2006 annual report published in May 2007 thus: "A key element in driving growth from one business cycle to the next is Countrywide's determination to dominate our core business, real estate finance."[4] At the same time, co-founder and CEO Angelo Mozillo told investors that Countrywide would "Come out stronger in the long run, just as we have often done in the past."[5]

However, domination in one particular segment, subprime mortgages to borrowers with weak credit, combined with the collapse of credit markets, forced the company into a fire sale to Bank of America just a year later.

Both GM and Countrywide bet on strategies that were undone by market changes that exposed inherent weaknesses in their chosen strategies. At Sears, which for almost half a century was the Wal-Mart, before Wal-Mart, of U.S. retailing, the 1980s ushered in a strategy of adding financial services to the core retail business. Between 1980 and 1985 the company added stock brokerage (Dean Witter), real estate brokerage (Coldwell Banker), and credit cards (Discover) to its existing insurance business (Allstate). By one measure the diversification was a success. In 1992 the financial services businesses had revenues of $59 billion. However, the potential synergies with the core retail operation were not so obvious. Few customers bought a few hundred shares of GE, insured their car and looked for a new house while shopping for a new leaf blower.

In 1993, the company began to divest itself of all the financial services businesses. But it was too late; the distractions had allowed Wal-Mart to blow by Sears as the largest retailer, first in the United States, and then the world. In 2005, Sears merged with another fallen star, Kmart, and by 2008, the combined company ranked as the eighth largest U.S. retailer with sales of $50 billion or just 13 percent of those at Wal-Mart, and less than those its former financial services arm alone had achieved sixteen years earlier.

Strategy has many similarities to those excessively complex financial instruments (think—credit default swaps and collateralized debt obligations). With strategy, if you don't understand it, you can't execute it. With a financial instrument, if you don't understand it, don't invest in it. Simplicity is key. I like the way General Electric described growth strategies in its 2003 Annual Report, "The best growth strategies take companies to places where only a few can follow." I understand that, and it provides a test I can apply to any strategy: Will this strategy create distance between our competitors and us?

A GE alumnus offered some of the best advice on strategy. Larry Bossidy was Jack Welch's number two at GE for many years before becoming Chairman and CEO of AlliedSignal and then Honeywell. I had the pleasure of working with him early in his tenure at AlliedSignal during the early 1990s, and his candor and clarity left you in no doubt what he was thinking. In the book *Execution* (Crown Business, 2002), co-authored with Ram Charan and Charles Burck, Bossidy described strategy thus: "It's a roadmap, lightly filled in, so it gives you plenty of room to maneuver."

I like that; it's simple and readily understandable. You have a destination in mind, and you've worked out a rough direction or route for getting there, but you haven't necessarily planned out every restroom break or constrained yourself to a single road. You have options to take alternative routes if needed and maybe even change the ultimate destination based upon events along the way.

Building upon this I would add one further dimension—speed. How fast do you want to get there? Strategies that clearly describe a direction, a destination, and a speed provide a solid foundation for planning. For example, the command, "Go west young man," offers information as to direction but provides little guidance for planning. If I am sitting in New York, will getting to Pittsburgh be good enough, or do I need to go all the way to San Francisco?

If the destination is defined as San Francisco, you now have more information to start building a plan to get there, but you still have a lot of choices—walk, ride a Harley, cruise in a Corvette, or fly on the Learjet. If speed is added to the equation in the form of "head west to San Francisco and try to get there in less than 24 hours," planning just got a whole lot easier. You can eliminate walking, riding your motorcycle, driving, or catching the train as options since none of these tactics will get you there in time. This is a key point of good strategy—it should simplify planning by taking certain options off the table. Often the most valuable section in a strategy is the one headed: "Things we will not do." Interestingly, it is often the one section in voluminous strategy documents that is missing.

Fatally Flawed

In the early 1990s, Green Tree Financial emerged as a leader in the business of providing financing for the booming mobile home or manufactured housing market. Green Tree financed almost 40 percent of all mobile homes sold. Its profits increased by 600 percent from 1991 to 1997, and its CEO took home more than $100 million in 1996 alone.[6] In 1998, Conseco bought Green Tree for $7.6 billion; in December 2002 Conseco filed for bankruptcy, largely driven by huge losses on the assets acquired in the Green Tree deal. So what drove such growth and then triggered the rapid decline? Green Tree had a fatally flawed strategy that sowed the seeds of its own destruction. Green Tree's major innovation was to offer 30-year mortgages to people wanting to buy manufactured homes as opposed to the more traditional 15-year loan. This reduced the monthly cost and, when combined with financing of up to 95 percent of the purchase price, made ownership possible for many people with less than stellar credit (does this sound familiar given the events of 2008?). Sounds wonderful except for five minor problems:

1. A mortgage uses the asset being bought as security for the loan; however, manufactured homes, unlike normal homes (or at least unlike normal homes until 2006), do not rise in value. They depreciate much like a car, so with a 30-year loan where principal payments are low in the early years, it does not take very long for the loan value to be greater than the underlying security.

2. Manufactured homes have a typical lifespan of 15 years yet the mortgage would not be repaid for 30 years.

3. Incentives for sales teams were based largely on the volume of new loans sold. Not surprisingly, sales people did not focus too much on the credit quality of the borrower.

4. Green Tree securitized the loans it made and sold the resulting securities to investors, pocketing the difference between the interest paid by borrowers and the interest paid to investors; however, when hit with increasing defaults as borrowers with suspect credit stopped repaying loans or high levels of refinancing as interest rates fell, Green Tree was left with a loss.

5. Green Tree used an accounting approach called "gain on sale" that recorded profits on the securitized loans when they were sold based upon its own internal forecast of repayments. As interest rates fell, more and more borrowers paid off their loans early and the projected profits never materialized.

Over time, many borrowers began to understand points 1 and 2 and simply walked away from the loan or filed for bankruptcy, as the payments became too great a burden. Conseco ended up writing off over $3 billion related to Green Tree after the acquisition. What is interesting is that Green Tree's problems were already obvious when Conseco bought the company. Green Tree wrote off almost $400 million just three months before Conseco made its move. At the time *BusinessWeek* commented, "Analysts say Green Tree is not likely to experience permanent damage."

Jumping forward ten years, the Green Tree saga provided a salutary but largely ignored warning of the subprime crisis as lenders relaxed credit standards and reduced down-payment requirements, essentially betting that ever-increasing property values would keep them whole should borrowers default. When prices first stagnated and then started falling, triggering the recession that started in late 2007, Wall Street, which had consumed vast quantities of these securitized mortgages, found values collapsing as lenders were hit with increasing defaults combined with property values that came nowhere near the value of the outstanding mortgages, thereby triggering a major economic meltdown. As Michael Lewis, author of *Liars Poker,* (Penguin, 1990), noted in a December 2008 article: "If you want to know what these Wall Street firms are really worth, take a hard look at the crappy assets they bought with huge sums of borrowed money, and imagine what they'd fetch in a fire sale."[7]

So What?

- Keep strategies simple.
- Effective strategies clarify not confuse.
- Describe what you are not going to do as well as what you are going to do.
- Strategies should be flexible—tactics can be adapted to the current environment without ditching the strategy.
- If your employees, customers, or shareholders don't get it, it is not an effective strategy.
- A strategy is only as good as the execution that follows.
- A five-year financial plan is not a strategy.

Notes

1. *Michael Porter Asks, and Answers: Why Do Good Managers Set Bad Strategies?* Published: November 01, 2006 in Knowledge@Wharton.

2. Simon Ghetti, Silvia Papini, and Laura Angelini, "The Development of the Memorability-Based Strategy: Insight from a Training Study." Department of Psychology, University of California, Davis, May 2005.

3. GM Annual Report 2006.

4. Countrywide Financial, Annual Report 2006.

5. "Countrywide's Collapse Complete—Lender Vowed It Could overcome Housing Struggles," *Columbus Dispatch,* January 13, 2008.

6. Andrew Osterland, "How Green Tree Got Pruned," *BusinessWeek,* November 1997.

7. Michael Lewis, "The End." Portfolio.com, December 2008.

Chapter 3

Gurus, Consultants, and Other Snake Oil Salesman

Midnight on December 31, 1999, did not just herald the dawn of a new millennium; it also marked the date at which total U.S. employment in professional services surpassed that in manufacturing for the first time. Today more people talk about stuff than make stuff.

When I started out as a consultant in 1985, the profession—and it was still a profession back then—was clearly focused on helping businesses improve their performance. In the years since, things have got a little blurry. Today, everyone seems to call him- or herself a consultant; just as in Los Angeles every waiter is really an actor, so every "resting" executive is really a consultant. According to the U.S. Economic Census, between 1997 and 2002, the number of management consulting firms increased by 54 percent, the number of consultants increased by

52 percent, and revenues increased by a whopping 73 percent to more than $90 billion. Those are pretty astonishing growth rates; consulting has become a very lucrative profession. For more than 25 years I have made my living by taking ideas from one company and selling them to another. A friend once described me as a prostitute of the brain, which is actually a good thing, since if I had to rely on my body to make a living I would have been destitute years ago. As we have already seen, Cruciant is a proud user of consultants, and Henry the CFO is determined to crack down on this profligacy.

Fiction: Henry's Office—October 2008

Henry is reviewing possible expense cuts with Kevin Na, his budget manager.

Henry: "We've already done all the usual things haven't we? Hiring freeze, cut all non-customer travel, stop all non-essential training . . ."

Kevin: "Yes, we have. That should save around $11 million this quarter."

Henry: "What are the other big discretionary items?"

Kevin: "Well, the largest by far is our spending on consultants; across all areas of the business it is running at close to $3 million a month."

Henry: "What? How the hell did it get that high?"

Kevin: "I've no idea, but I put together a list of where we are spending the money."

He passes a piece of paper across to Henry—(see Table 3.1).

Kevin: "These are the top ten individual projects. You can see that our total spend in just those is estimated to be $6.2 million this quarter, with another $400,000 in smaller projects."

Henry: "Which ones can we cut? The White Hot is untouchable, that's Borden's and things will have to get a whole lot worse for him to cut them out."

Kevin: "Well, as you can see, most of the spend is related to the Asia launch—almost $3 million this quarter. Given that we are slowing down the rollout there, much of that could be delayed, don't you think?"

Table 3.1 Project Expenses

Project	Firm	Q4 Estimate	YTD Spend
Corporate strategy	White Hot	$ 525,000	$ 1,575,000
Corporate mission and vision	Innovisions	$ 75,000	$ 375,000
Project Green Cruciant	EcoTransformation	$ 400,000	$ 0
ERP system implementation	TechStars	$ 1,500,000	$ 4,500,000
Asian launch	Cool, Hip & Trendy	$ 750,000	$ 2,500,000
	Ling & Fu	$ 500,000	$ 950,000
	Oliver James Inc.	$ 600,000	$ 2,400,000
	Dynamic Marketing Inc.	$ 1,000,000	$ 3,150,000
Brand strategy	Cool, Hip & Trendy	$ 250,000	$ 2,100,000
Executive compensation plan	SeriousRewards Inc.	$ 600,000	$ 300,000
All other projects		$ 400,000	$ 2,000,000
TOTAL		**$6,600,000**	**$19,850,000**

Henry: "Probably—although Marketing will give us the usual 'BS' about how it's a campaign that builds and therefore you have to keep it going or you lose the value of all the money spent so far. Still they are just going to have to deal with it. Same with IT and HR—I want their spending cut by at least 25 percent—their projects are always late and over budget anyway. From now on no new consulting contracts are to be signed without my approval."

Kevin: "OK. What do you want to do about our benchmarking program? It's not listed separately, but it's there for $400,000 in the budget for the fourth quarter."

Henry: "Leave that in there. If anything, it is even more important to identify cost savings opportunities with everything that's going on out there. However, have Stephanie go back and tell the firm that they must get it done for $350K."

Four Months Later . . .

Henry: "So how did we do on the expense side during Q4?"

Kevin: "Not bad. The projected spend was $6.6 million and we came in at $4.3 million. Most of the savings were in deferring the Asian rollout; although I'm a little concerned that Marketing is now saying that it will cost an extra $1 million to complete the work because of the lost momentum. The other worrying trend is that it seems a lot of functions took part of their consulting budget and used it to rehire employees we let go during the reduction in force, the argument being that service levels were being materially impacted. Overall with all that going on, I think we saved about $1.5 million in the fourth quarter."

Henry: "Yes, but what are the real savings? Simply pushing spending out does not save us anything in the long term."

Kevin: "I know, and I think we will be lucky if we save $250,000 overall."

Henry: "That's a lot of work for not much result. When we get the time, we need to fix the whole process. Our culture is to hire outsiders whenever we want to, not just when we really need them. By the way, did you see the benchmarking results? We can save about $3 million over the next two years, and the payback is about one year. Has The Benchmark Brotherhood got their proposal in yet?"

Kevin: "Yes, they have. It is for $1.5 million plus 10 percent of the savings."

Henry: "OK—let's get it signed then."

Facts: Are You Renting Bodies or Brains?

In the spirit of full disclosure, I have been a consultant for all but three years of my working life. My success rate over that time has probably been a little better than that of an economist's forecasts, so I've had my share of failures, although I can honestly say none of them were intentional. So my musings on the value of consultants have both the benefit and bias of experience.

The best consultants bring unique knowledge and experience to bear; however, in many organizations the mere mention of consultants is met with cynicism at best, and downright ridicule at worst. The tales of consulting nightmares are legion; just a few of the more popular blood-sucking, sorry, fee-generating tactics include:

- **The Kindergarten**. Hordes of newly minted, highly paid MBAs descend on an organization for months on end at an hourly rate of about $300 or about five times that of the experienced client staff who are assigned to work with them. They proceed to flowchart, graph, and spreadsheet everything that moves, gaining tremendous knowledge of the business but offering little practical output other than numerous neatly tabbed ring binders containing the afore-mentioned documentation. Suddenly, one day they all leave, ready to be sold to another unsuspecting client as experienced "senior" consultants at a bargain rate of $350 an hour. Two recent kinder-garten waves to wash over business have been the ERP implemen-tation wave where hordes of consultants fresh out of a six-week training program helped large companies spend $100 million or so implementing SAP, Orcale, or some other Enterprise system; and the Sarbanes-Oxley wave, where corporate finance staffs, auditors, and consultants sat down and tried to interpret the mass of new legislation passed in the wake of Enron.

- **The Bait and Switch.** One of the oldest tricks in the consultant's arsenal, the bait and switch starts with highly impressive partners and associates spending a few days "scoping" out the engagement and defining the "problem statement" before developing their proposal emphasizing their "value proposition." Management becomes enam-ored with the insight and expertise these "thought leaders" bring to the table and sign on for a sizable engagement. After the initial kick-off meeting, the high-powered talent disappears to be replaced by a few of the aforementioned MBA intake and the Kindergarten reas-serts its presence.

- **The Body Shop.** Business is booming and the organization must install massive new computer systems to "scale" to meet the company's growth targets and take advantage of all the latest "best practices." A respected "integrator" is chosen as a "partner" to assist in this immense undertaking, and dozens of consultants descend on the company for a couple of years as millions are spent on global deployment. The internal IT staff marvel at the ability of these "youngsters." Apparently, these consultants, not even MBA's in this case, but computer science graduates and liberal arts majors, have spent a few weeks at an intensive training school and are now miraculously transformed into fully fledged implementation con-sultants. Thankfully, no one ever conducts a post-implementation review to see if the benefits touted in the original business case were ever realized. Fortunately, the combination of the dot.com blowout in 2000/2001 and the rise of off-shoring pretty much made the body shop extinct for large-scale systems development projects. Hourly rates plummeted from the $250–350 range in 1999 to less than $50 just two years later, often with an increase in the skills of the assigned consultants as Indian PhDs replaced graduates from an SAP school in South Florida.

- **The Strategy.** A new CEO has just been appointed, and it is imperative that he or she has a new vision and strategy for the business. However, this person only has the standard "first 100 days" to get the job done. Don't worry; simply call one of the premier strategy consulting firms, probably the one the CEO used to work for, and have it help out. For a modest $2 million, a beautifully pre-sented strategy replete with bullet points, scatter diagrams, and two-by-two matrices will set out the clear path to greatness. After the initial excitement of board presentations, investor presentations, and employee all-hands meetings, the strategy takes its rightful place on a shelf next to its forebears—never again to see the light of day.

- **The Slash and Burn.** Expenses are out of control and revenues are slumping. It's time to bring in the hatchet men (and women). Organizational charts are scrutinized, and numerous layers and boxes are eliminated. Budgets are slashed and projects cancelled. A thick report details the millions that will be saved after imple-mentation. The consultants' fee is fattened by a nice percentage of the savings identified and then they leave town—well before any actual savings have been realized. About 18 months later another firm is hired to repeat the exercise, because for some reason the previous recommendations never got implemented.

- **The Underground Rehire.** During the last downturn, numerous highly paid and very experienced workers were fired. They were either replaced by younger and therefore much cheaper personnel or not replaced at all in order to reduce costs. To ensure that costs are tightly controlled, a hiring freeze is instituted. After a short period, the business begins to suffer through the loss of experi-enced talent, but managers are hamstrung by the hiring freeze. No problem—simply hire a few former workers back as consultants.

While the hiring freeze was in place, there were budget dollars that could be pulled from elsewhere to fund these consultants. A number of former workers reappear at significantly higher hourly rates and life goes on.

Fortunately, the majority of consultants are out to do the right thing and to do it ethically, but the occurrence of these six diseases is far too common and it poisons the water.

Mythbuster Wisdom: What's Your ROCF (Return On Consulting Fees)?
Is your return on consulting investment at least equal to the price/earnings multiple of your stock? So if your enterprise P/E ratio is 15 and you spend $250,000 on consultants you should at a minimum realize a return in excess of $3.75 million. If the answer is no, you better be able to justify the investment in terms of reduced enterprise risk.

Probably the first true management consultant, and perhaps the best, was Peter Drucker. Born in Vienna in 1909, Drucker immigrated to the United States in the 1930s. His 1946 book *The Concept of the Corporation (Transaction, reprinted in 1993),* based upon observations at General Motors, laid out much of the thinking that would dominate management for half a century. Unlike many others who followed, he did not rest on his laurels but remained an astute observer of both good and bad business practices right up to his death in 2005.

Drucker epitomized the essence of what a good consultant should be able to do—explain seemingly complicated ideas in very simple terms. If you read any of his many books, you will spend most of your time thinking, well, that's obvious isn't it? Of course, the true worth of a consultant is not when other consultants like me laud him or her, but when people who have real jobs praise his or her advice and counsel. In the May 2009 issue of the *Harvard Business Review,* A.G. Lafley, then the CEO of Procter & Gamble, praised Drucker's insights on the unique role of the CEO[1] and how those insights had helped him in his tenure at the helm of one of the world's great companies. Lafley reaffirmed the value of answering the question: "What business are you in?" but also cited Drucker's additional question as being equally important: "What business are you not in?" Sounds simple, and it is— but how many companies have actually answered that question?

Drucker hated the increasing use of the word *guru* as applied to himself and others, and to his credit commented, "We are using the word 'guru' only because 'charlatan' is too long to fit into a headline."[2]

Objectivity and Independence—No, Not Really!

One of the top reasons cited for seeking expert counsel, be it legal, financial, technological, or managerial, is to secure independent and objective advice. But that's a myth. Advice is a complex web of self-interest designed to fuel future revenues. How often has a lawyer told a client that he or she doesn't really need legal advice? Has a consultant ever gone to a client and said, "There is no role for me beyond this phase"?

Three recent examples of the questionable independence of supposedly objective bodies illustrate the point. Some of the blame for the financial meltdown in 2008 has been laid at the door of the ratings agencies that make money by charging fees to banks that issue the bonds that the agencies rate for credit quality. Does a triple-A rating increase the future flow of business from an issuing bank? Well, it probably doesn't do any harm. This comes just a few years after the security analyst community on Wall Street was blamed for the dot.com collapse for cheerleading stocks that their investment banking colleagues were leading to lucrative IPO and financing fees. How embarrassing for a banker to have his or her colleagues in the research department post a "sell" rating on their prized client. Finally, there has been some chatter about the close relationship between compensation consultants and CEO's who are their clients. These supposedly independent advisors are often hired by a firm's board of directors to offer advice on the design of executive compensation plans. Clearly, a rising executive star is going to look kindly on the firm who secures him or her a lucrative compensation package upon the move into the corner office. As journalist Harris

Collingwood noted in *Atlantic Monthly,* "Compensation consultants know that if they win big pay packages for their CEO clients, they'll be rewarded with lucrative contracts to administer employee-benefits plans and the like."[3]

The lack of independence inevitably colors some advisors. One way to identify those advisors who really are credible is when they do admit that their role no longer makes sense or they offer advice that leads you to move in a direction that offers no benefit to themselves. Ironically, on the occasions when I have offered such advice, I have almost always got a call a few weeks later offering me further work. For the professional advisor, the best thing you can do is to make yourself expendable; it is actually the easiest way to make yourself indispensable. However, all advisors, consultants, and CEOs for that matter should remember DeGaulle's admonition, that "the graveyards are full of indispensable men."

So What?

- Are you sourcing distinctive expertise that you cannot find internally or justify employing on a full-time basis? If not, you are just augmenting current staff due to a temporary resource shortage. Depending on your answer, make sure you pay appropriately.
- Are you buying the people who sell the work or those who will actually be doing it? Those who sell the work are rarely those who will be on the ground doing the day-to-day work. Make sure the promise matches the reality.
- Will the use of consultants demonstrably increase the value of your business or reduce risk in some tangible way? For example, will a new strategy provide insight into new, untapped markets? Will the reorganization of the finance function result in shorter cycle times for building budgets, earlier identification of credit risks, or reduced errors in the accounting close process?
- Will the use of external advisors result in a change that delivers on at least one and preferably all three of the following promises:
  a. Better?
  b. Faster?
  c. Cheaper?

- Ask the consultants to describe the criteria for defining when the advisor's job is done and when is help no longer needed. Watching them squirm as they try to answer this question is hugely entertaining.

Notes

1. A.G. Lafley, "What Only the CEO Can Do," *Harvard Business Review*, May 2009.
2. "Peter Drucker, the Man Who Changed the World," *Business Review Weekly*, 15 September 1997.
3. Harris Collingwood, "Do CEOs Matter?" *Atlantic Monthly*, June 2009.

Chapter 4

Forget Success, Focus on Failure

One of the great strengths of the American psyche is that there is little stigma associated with failing. In fact, failure is celebrated. To an American, everything is a learning experience, and there is no better story than a great comeback. Yet the landscape is littered with the burned-out carcasses of once-proud businesses. Numerous iconic names have simply disappeared or been mortally wounded: Bear Stearns, Chrysler, Digital Equipment, Enron, General Motors, Kmart, Kodak, Lehman Brothers, MCI WorldCom, Montgomery Ward, Motorola, Pan Am, Polaroid, Sears, Sunbeam, TWA, Wang, Westinghouse, and Woolworth. All were once leaders in their industry, yet one-time leadership is no protection from future irrelevance. The causes of their demise were diverse. Enron and WorldCom cheated while Polaroid and Wang failed to adapt to a rapidly changing world. How well are the lessons learned? After all, we have seen bubbles in everything from tulips to technology stocks over the last 400 years. While many talk about how the best lessons are those learned through failure, how many managers actually contemplate failure? Does anyone ever ask the question: What if we are wrong? Or what events or trends could cause our demise? The answer is rarely. Much more likely, you rationalize the demise of another by emphasizing how unique and different you are and boldly stating that there is no way that could ever happen to us. In today's turbulent world that's naïve; asking such questions is crucial. Of course, the team at Cruciant cannot contemplate failure.

Fiction: Sustained High Growth in Revenues and Earnings

Early in 2002 the team at Cruciant was on a roll. In the three years since it had been spun off from United Integrated (UI), revenues had been growing 17 percent a year while earnings had averaged 19 percent growth. Cruciant's share price had increased from $17 a share at the time of the spinoff to $57 a share. Such was the company's success that UI had sold off its remaining 32 percent stake in the company, netting a tidy $1.8 billion profit. The dot.com blowout and 9/11 had been merely blips in the company's growth path. Cruciant's management team was being lauded in the business press for unlocking the vast potential that had been buried deep in the bowels of UI for so many years.

With confidence at an all time high, the company decided that 2003 would be the year that Cruciant took its performance to another level. CEO Steve Borden set targets of 25 percent sales growth and 30 percent earnings growth predicated upon a raft of new product launches, entry into numerous new markets, the opening of the company's first retail outlets, and the implementation of a new enterprise-wide computer system that would automate all the basic transaction processing of the company and reduce costs by more than $15 million. Throughout the balance of 2002 the planning was intense. A "war room" was set up in a rented office not far from Cruciant's headquarters, and fifty staffers from across the company were brought to together to form "Team Turbo." Team Turbo was charged with planning, coordinating, and managing all the programs that were going to "turbocharge" Cruciant's growth in 2003. A fully staffed Program Management Office, or PMO in the jargon, was launched with considerable help from a number of different consulting firms. Project charters, service level agreements, Gantt charts, PERT charts, and critical path analyses papered the walls. The executive steering committee, chaired by Steve, started off with monthly meetings, but as the level of activity increased, they moved to a biweekly cycle. At its peak, during the second quarter of 2003, more than 500 staff and consultants were working on the various initiatives; spending was running at $4 million a week.

Executive Steering Committee—May 2003

Cameron Brown, the program manager for Turbo, is reviewing progress with the executive committee. Each committee member has a thick stack of reports in front of him or her.

Cameron: "In your briefing packs you have the overall project plan and detailed status reports from all the initiatives. I do not propose to review them all today (there are many relieved looks around the table), but feel free to review them at your leisure. I will focus on the program dashboard that you can find behind tab one in your binders."

Each member of the committee dutifully flips to tab one where there is a single sheet of paper that lists all the programs that make up Turbo down the left-hand side. The next three columns give the Percentage Complete, Open Issues, and an Overall Status, which is represented by a red, yellow, or green flag. Given the number of projects, the font size is really small, but it is easy to see that all but three programs have green status lights.

Cameron: "As you can see from the dashboard, we only have three projects whose status is not green, and they are all yellow. I have reviewed all three with the respective project managers and each of them assures me that these are merely temporary blips and that by our next meeting all will be back to green. At this time there are no major decisions required of the executive committee, so I propose we adjourn the meeting."

Steve: "Agreed and nice job, Cameron."

As the committee members file out of the room, Sarah turns to Phil and says, "I hope all our meetings are as short as that—I can now get some real work done!"

"Me too," responds Phil.

Two Weeks Later . . .

The meeting enters its fifth hour. Cameron is explaining the reasons why the seventeenth of twenty-three projects that has a yellow or red status indicator is not on track.

Cameron: "We have had a rough couple of weeks—the dependencies between all the different programs are driving these issues. The new computer system is on the critical path for all the other programs, and we are finding big problems with the quality of the data in all the legacy systems that we are replacing."

Steve interrupts: "How can this have happened in just two weeks? Everything looked great at our last meeting."

Cameron: "As far as the individual projects were concerned, everything was looking good, but it was only at our two-day program management meeting last week that each team began to evaluate the impact of the systems project being behind schedule. This is by far the biggest systems project the company has ever attempted, and our consultants tell us its one of the biggest they are aware of in the world."

Steve: "So are you telling me it's failing?"

Cameron: "Well not exactly. With sufficient time and resources we can get the job done. It is just going to take longer and cost more than expected."

Steve: "Bloody typical—anything can be solved with time and money. Well, we will see how things play out over the next two weeks and then we may have to make some tough calls."

Another Two Weeks Later . . .

Steve addresses the committee: "As of 7 PM last night, Turbo has been shut down. Not only did we find that the issues with the system were probably insurmountable, but Henry has gone back and looked at the business case for the overall program, and it transpires that the original business rationale for Turbo has evaporated. While it made great sense a year ago, when we approved it, the shifts in the market and the changes in technology make much of what we were attempting pointless today. In fact, the rationale fell apart about six months ago. So, while at that time all the projects were green, the reason for doing them had already disappeared! Why it took us six months to find out I will never know. We will be issuing a press release in the morning announcing the abandonment and telling investors that we are taking a $45 million write-down on the program. Needless to say I am not happy. This is embarrassing—we cannot afford any more screw-ups."

In the days that follow, Cameron clears out his desk, Cruciant's stock price drops $12 and a leading business magazine runs a story under the headline, "Cruciant's Big Blunder—Can They Get Their Mojo Back?"

Facts: Accept Failure, Fear Success

English book publisher and cataloguer Henry Bohn commented in the nineteenth century, "Success makes a fool seem wise." At no time has this been more evident than over the last few years. A few quarters of rising profits in a booming economy can convince even the mediocre that they are something special. Numerous highly intelligent and previously successful leaders have run aground such as Carly Fiorina at Hewlett-Packard, George Fisher at Kodak, and Michael Armstrong at AT&T. Some have steered their businesses over a precipice, undone by changing markets or simple hubris. Many executives talk about the need to learn from mistakes, but how many actually contemplate the fact that they might screw up? After all, they did not make it to the corner office by failing.

Gene Kranz, flight controller for the ill-starred Apollo 13 mission, uttered the phrase "Failure is not an option" in April 1970. Since then many managers have adopted the phrase as part of their management mantra, and it is ridiculous. While Kranz was right about the situation on board Apollo 13, the homily has no place in the business world. Failure is an inevitable part of any enterprise both for-profit and not-for-profit. Yet so much of management's time is fixated on success with little consideration of the potential for failure.

Strategic plans lay out, often in mind-numbing detail, the reasons for success; investment proposals list the critical success factors necessary to realize the payoff; managers enthusiastically present business plans and exude confidence in their ability to deliver. Discussion of the likely causes of failure are usually confined to a pedestrian risk analysis that poses a few "what-if" questions and then discounts each scenario as not material or not probable. Frankly, in today's increasingly volatile and uncertain world, this is not just stupid, it is negligent.

Risk-taking and the acceptance of failure are fundamental to the economic system. Harvard professor Clayton Christensen predicates much of his book *The Innovators' Dilemma* on an understanding of why companies fail. He even entitles one section "Building a Failure Framework."[1]

Managers who avoid failure are bad managers. The pressure never to fail or never to make a poor decision is wrong headed and dangerous. Many industries routinely tolerate very high failure rates: How many drugs make it to market; how many holes drilled yield oil; or how many movies make money? Other industries such as fashion and consumer electronics consciously obsolete their own products for the sake of sustainability and growth. Failure is a vital element of the economic system and, as the events of 2008 showed, it is a thriving business.

Cataloging Failure
- Since 1980, 1,850 companies that went public have gone out of business.
- 90 percent of oil wells drilled are dry.
- 70 percent of pharmaceutical compounds fail to result in new drugs.
- 59 percent of new restaurants close within three years.[2]
- 56 percent of all business fail during their first four years.[3]
- 60 percent of all acquisitions fail to add any value.
- 70 percent of re-engineering projects fail.
- 37 percent of companies abandoned a major business change project between 2005 and 2007.[4]
- 60 percent of all businesses never make a profit—ever.[5]

- Only 1 out every 4 consumer products in development make it to the market—of those launched, more than 1 in 3 fail.[6]
- The failure rate for new products in the retail grocery industry is over 70 percent.

Success Can Be Dangerous for Your Health

Success can be very dangerous; it breeds arrogance. Witness the inflated egos that preceded the dot.com bust, or the demise of Long-Term Capital Management—after all, Nobel economists can't be stupid, can they? Beyond arrogance, success creates intense pressure to sustain itself or at least appear to sustain itself as was demonstrated by Enron, Worldcom, Bernard Madoff Securities, and The Stanford Group. Success also fuels a culture of entitlement, or just plain greed, where rewards no longer need to be earned as at Tyco and Adelphia Communications. It is a pretty potent combination: arrogance, ego, invincibility, and entitlement. No wonder so many titans fall so far.

Mythbuster Wisdom: The Top Five Danger Signs of Corporate Hubris
- Building an ostentatious new headquarters. There are numerous examples including Chrysler, GM, AT&T, Sprint, and Pan Am.
- Being named to the top 20 of *Fortune* Magazine's most admired list (Rubbermaid, Motorola, Enron, Daimler-Chrysler, Lucent, and Ford)
- The CEO is on the cover of *Forbes, Fortune,* and *Business Week* with alarming regularity (Al Dunlap—Sunbeam, Carly Fiorina—Hewlett-Packard, Dennis Kowlowski—Tyco, Jeff Skilling—Enron).
- The company consummates a massive acquisition that promises to "redefine markets," "create unprecedented value,"

or "deliver tremendous synergies" (AOL–Time Warner, Sears–Kmart, Citibank–Travelers, Daimler–Chrysler).
- Hire a high-profile CEO from outside the company (John Sculley—Apple, Michael Armstrong—AT&T, George Fisher—Kodak, Bob Nardelli—Home Depot and Chrysler, Gary Wendt—Conseco).

For America On-Line (AOL) success caused the press to rename the company, America On Hold. In 1996, America On-Line was the dominant online service provider allowing millions of users to send email and access both proprietary AOL content and the burgeoning Internet through dial-up access over telephone lines. But the company wanted more. Having vanquished early rivals such as Compuserve and Prodigy, it wanted to secure its leadership position in the face of emerging competitors such as AT&T and Microsoft. AOL flooded the market with aggressive promotions and free software offering access to the AOL service. Thousands of new subscribers signed up even as early signs of service problems began to emerge. Buoyed by its initial success, AOL ramped up its efforts by introducing a flat-rate pricing plan. This allowed users to stay online for as long as they wished all for one flat rate. Not surprisingly, with no incentive to log off, AOL's capacity was rapidly exhausted; millions of users heard busy signals when trying to connect even as AOL continued to sign up new customers—hence the sobriquet, America On Hold.

For Hoover, success cost the company $75 million. In 1992, the Hoover appliance company in the UK, a division of Maytag, ran a promotion that offered two free trans-Atlantic airline tickets with the purchase of a vacuum cleaner. For purchasing a £100 ($150) Hoover appliance a customer could get two free round trip plane tickets to the United States, then valued at more than $600—how good a deal was that? Not surprisingly, over 200,000 people bought inexpensive appliances and demanded their tickets. In fact the number of tickets that could theoretically be reclaimed exceeded the total airline seat capacity across the Atlantic! Hoover tried to extricate itself from a dangerous situation by offering vouchers or refunds, but consumers and, more important, England's notorious tabloid press, were having none of it. Hoover became front-page news, and the company was facing a pubic relations disaster. By the time all the lawsuits were settled in 1998, the debacle had cost Hoover over £50 million ($75 million).

Numerous companies from Apple with the first iPhone to Amazon with its Kindle have experienced negative press when excessive demand for new products has exceeded supply. Sometimes scarcity creates prestige; more often it creates anger and frustration.

The Perils of Being Number One

Which company was ranked number one in *Fortune* magazine's Most Admired Companies list in both 1994 and 1995 after holding down the number two spot for the previous five years? No, it wasn't Apple, Coca-Cola, or General Electric.

Fortune Most Admired Companies of 1994

1. Rubbermaid
2. Home Depot
3. Microsoft
3. Coca-Cola
5. 3M
6 Motorola
6. Disney
8. Procter & Gamble
8. J.P. Morgan
10. UPS

Source: Fortune

The number one company in both years was—Rubbermaid. Where is Rubbermaid now? Just five years after reaching the lofty heights of being the most admired company in the United States, Rubbermaid was bought by Newell for $6 billion. This was supposed to be a merger of titans. Newell had consistently delivered annual shareholder returns of over 20 percent. When the deal closed, the combined companies had a combined stock market value of $12 billion, and Newell's stock stood to close to an all-time high of $48. How the mighty have fallen! Since the acquisition, stock of the renamed Newell Rubbermaid has never again approached those lofty levels. By the end of 2008 the stock was trading below $9 a share and the company's total market capitalization was under $2.5 billion, an 80 percent decline. Of the other nine members of the 1994 top ten, only Procter & Gamble and Microsoft remained by 2008.

Forget "In Search of Excellence," How About Excellence Lost?

In 1982, Tom Peters and Robert Waterman's seminal business book, *In Search of Excellence* (HarperCollins, reprinted in 2004), was published. The authors identified 36 companies that they defined as excellent by having met their criteria of superior performance over a 20-year period from 1961 to 1980. The criteria included measures such as asset growth, return on capital, and return on equity. By all accounts these were tremendously successful businesses over an extended period of time. However, the widely varying fortunes of these stars over the next thirty years offer a cautionary tale of the fragility of success. Of the original 36 companies, seven no longer exist: Amdahl, Cheseborough-Ponds, Data General, Digital Equipment, Raychem, and Wang Labs. Three have endured bankruptcy, Revlon, Kmart, and Delta Airlines. Levi Strauss, Kodak, and DuPont all lost market leading positions and have underperformed financially. Many of the others, including Avon, Boeing, Bristol Myers, Caterpillar, Disney, Dow Chemical, Hewlett-Packard, IBM, McDonald's, Maytag, and Merck, have found the intervening 25 years to be anything but a smooth ride. Of the original 36 companies, not one rated in the top 10 in terms of 10-year shareholder returns on the Fortune 500 of 2008.

Preparing to Fail

So how do you prepare for failure? A good start is to be paranoid. After all, former Intel CEO Andy Grove entitled his biography *Only the Paranoid Survive* (Currency, 1995). After paranoia, the most practical step you can take is to ensure that every plan or project proposal defines the factors that could cause it to fail and, even more useful, defines the criteria under which it should be abandoned. Most plans do a fine job of defining their critical success factors, but understanding the possible causes of failure or irrelevance is far more useful. Smart investors have used stop-loss limits for years to minimize the impact of a falling stock price. Why not institute a series of "stop-project" limits that define the criteria for abandonment?

Approval of plans or budgets should not mean the end of scrutiny; even projects that are on time and on budget may become irrelevant if the original business rationale ceases to be valid. Peter Drucker suggested that the key question for managers is, "When do you stop pouring resources into things that have run their course?" A related and potentially more important question is, "Do you know when things have run their course?" Throwing good money and resources at ideas or initiatives that no longer make sense is more common than you may believe. All too often failing propositions limp along well after they have run their course. In both the canal and railway booms of the nineteenth century, investors kept pouring money into new projects long after the businesses had ceased to be profitable. Investors kept funding new condo developments in Miami and Las Vegas long after the housing market had peaked. Could General Motors have reduced its dependence on gas-guzzling SUVs before gasoline hit $4 a gallon? Could Palm have foreseen the rapid adoption of the smart phone, which decimated its once dominant share of the market for personal digital assistants (PDAs)? Could any of the hundreds of banks investing in mortgage-backed securities have foreseen a day when house prices did not go up at least 10 percent every year? I suspect the answer is yes.

Some industries have well-developed measures of failure. A television show with low ratings, a share price that falls below a stop-loss limit, a consumer product that tests poorly, or a new drug that fails to secure FDA approval are all examples of measures of failure. Some companies define failure as a criterion for survival, as in General Electric's famous objective to be number one or number two in all of its markets. However, in many areas of business the criteria are not well understood because they are not well defined. Organizations that can identify possible failure early have a distinct advantage. But that advantage will only be realized if they have the courage to act. There are many investors who carefully set stop-loss limits only to ignore them in the hope of a rebound—it rarely pays off.

Even the Best Screw Up

Failure is not solely the preserve of the stupid. Even the most successful organizations fail and it's not all bad. In fact failure can be very healthy providing the lessons are learned.

- New Coke
- Apple's Newton and Lisa
- Steven Spielberg's *1941*
- AT&T Video Phone
- McDonald's McLean Deluxe
- Levi's on-line
- Wal-Mart Japan
- Virgin Cola
- Honda's Formula 1 team
- Sony's Betamax video recorder

Having the courage to kill a once-cherished project is a hallmark of a great company. In early 2005, Intuit, the accounting and tax preparation software company, based in Mountain View, CA, launched an effort to target young tax filers through a website called RockYourRefund. com. No doubt the name was supposed to be seen as cool by Intuit's target market, but since when have taxes been cool? Anyway, Intuit offered young people discounts for travel and consumer electronics and provided a service that allowed for tax refunds to be converted into prepaid Visa cards. The promotion bombed and the company processed very few returns, yet later that year the team behind the campaign received an award from Chairman Scott Cook, who commented, "It's only a failure if we fail to get the learning."[7]

Giving Up on Success

Sometimes apparent failure hinders future success. Taking a short-term view can lead to decisions that in retrospect seem shortsighted. In 1996, General Motors launched the EV1, an electric car designed to help the company meet California's increasingly strict emissions standards. Just over 2,000 EV1's were built, and GM withdrew the vehicle in 1999. Conservative estimates put the vehicle's cost at roughly twice that of the revenue generated from the leases, and the car was never made available for sale. Based upon the initial launch, the EV1 was a failure, but in late 2008, then GM CEO Rick Wagoner commented that canceling the program was one of his worst decisions. GM R&D chief Larry Burns commented that if the company had continued the program it could "have had the Chevy Volt ten years earlier."[8] The EV1 may have been a commercial failure, but it would not have taken a rocket scientist to envision a plausible future scenario where alternative fuel technologies would be an important element of any competitive vehicle maker. Would the EV1 have saved GM? Probably not, but building on the experience may have allowed the company to compete more effectively in today's increasingly green world.

The first step is to identify failure early, and the second and more important step is to learn from failure. In 2000, Virgin Atlantic Airways made a $67 million investment to create new sleeper seats for the airline's "Upper-Class" cabin, the airline's equivalent of business class. Less than a year later, British Airways, Virgin's chief competitor, launched a superior offering with a true, lie-flat bed. Virgin was immediately at a competitive disadvantage. In a lesson that many others could learn from, Virgin handed the task of how to respond to British Airways to the very same person who led the original design. The company showed faith and a tolerance for failure. Not even 9/11 distracted the company; Virgin stuck with the project and in 2003, after spending

$127 million, it launched a new "upper-class suite" to wide acclaim. Having sampled both the British Airways offering on a Los Angeles to London flight and Virgin's on a 24-hour hop from London to Sydney via Singapore, I can confirm that Virgin's investment was well worth it.

Another example comes from Home Depot. On April 30, 2009, Home Depot closed down its Spanish language website after just four months.[9] The site offered 40,000 products for sale and was launched based upon research showing that Spanish-speaking customers preferred to shop in Spanish even if they were bi-lingual; however, sales were disappointing, and Home Depot found that over half the site's visitors were from countries where the company had no stores or to which they did not ship. Rightly, they shut the site down before further resources were wasted.

During the near collapse of the telecommunications market in 2001, overly optimistic forecasts of the growth in demand for bandwidth saw revenues at the specialty glass maker, Corning, shrink from $7 billion to $3 billion in a matter of months—a catastrophic decline by any measure. Corning had profited nicely from the demand for its high-tech fibers, but how many companies can absorb a 57 percent decline in revenues? In the aftermath of the collapse, senior management resolved not to get caught out again so they developed a new set of management processes to aid in the detection and management of future downturns. Their approach combined a series of early warning mechanisms designed to provide management with time to prepare for a downturn with a series of tactics to manage through the downturn. The recession of 2008 put its plans to the test. While Corning was not immune to the effects—it laid off 13 percent of its staff—the company's management team felt far better equipped to cope with the rapid decline in prospects. By combining research that looked not just at the health of the company's customers but also at its customers' customers to detect early signs of market stress with contingency plans that modeled tactics the company could employ under a variety of dire scenarios, managers were able to act with confidence and speed to mitigate the effects of the global recession—a very different story than 2001 when nearly 50 percent of the company's employees had to be fired.

The development of early warning systems combined with disaster recovery plans offers a potent tool for managers to deal with the unexpected but increasingly frequent events that send shock waves through the global economy. The use of such systems is increasing across many different fields from hurricane warning and evacuation planning systems developed in the wake of Hurricanes Katrina and Rita in 2005 to the World Health Organization's pandemic alert system that was used to manage the H1N1 influenza outbreak in 2009.

Planning for success first involves the recognition of possible failure. Ensuring that can't-miss projects are not given open-ended budgets is one step in smart management. Microsoft has created a rapid development web research laboratory called Live Labs, which adopts a progressive approach to funding its projects. Initial funding is no guarantee of further funding. Projects must continually demonstrate their relevance and potential in order to secure ongoing funding similar to the venture capital model. This constant harvesting of sub-par investments serves both to motivate project sponsors to continually deliver value but also avoids pouring money and resources into programs that no longer make sense. American Express uses a similar process of regularly reviewing projects for continued relevance. A project may be on track by all the usual measures (time, budget, quality), but if the original rationale for approving the investment no longer holds true, it should be killed.

New Coke—A Lesson in Management Excellence—Honestly

The battle for supremacy in the cola wars has been going on for decades as Coca-Cola and PepsiCo have slugged it out for every point of market share. This has been a heavyweight fight that makes the "Rumble in the Jungle" seem like a little local skirmish. By 1985, Coca-Cola, while still the overall market leader, had seen its market share decline for fifteen straight years. Pepsi had taken the lead in supermarket sales in the 1970s and was closing the gap in overall sales. If Pepsi could persuade one large customer, such as McDonald's, to switch to its products, it would take the top spot.

Pepsi's success came on the back of an aggressive marketing program that positioned Pepsi as the more youthful and cooler product for "The Pepsi Generation." Integral to the marketing campaign was

The Pepsi Challenge, a blind taste test that consistently demonstrated that customers preferred the taste of Pepsi to that of Coke. Obviously, Coca-Cola had a problem, but CEO Robert Goizueta had a solution— a new formula for Coke. A series of taste tests in twenty markets showed the new formula soundly beating Pepsi with the 99-year-old original Coke in last place. The potential market share gains from the new formula were estimated to be worth $760 million in additional sales. The data was convincing so the decision was made—New Coke would launch on April 23, 1985, replacing the iconic original.

As news of the launch leaked, Pepsi responded by taking out full-page newspaper advertisements with the mocking headline, "The Other Guy Just Blinked."

Coke pressed on, but a backlash was building. Just weeks after the launch, the company had received 400,000 negative letters; call volume on Coke's customer service hotline rose from 400 a day to 1,500 a day, and one angry customer formed a group called Old Cola Drinkers of America to campaign for the return of the original formula. In the face of mounting pressure and lackluster sales, the company announced on July 10 that the original formula would be brought back—only 79 days after New Coke's launch. Coke admitted it was wrong. One of America's most successful companies led by one of its most admired CEOs had the courage to admit that one of the biggest bets in consumer marketing history had spectacularly failed.

But Was It Really a Failure?

Success in business is all about taking risks, and that by definition implies that you will sometimes fail. My own take is that the story of New Coke is an excellent case study of fast and effective management decision making. Rather than arrogantly pursuing a failing strategy, Coke's managers took the decision to reverse course and admit failure. How much more damage would have been done if management had stubbornly pursued a failing strategy? Even Pepsi's then CEO, Roger Enrico, acknowledged that Coke's reaction showed the company's acceptance of risk taking and failure. No executives were fired after the debacle, sending a powerful message about Coke's willingness to embrace risk-taking and accept failure.

The aftermath of the New Coke saga is interesting to note. By the end of 1985, Coke was again outselling Pepsi, a position it has maintained ever since. Ironically, even after Classic Coke was brought back, New Coke continued to win blind taste tests against both Pepsi and Classic Coke. Ten years on, Coke had the self-confidence to hold an anniversary celebration of the launch of New Coke at which Chairman and Chief Executive, Robert Goizuetta commented, "We set out to change the dynamics of sugar colas in the United States, and we did exactly that—albeit not in the way we had planned." He went on to say that the story of New Coke was a prime example of "taking intelligent risks." Revisionist history? Maybe, but there are lessons for us all in the decisive and honest way Coke handled its failure.

In a similar move, former Boeing executive Alan Mulally, on taking the job of CEO at Ford, was incredulous that the company had ditched the Taurus brand name after it had graced the best-selling car in the world for more than a decade. Ford had replaced it with the ever-so-sexy moniker "Five Hundred." Mulally demanded that the brand name be reinstated, and the new Taurus was launched in 2009.

IBM—From Survival to Leadership

Lou Gerstner is widely credited with saving IBM. He took over as Chairman and CEO on April Fools Day in 1993. At the time the jury was still out on whether IBM would survive despite its storied history. In his first year in charge the company recorded an $8 billion loss. As an outsider, he was not steeped in IBM's culture—this can be both an advantage and a disadvantage. Gerstner was a former McKinsey management consultant who joined IBM from the tobacco company R.J. Reynolds. As an outsider, he was able to dispassionately review IBM's business. For example, he quickly killed off IBM's ill-fated PC operating system, OS/2, which had never threatened Microsoft's dominance despite being a technically superior product (OS/2 was Betamax to Microsoft's VHS). IBM's engineers, with years vested in creating the product, could not countenance such a decision, yet the market had spoken—OS/2 was a failure and a drain on resources.

With such commonsense decision making, Gerstner revived IBM. By the time he retired in 2002, the company was back on track reporting profits of $7.7 billion—but that was only Act One. New CEO Sam Palmisano wanted to build on Gerstner's legacy, but he also recognized that for IBM to regain its market leadership position, more work was needed. Between 1995 and 2004 IBM had successfully grown its revenues from $70 billion to more than $96 billion but saw its gross profit margins shrink by 5 percent as some of its businesses became commoditized. Given its business portfolio at the time, the company was forced to seek ever-greater expense reductions in order to grow earnings—not a sustainable long-term strategy. The solution was to reposition the company. Palmisano shed lower margin businesses such as personal computers and hard disk drives while adding higher margin consulting and software businesses such as PriceWatehouseCoopers and Cognos. The results were clear. While revenues in 2007 were only marginally higher than in 2004, net income increased by more than 38 percent from $7.5 billion to $10.4 billion, and gross profit margins increased from 36.9 to 44.1 percent. Despite the global economic crisis, 2008 proved to be even better: Revenues grew to $103.6 billion and net income rose to $12.3 billion. Again the sale of the PC business, an industry that IBM helped create, was gut wrenching. After all, the story of the "skunk works" development of the IBM PC has entered business mythology—but selling it was the right decision, much like Gerstner killing OS/2 fifteen years earlier.

Now IBM touts its abilities far beyond the sale of computers and software—it is helping the cities of Stockholm and Singapore fight traffic congestion, developing systems to reduce waste in the electricity grid, and investing heavily in its bold Smarter Planet initiative, which was launched in late 2008.

Mythbuster Wisdom
In 1982, IBM, Commodore, Apple and Radio Shack had a 75 percent share of the PC market. Today, only Apple is still in the PC business.

The ability to anticipate failure and take decisive action is one of the defining attributes of a great organization. Not only are precious resources conserved but the learning experience equips a generation of managers with invaluable experience about effective risk taking. Would Chrysler have had the courage to launch the minivan without having suffered its first near-death experience in the 1980s? Did Sony's Betamax experience help instill the importance of marrying cool technology with excellent marketing that gave the world the Sony Walkman? How much did Apple learn from the relative failure of the Newton that could be applied to the success of the iPod?

So What?

- Pay as much attention to identifying the critical failure factors of any strategy, plan, project, or initiative as in identifying the critical success factors.
- Define the criteria for abandonment for every product, project, or investment. Ask the question: Under what circumstances does it make sense to just give up?
- The right to succeed is earned; it is not an entitlement.
- Be careful: Rock star CEOs may be more lucky than good.
- By all means benchmark the leaders. Just remember you may learn more from the companies that are trying to usurp them or those that fell by the wayside.
- Punishing failure (as opposed to stupidity) encourages mediocrity.
- The biggest sin is not to fail but to fail to learn (Benjamin Franklin).
- Spend less time avoiding mistakes and more time identifying mistakes in order to minimize their impact.
- Sensing failure but not acting is a bigger sin than being taken by surprise.

Notes

1. Clayton M. Christensen, *The Innovator's Dilemma* (Cambridge, MA: Harvard Business School Press, 1997).

2. H.G. Parsa, "New Restaurants Openings 1996–1999," Ohio State University.

3. U.S. Small Business Administration. www.sba.gov, (accessed March 2009).

4. "Securing the Value of Business Process Change," report produced by Logica Management Consulting and The Economist Intelligence Unit, 2008.

5. National Federation of Independent Businesses, nfib.com, March 2009.

6. Stevens, G.A. and Burley, J., "3,000 Raw Ideas = 1 Commercial Success!," *Research Technology Management,* May/June 1997.

7. Jena McGregor, William C. Symonds, Dean Foust, Diane Brady and Moira Herbst, "How Failure Breeds Success," *BusinessWeek,* July 10, 2006.

8. Keith Naughton and Allan Sloan, "Comin' Through," *Newsweek,* March 12, 2007.

9. Ann Zimmerman, "Home Depot Spanish Site Is Shuttered," *Wall Street Journal,* May 2, 2009.

Chapter 5

Budgeting—A Modern Vision of Hell (Well, Purgatory at Least)

I s budgeting your most loved and valued management process? Well, it should be. Given all the time, effort, and focus that is placed on creating budgets, it is not just sad that it is probably the most loathed of all management processes—it is a crime. For all the effort put into their creation, the value derived is pitiful.

Creating budgets takes too long, is mired in useless detail, and the results are frequently made immediately obsolete by real-world events. Yet the budget defines an organization. It sets resource allocations; is used as a basis for measuring performance; has a big influence on compensation; defines an individual's stature and power—the bigger your budget, the more important you are; is the basis for management reporting; and governs almost all management behavior and decision making. Like most companies, Cruciant's budget process is fatally flawed.

Fiction: Henry Pritchett's Office—Early September 2007

Henry Pritchett, Cruciant's CFO, is meeting with his Director of Budgets, Kevin Na. "Kevin, we need to get the budget template out in the next week or so. How do we stand?"

Kevin looks a little concerned, "My team has been working hard to update last year's model for all the organizational changes that have taken place, but it's been a little challenging to do that while also trying to integrate the spreadsheets that Marketing and Product Development have developed for all their new initiatives for next year. Unfortunately, they created their own template, so Martha has spent much of the last month working to convert each spreadsheet into the same format as our budget. There is quite a bit left to do, but I think we can probably target next Wednesday to be done."

Henry replies, "Let's shoot for Monday. You know how long the field takes to fill the damn thing out. Now in the budget instructions I want you to emphasize that for this cycle we are going to pay particular attention to spending on outside labor. We need to take the total spending on outside labor and break it into two parts, one for consulting and the other for temporary staffing. I want visibility to spending every month. OK?"

"We can do that." Kevin responds. "I'm not sure how good the data will be; people in the field are terrible at getting the expenses right beyond the first quarter."

"Well, this year it is going to be different," states Henry. "I am having White Hot work on some planning accuracy metrics to put on everyone's scorecard. That should focus their attention. People have to understand that the budget is the most valuable management tool we have, and this year we are going to be holding everyone accountable." Kevin nods his head and thinks better of debating the point further.

As he makes his way back to his office, he thinks back to a discussion he had with a group of sales managers earlier in the day. They were bitching and moaning about the budget process. It took too long, and the level of detail that corporate asked for was, in their opinion, absurd. One of them went so far as to say that after the first quarter they basically just made the numbers up with the objective of trying to get away with the lowest possible sales target; another said that he didn't really bother much with the budget, as long as the overall number looked about right he let his finance support person fill the rest out. A third manager commented that the whole process was a waste of time because corporate never liked the numbers and always ended up inflating the sales target and reducing the expense target. He wondered why corporate didn't just fill in the template themselves and send it out. Sometimes Kevin himself questioned the value of the whole process. He and his team spent almost five months working on the process. They sent out over a hundred spreadsheet templates that they then consolidated and analyzed before each management review. In a good year this would happen two or three times—in a bad year, six or seven times. This looked like it would be a bad year and that was before the usual last-minute panic.

Typically there was always a budget crisis towards the end of the year and either Steve or Henry would make some arbitrary adjustments such as reducing all expense budgets by 5 percent. Typically, this happened on Christmas Eve, so Kevin and his team spent much of the holiday period scrambling to redo all the budgets and send them out to each manager before the New Year began. January was then consumed with questions about the new numbers, and typically some managers would cut side deals with Steve or Henry to rescind some of the cuts. If he were lucky, Kevin would have a finalized budget by early February so he could report comparisons to the actual results for January. By early March the big variances would start to emerge, and managers began to ignore all the detail in the budget and simply focus on how to hit their overall budget number, which dictated their bonus.

Upon arriving back at his office, he called Martha in. They discussed Henry's request and agreed that this meant a Saturday in the office for the team. Neither of them was happy about the prospect, but at least they were used to it.

Creating the budget at Cruciant was a painful process, but then, it always had been. Managers dreaded the approach of budget season. For four or five months there would be a seemingly endless round of meetings between managers from different departments seeking to construct a very detailed but usually inaccurate view of next year's business. Kevin and Martha would prepare long emails providing instructions as to how to fill in complex spreadsheets detailing everything from exactly when new employees would be hired to how many new computers would be needed by each department. After a few weeks of PNIB (putting numbers in boxes), the spreadsheets would be emailed back to Martha who would spend many long hours consolidating them into a series of different views—by department, by country, and by business unit. Of course, there would be numerous errors that had to be chased down and corrected. Once a solid baseline had been created, the process of cost allocations could begin. Allocating costs was the most complicated part of the whole process. The objective had once been laudable. Senior management wanted each manager to have visibility to the total cost of his or her operations, not just the direct costs like salaries, travel, and training, but also their share of the cost of facilities, IT, human resources, and the other functions that make up Cruciant. Effectively, each manager would be able to see a total profit and loss account for his or her area of responsibility. The allocation rules had been developed a few years ago by a team of outside consultants who had spent many weeks analyzing different aspects of Cruciant's business to identify what they called drivers, that could be used for dividing up the budgets of central departments and support functions among the different business units. Some of the allocation rules were straightforward; floor space was used to allocate facilities cost; headcount was used to allocate human resources costs. Others were less obvious—IT costs were allocated using a formula that included headcount, number of computers used, and amount of disk storage space consumed. No one really understood the formulas because they had been tweaked many times over the years.

After all the cost allocations have been completed, the management team reviewed the updated budgets. At this point, Henry usually found that the growth in expenses was unacceptable so he would issue instructions that all departments were to reduce their expense budgets by a few percentage points. Of course, no similar reductions were ordered to the revenue targets.

The Target Negotiation: VP of Sales Sarah Coombs' Office— October 2007

James, a regional sales director, walks into Sarah's office to discuss next year's plan. Sarah opens the discussion by congratulating him on last year's results and comments that it provides a sound foundation for further growth next year. James sort of agrees, but cautions Sarah on the one-time factors that helped his team succeed. The discussion progresses from there and Sarah goes on to outline the bonus program for next year. As in prior years, the majority of James' bonus will be driven by his team's performance relative to the agreed plan with a small percentage determined by the performance of the company as a whole. Sarah asks James to take a couple of weeks and work up some preliminary numbers for their next meeting. She reinforces the overall company targets of sales growth in the range of 8 to 10 percent and earnings growth in the 13–15 percent range. (The targets that the management team communicates are always higher than what is actually needed. After all, you need some cushion as one or more teams are bound to miss.)

Over the next two weeks, James works hard with his team developing a range of different scenarios. Toward the end of the process he gathers his managers together and they discuss the probability that they can meet each scenario. Two are immediately discounted, one because it will never fly with Sarah and the other because it exceeds the target range Sarah provided and would need execution to be flawless. After all why commit to a target higher than needed? The debate centers on three scenarios, the first of which delivers performance at the top of the target range. The consensus is that this is the one the team feels is most likely based upon their current understanding. The second scenario is what the team calls the "slam-dunk" case. If they can get this one agreed, they can start spending next year's bonus immediately. The third scenario sits between the two and offers what James' describes as the "Well if you insist, we think we can get there if we pull out all the stops" scenario. All agree that this is the most likely end result of the target negotiation. The decision is unanimous: James will present the slam-dunk case to Sarah, and if she pushes back, he will reluctantly propose the middle case, all the time stressing that this is really a stretch.

At his next meeting with Sarah, James presents his plan. Sarah appears a little disappointed. While the numbers are within the target range, she had expected more based upon "the momentum we have going into next year." James cautiously agrees and promises to "review the numbers with a sharp pencil" and get back to her in a couple of days. He reconvenes his team and triumphantly reports that while

Sarah was not happy with the "slam dunk case," he is sure she will buy the middle option. A few days later, he presents this to Sarah, who readily agrees. Come year-end the team easily beat the target. Sarah is delighted and James and his team all receive nice bonuses. Cruciant's sales growth for the year reaches 8 percent, but the markets are disappointed because all their major competitors had logged double-digit gains. James is unconcerned; his new Porsche should be delivered at the end of the month.

The Budget Review: Henry's Office—October 2007

Steve Borden storms into Henry's office. Henry quickly ends his call and looks up. Before he can say a word, Steve lets rip, "Henry, what is this? This budget is worse than useless. They have sandbagged every damn line item. How can Rich ask for 15 percent more for Marketing than we agreed back on Nevis? What's he thinking? As for Phil, doesn't he know that capital is going to be tight next year with all the new product development we have to do, and he wants to spend $3 million on a new purchasing system? This is a joke; I should just fire the lot of them!"

Henry sits and waits for Steve for run out of steam, then calmly says, "Steve, this is just the first roll-up. Remember last year? We were $120 million off in the first run-through. I am putting together a memo to each of the team reminding everyone about the commitments we made on Nevis. Then Tom from White Hat is putting together an all-day session next week where each functional leader is going to lay out his or her needs from each other function so we can synchronize all the intercompany stuff that is double-counted in there at the moment. I expect that by the end of the month we will be a lot closer to the numbers you need."

Somewhat mollified, Steve comments, "We'd better be. Keep me posted on the outcome of next week's meeting. Now, what about the forecast for the fourth quarter of this year?"

Henry sighs, "Well, that is proving a little challenging. We have just closed the books for September and I saw the actuals yesterday. There's some real noise in the receivables that I am trying to get to the bottom of, but overall we should be within $2 million of the last forecast.

Earnings look like being a penny ahead of the guidance we gave The Street. I was able to write back a couple of reserves that got us back on track. There is clearly some softness in Europe that we need to get to the bottom of, but as you know, they report on a one-month lag so we won't know the true picture for a few weeks yet. Maybe you can shake them up a bit when you are over there next week?"

"I certainly will. I told the Board we would be two cents ahead but I can live with one, provided Q4 comes in on the mark." Henry responds, "December is always tricky, but Sarah tells me the pipeline looks solid so we just need to close the deals."

Steve gets up to leave, commenting: "I am having daily reviews with Sarah to make sure we stay on top of all the deals."

Early November 2007

Wanda Coombes is the manager of Cruciant's direct sales organization. She supervises a team of fifty direct sales associates who handle orders from small and medium size customers who are not assigned a full-time Cruciant account representative. She has been working for the last few weeks on her team's budget for 2008, and it has been challenging. Her sales target has been increased by 12 percent, but she is being told to keep her overall expenses flat. If she wants to hire additional representatives to help meet the higher sales target, she must make cuts elsewhere in her budget. Her team have hacked the training and travel budgets to the bone but still need to find a few thousand more if they are going to be able to hire a couple of extra sales representatives. Today Wanda is meeting with the IT and HR functions. These meetings occur across Cruciant and are intended to allow the buyers and suppliers of central services to agree on service levels for the following year. Both IT and HR supply services to Wanda's team such as computers, printers, recruitment, and training. Wanda opens the meeting by stating her goals: "I need to get our allocations from your two groups down by $75,000 next year if I am going to be able to meet the sales targets we have been given. What can we do to achieve that?"

The IT representative explains that there is very little fat left to cut in IT's budget, so any reductions must come at the expense of service levels. The HR representative makes much the same comments. Wanda is not happy, but she is prepared. "I know we are all under pressure to drive profitability up next year, but it seems that my team is paying rather a lot for some of the services you folks provide. For example, each of the PCs I have costs me close to $6,500 a year; I can go down to Best Buy and get one for $600, so why is it so expensive? And as for HR, you charge me $20,000 to recruit each new employee. That is 40 percent of the starting salary; even the best outside recruiters only charge 33 percent." The IT representative tries to explain that the charge is for a lot more than the PC; it includes all the software, the costs of the help desk, maintenance, networking, and security. HR mumbles something about the need to spread the total cost over all the business units, but Wanda brushes away their concerns. She demands cuts in the allocations and sends them on their way. A few days later she receives her updated allocations and is pleased to see the changes she requested have been made.

A few days later, Candice, the CIO, is reviewing her budget with Henry. She explains that the only way she has been able to manage to the target she was given has been to suspend a number of important upgrades to the core order entry and billing systems. She also explains that her team has been under great pressure to reduce the cost allocations back to the revenue-producing units. She is pleased to report that her team has been able to pass on a 15 percent reduction in these costs by reviewing the cost allocation algorithms used in the chargeback system. This has resulted in a 7 percent increase in central IT costs, but she has been able to keep the overall effect flat by delaying the PC upgrade until next year. Henry asks a couple of questions about the accounting but signs off on Candice's revised budget.

Five Months Later . . .

Wanda is reviewing her team's performance with Sarah, the VP of Sales. She explains that while her team was ahead of plan during the first three months of the year, there have been major operational issues in the last two months. She explains, "In early April the order entry system started to crash as we pushed through more volume. IT told me they had delayed the planned software upgrade due to budget issues, but the effect has been terrible. We have had to tell customers that we cannot process their orders or give them a definite delivery date and ask them if we can call them back later with the details. Not surprisingly, they were not pleased. When we do call back, most of them have ordered from one of our competitors. IT managed to get some sort of workaround that got us back up after a couple of weeks, but it's not ideal. We have also seen a much higher number of PC problems. Apparently, the workaround maxed out the memory and so PCs kept crashing. I ended up having to go out and buy ten new machines out of my budget. To pay for them I have had to delay two new hires until the fourth quarter. The overall effect is that we are 8 percent behind plan."

The Boardroom—Mid-November 2007

Henry opens the meeting: "Well, the third iteration of the budget is a lot better, but we still have a $15 million gap. Steve has to present to the Board next week, so we have decided to take a few decisions to close the gap. Rich, you need to cut $2 million from your advertising budget in both Q3 and Q4. Sarah, you should delay the hiring of the Indian sales team from Q1 to Q3 and cut the travel budget by 10 percent. Phil, we just cannot do the purchasing system next year so that's out, and Candice (the CIO), you will have to go back to MegaOffshore and get them to take their monthly fees down by $250K."

Sarah asks, "What about the sales targets?" Henry looks at her and replies, "Steve will not reduce the sales targets. Both he and I are convinced there's plenty of fat left in the operating budgets, so these decisions simply cut that out. Martha will send out revised budgets to each of you later this afternoon. Each of you needs to make sure your team updates their individual budgets to reflect these changes and submit by the end of the week. Thanks, we are done here."

Facts: Not Just a Waste of Time

The average organization spends anywhere from three to six months creating the annual budget. As Jeffrey Pfeffer commented in his book *What Were They Thinking* (Harvard Business School Press, 2007), "All this expenditure of time and effort seldom produces anything of much use to anyone." Thousands of hours of staff time are consumed as staff members diligently take last year's budget or the current year's actual results and tweak them to try and create an acceptable budget for the coming year. Budgets are almost always annual with the time horizon inextricably linked to the accounting calendar. Detail is the name of the game with numerous line items, often more than 200, having to be laid out by month for the coming fiscal year. After the budget is completed, hopefully but not always, before the fiscal year actually starts, it has a useful life that can be measured in weeks. For many companies the budget ceases to be relevant in less time than it took to create as market events make the original assumptions obsolete. For companies operating on a calendar-year basis, the fourth quarter of 2008 was like a scene from the film *Groundhog Day:* As financial markets entered freefall, credit dried up, and consumer spending slumped, companies were forced to rebudget 2009 on an almost weekly basis. Many late nights were spent poring over sales and expenses estimates that had virtually no chance of becoming reality.

By the end of the first quarter of 2009 most companies had already abandoned the original budget and were explaining to investors why they were sharply lowering expectations for the rest of the year. In February 2009, Deutsche Telecom forecast that its earnings for 2009 would be 19.5 billion Euros; eight weeks later it issued a profit warning and revised its forecast to a range of 18.7 to 19.1 billion Euros.[1] The company blamed the change on the global economic slowdown, heightened competition, and weak currencies in certain markets. There are a number of lessons to be learned from this episode. First, the original forecast was expressed as a single point estimate (very precise but not very accurate). Second, the updated forecast was expressed as a range (less precise but much more realistic). Third, the excuses the company gave for lowering expectations—economic slowdown, competition, and currencies—were not exactly new news in the eight weeks since the previous forecast. Finally, Deutsche Telecom's shares fell 7.2 percent on the news, roughly three times the percentage change in the forecast. It is likely that Deutsche Telecom's finance team spent considerable time reworking detailed budgets to reflect the changes in the forecast.

Mythbuster Wisdom
With budgeting the devil is not in the details, it is the detail.

Detail Does Not Equal Accuracy

The only guarantee with respect to budgeting is that the more detailed the budget is, the more wrong it will be. We do not have a crystal ball, therefore detail does not equal accuracy, yet we keep

---

Yes—That Was Me

One of the most widely quoted statistics about the budget process is that the average company devotes 25,000 days of effort per billion dollars in revenue to the budget process. It has been quoted in many articles and at least four books, and I was the guy who calculated it! Back in 1998 I was working for The Hackett Group, a company I helped to found back in 1991, and we were analyzing the results of our latest benchmark study on the planning process. One day, I was sitting in my office surrounded by data. On my computer was one of those enormous spreadsheets that dominated my life at that time. I was looking for inspiration—how do you make statistics about the budget process exciting or, at the very least, interesting? As I dug through the numbers, I started to map out the total amount of effort that different functions dedicated to the budget process. After trying a few different ways of representing the data, the 25,000-day statistic seemed to work. I went back and recalculated it a few times just to make sure it was correct and, as they say, the rest is history.

Is it still valid? After all, that was more than ten years ago. Probably not, although I suspect any improvement is far less than many would hope. While technology has helped companies streamline many business processes, the budget does not seem to be one of them. If anything, budgets have become even more detailed (and hence even more inaccurate) in the last few years. My own estimate is that the 25,000-day number is probably more like 20,000 today. However, as labor costs have risen, that still equates to a cost of almost $10 million per billion dollars of revenue to create something that in most cases is irrelevant, if not downright dangerous. Let's see if that statistic goes viral as well.

asking for more detail in the vain hope that we will suddenly become more prescient about the future. It is not only a waste of time; it is downright dangerous. The precision and detail in budgets gives the illusion of accuracy.

Imagine calling up the weather service and asking for a detailed forecast of what the weather will be like next November 5th. How much confidence would you place in the results? About the only item I would trust would be a comment that it will probably (but not necessarily) be colder than it was in June, always assuming, of course, that you live in the Northern Hemisphere. Yet we ask departmental managers to develop detailed estimates of spending on numerous items for every month of the budget year. When looking that far into the future, the budget developer faces much the same predicament as the weather forecaster: The only reliable source of data upon which to base a prediction is what happened in previous years. Well, that worked very well during 2008, didn't it?

Creating excessively detailed budgets has become a disease. Managers take pride in the complexity of their budgets and consider the phrase, "That's a very detailed budget" to be a compliment. In reality, it is more a commentary on the incredible waste of valuable staff time, but that is not the real problem.

Most budgets describe in detail how an organization is going to deliver a planned level of performance. For example, a budget sets out details as to how an organization will deliver precisely $117.35 million in profit next year. What are the odds that the actual results will meet that target? Not very high, and even if the bottom line does come close, it is usually the result of the positive and negative variances in the plan neatly canceling each other out. Yet numerous business decisions will be taken based upon the numbers in the budget, and that can be very dangerous.

Suppose your budget defines that sales next year are expected to be €241.36 million. How might that information be used to make decisions? Assume you are the manufacturing manager for the company. It would be logical to use the budget number as the basis for ensuring you have sufficient manufacturing capacity to produce at least €241.36 million worth of product. But what happens if next year's sales fall short? If sales only total €211 million or 87 percent of budget, you will be sitting with excess capacity that you have paid for but that you did not use.

Consider how your decision making might have changed if the budget had taken greater account of the likely variability in next year's performance—in other words, had given a more realistic view of the uncertainty about future sales. Suppose that instead of setting the budget at a very precise €241.36 million, it had been set as a range of sales expectations between €210 and €250 million? As manufacturing manager, you could look at the budget and conclude that there is a fairly high degree of confidence that sales will be at least €210 million. Given that information, you may choose to develop a more flexible manufacturing plan that establishes internal capacity at, say €215 million, at the lower end of the range thereby minimizing the risk of being left with unused capacity. Then, in order to support potentially higher levels of sales, you decide to enter into supply contracts with third parties to provide for sales in excess of €215 million. You may pay a slightly higher price for such arrangements, but you only pay if you need the product, thereby building cost flexibility into your plans that offer a broader range of successful outcomes. I know this is overly simplistic, but it does illustrate how setting rational confidence levels and ranges around future plans and budgets can lead to more intelligent decision making. Of course, your predictive ability varies by the type of item you are trying to budget. If you entered into a long-term lease for office space, you will have a much higher level of confidence in the accuracy of the budget line item for rent, hence you can be much more precise in estimating your spending on rent. An intelligently built budget will communicate not just the magnitude of the item being budgeted but also the confidence level in the estimate. One way to do this is by expressing the budget as a range as described earlier. In general terms, the broader the range, the lower the confidence level or predictive ability.

A second approach is to set the budget number but also communicate the confidence level around that number. For example, you may set the budget for rent at $150,000 with a confidence level of 99 percent because of the existence of a long-term lease; conversely, you may set the budget for heating at $35,000 with a confidence level of 50 percent because you have not entered into a fixed price contract for gas and electricity but have chosen to ride the market price, which can be very volatile. Using the budget as a vehicle for communicating the level of certainty (or uncertainty) in a particular item is an incredibly important step if budgets are to be relevant in today's turbulent world.

Why Do We Plan the Wrong Stuff?

Excessive detail is not the only problem. Most budgets provide great detail about things that have little or no relevance to the important things an organization must do in order to be successful.

When leaders talk about what will make their organization great, they talk about things like innovation, customer focus, and talent, yet try finding the line items in the budget that explain how much the organization is investing in these supposedly critical capabilities. There will be lots of lovely detail telling you the expected cost of office supplies, rent, and travel, but you will have a tough time finding the amount that is being invested in retaining the organization's best customers or attracting talented employees.

The only logical explanation for this state of affairs is that the things that are in the budget are what are really important and those other things are not really important—they are just CEO blather. After all, you surely don't think that the finance team would structure the budget to omit things that were important, do you? After all, they've been doing it the same way for more than half a century.

Unfortunately, we persist in planning and reporting our businesses the way accountants view them rather than the way we manage them. We need to start budgeting (and planning and reporting) the way managers think, not the way accountants count.

Over the last two decades, there have been some attempts to increase the relevance of the content of plans, budgets, and reports, but all too often they have simply repeated the sins of excessive detail and complexity that characterize so much of traditional accounting. An obvious example is the use of activity-based costing or ABC. ABC was introduced in the 1980s and attempted to provide a clearer representation of the true costs of business activities by adopting more rational rules for allocating different costs to products, processes, or other elements of a business. The intention was laudable, but most implementations have been lamentable—strangled by detail and complexity and

> **Mythbuster Wisdom: Twenty Reasons to Hate Budgeting**
> 1. Time consuming.
> 2. Too much detail.
> 3. Always sandbagged.
> 4. Bogged down by allocations.
> 5. Rewards the best "games" players.
> 6. Tied to the calendar not the business.
> 7. Run by the accountants.
> 8. Solely focused on the financials.
> 9. No sense of materiality.
> 10. Ignores risk.
> 11. Weak ownership.
> 12. Poor accountability.
> 13. Focused on the wrong stuff.
> 14. More a negotiation than a plan.
> 15. Bears little relation to the business strategy.
> 16. Give a false sense of accuracy.
> 17. Too internally focused.
> 18. Largely obsolete the day it is created.
> 19. Difficult to update.
> 20. Created using thousands of spreadsheets.

creating yet another bureaucratic accounting process. There seems to be something in the DNA of accountants that while the stated goals are transparency and simplicity, the results are usually opaque and complex.

In the United States the statutory body charged with setting accounting standards is the Financial Accounting Standards Board or FASB. FASB, or FAS-B to those in the know, states that its mission

"is to establish and improve standards of financial accounting and reporting for the guidance and education of the public, including issuers, auditors, and users of financial information."

So next time you pick up a company's annual report, you know whom to thank for the clarity with which the information is presented. Those sections describing intangible assets, minority interest in equity of consolidated affiliates, and deferred income taxes (I wish I could defer some income tax) all add to the clear and concise picture of corporate health.

But FASB is not done. It goes further by stating that in order to fulfill its mission it must act to "improve the usefulness of financial reporting by focusing on the primary characteristics of relevance and reliability and on the qualities of comparability and consistency and keep standards current to reflect changes in methods of doing business and changes in the economic environment."

Again, it's interesting to compare the results with the objectives. Are public financial reports characterized by relevance and reliability and do they accurately reflect the methods of doing business in the twenty-first century?

Don't get me wrong. FASB has an almost impossible job when one considers the diversity of economic activity that has to be distilled down into a manageable set of financial statements—but the lack of clarity and transparency has been blamed as one of the causes of every financial crisis of the last fifty years.

Mythbuster Wisdom: The Myth of the Balanced Budget
The U.S. government has a whole department called the Office of Management and Budget (OMB). The OMB is the largest cabinet level department with 500 staff and has its very own budget (almost $80 million in 2007). Of course, the U.S. government has talked a lot about balancing its budget, but apart from one year during the Clinton administration, you have to go back to Eisenhower in 1957 to find a truly balanced budget. The economic stimulus spending of 2009 ensures it will be many more years before the words balanced, budget and government can be used together.

Sadly, external reporting is not the real problem. I am not advocating we throw away the entire regulatory reporting infrastructure that has been painstakingly built up over decades. Well, actually I am, but it is not the subject of this book. No, the real problem is that the information that management typically uses to run the business is the same as that used for external reporting, hence the focus on rent and depreciation at the expense of customer acquisition and employee retention. We use an external accounting view of organizations as the vehicle for making internal decisions, and it makes no sense. Don't believe me? Well, go to your accounting department and ask someone to give you a copy of the "chart of accounts," which defines how data is aggregated for accounting purposes across your company. Do you understand it? That's my point. We have to develop a view of our business that is relevant to the people in our business if faster, more confident decision making is to result.

Are You on the Road to Hell?

Does your budget process help your organization optimally allocate resources and rapidly adjust tactics to changing market conditions, or is it a tortuous exercise that develops vast amounts of detail that bears little relevance to what will actually happen? Answer yes if you agree or no if you disagree with each of the following statements to find out your destiny. Does management nirvana await you, where earnings always grow and retirement comes whenever you choose? Or is your destiny the fiery pit of variance analysis and excuse management?

1. Budget targets are not clearly understood or communicated at the beginning of the process.
2. Creating the budget takes more than three months.
3. There are at least three iterations of the budget.
4. Senior management regularly initiates arbitrary last-minute adjustments or cuts.
5. Budgets are developed using the same account structure that is in the general ledger.
6. Considerable time is spent arguing over the basis for allocating costs to different business units or departments.

7. Incentive compensation is directly tied to making the budget.
8. The budget serves as a vehicle for managers to negotiate perform-ance targets rather than develop a rational resource allocation plan.
9. All time periods are budgeted in the same level of detail.
10. Last year's budget or the current year's actual results are the only useful input managers have when starting the budget process.
11. The spreadsheet is the tool of choice for developing budgets.
12. Very few non-financial items are included in the budget.
13. Once completed, the budget is sacrosanct; no changes are allowed regardless of what happens in the outside world.
14. Analysis of budget variances rarely isolates the root cause.
15. Most business managers view the budget as solely a financial proc-ess over which they have little control or ownership.
How did you do?

Number of Yes Answers	Explanation
0	You are truly blessed (or a good liar).
1 to 5	While maybe not loved, budgets are valued.
6 to 10	Your pain is real.
11 or more	The flames are lapping at your ankles.

Learn to Love the Budget

It usually starts in early September with an email from the Director of Budgets heralding the beginning of budget season. You can hear the collective groan from the management ranks at the memories of budget seasons past. The next few months will be consumed by a mind-numbing death march to complete next year's operating budget. The result will be a very detailed financial plan that has about as much chance of becoming reality as a politician's election promises. As man-agement legend Jack Welch commented in his 2005 book *Winning*, ". . . the budgeting process at most companies has to be the most ineffective process in management."[2]

Most managers view the budget process as a painful distraction from their real jobs. How sad is that? Organizations spend thousands of hours building, consolidating, and arguing over budgets, only for most managers to see them as irrelevant once the exercise is completed. The typical reaction when the budget is finally put to bed is to breathe a sigh of relief and comment: "Thank God that's over with for another year. Now I can get back to my real job."

Jack Welch summed it up nicely (see sidebar): Most budgets are disconnected from reality. The irony is that the fix is not that complicated. Five simple steps can transform the budget from a bureaucratic and political mess into a valuable tool for translating strategy into action and results.

1. Budget the way you run the business, not the way you account for it.
2. Decouple budgets from the incentive compensation process.
3. Match the level of detail with your predictive ability.
4. Update budgets regularly so they reflect the latest and greatest insights about your business and the markets in which you operate.
5. Use the budget as a decision-making tool, not as a negotiation process.

Jack Welch on Budgeting[3]

Is budgeting necessary?

"Some form of financial planning is obviously necessary: Companies have to keep track of the numbers."

On budgeting today:

"The budgeting process as it currently stands at most companies does exactly what you'd never want. It hides growth opportunities. It promotes bad behavior—especially when market conditions change midstream and people still try to 'make the number.'"

The problem:

"Most budgeting is disconnected from reality."

Fixed budgets paralyze organizations and motivate behaviors that are the exact opposite of those needed for effective management. The language of the budget is not the language of a high-performing organization. Popular phrases such as "It's not in the budget" or "We have a 'use it or lose it' mentality" or "Talk to her, she has a bigger budget than me" or "Make sure to put that in next year's budget" or "Once approved, we can't change the budget" reflect an organization that has lost the plot.

Budgets are a huge impediment to agile decision making. Opportunities or threats emerge that were not envisioned in the budget and can paralyze decision making. Managers fret that the money or resources to exploit the opportunity or mitigate the risk are not in their budget—so they do nothing. For decades, a manager's response to uncertainty about the future has been to ask for more detail about things that cannot be accurately predicted. Far more valuable is to focus precious time and effort on understanding how a range of different future scenarios will impact the organization. What are the upside opportunities and downside risks? How will changes in markets impact future performance? What leading indicators will provide an advance warning and buy time to adjust plans to a change in future expectations? These are the questions that increase confidence and hence decision-making speed.

Unfortunately, agility, speed, and decisiveness are not adjectives often applied to the budget process; however, done right, budgeting has the potential to be a dynamic process of evaluating opportunities and threats and discussing different options for optimally allocating resources to drive exceptional performance, but a lot needs to change. It may not become loved, but it can certainly become valued.

So What?

- If it takes more than 30 days to build the budget, it is taking too long.
- Budget the way you manage the business, not just the way you account for it.
- You should be able to look at a budget and identify all the major elements of the business and the strategies and tactics that the business plans to execute.
- Budgets should describe how the business will change under different market scenarios so managers can rapidly adapt to changing circumstances.

- Incentives should never be tied to making budget.
- Detail does not equal accuracy when building plans, budgets, or forecasts.
- Budget in less detail the further out you look—match your desire for detail to your predictive ability.
- Always seek to update the budget to reflect the latest and greatest intelligence about what is happening now; resist the temptation to stick with assumptions that may have made sense when the budget was created months ago but which have been made obsolete by events.
- Sacrifice detail for scenarios; the more "what-ifs" you can evaluate, the better prepared you will be to respond to events.
- Remember the real value of planning and budgeting "is not about getting it right. . . but in making better decisions about the future." Peter Schwartz, *The Art of the Long View* (Doubleday, 1991).
- Expect the unexpected; the extraordinary is now ordinary. Is your budget ready?

Notes

1. "Deutsche Telecom Retreats from Earnings Claim," *Financial Times,* April 27, 2009.
2. Jack Welch and Suzy Welch, *Winning* (New York: Harper Business 2005), p. 189.
3. Jack and Suzy Welch, "Stop the B.S. Budgets," *Business Week,* June 26, 2006.

Chapter 6

The Futility
of Forecasting

Imagine you were sitting at your desk in October 2007 trying to develop a forecast for the price of oil (or house prices, unemployment, or car sales for that matter) as an input to your 2008 planning process. After a few iterations, you draw a graph that shows a steep climb from $45 a barrel to $147 by the middle of 2008, followed by an even steeper decline to $35 by the end of the year and then a steady rise back up to $70 six months later. What do you think the reaction of your boss would have been if you had presented him with such a scenario as a basis for building your 2008 plan? Incredulity might be too polite a term. Yes, today fact is stranger than fiction.

We need to acknowledge that material unexpected events are normal and are likely to remain so. As I write these words, the news is dominated by coverage of the outbreak of swine flu in Mexico, which in a matter of days has spread to the UK, Finland, New Zealand, and

Korea among others. Just recently the Mexican economy effectively shut down for a whole week, and this comes a few weeks after numerous cargo ships were highjacked off the coast of Somalia, Bangkok airport was closed for five days, and terrorist attacks rocked Mumbai. Years ago such events would have simply been interesting items on the evening news; now they are material events that impact organizations across the globe as markets, supply chains, and economies become ever more tightly connected. When are we going to realize that planning and managing through these type of events is part of our job? Of course, Cruciant is not exempt from the effects of unprecedented events but is confident in its ability to manage any challenge.

Fiction: September 2007

Alan Parkes, Cruciant's VP of Strategic Planning, is sitting at his desk trying to develop the baseline assumptions that the company will use in building its plan for 2008. He has a stack of economic forecasts from all the major banks in front of him and is checking the latest economic data online for each of Cruciant's key markets. While all the forecasts are different, there seems to be a common theme. Global economic growth will slow a little during 2008 but remain strong in China and most other emerging markets; inflation will pick up slightly; and the dollar will stay roughly at $1.20 to the Euro and $1.50 to the pound. Oil prices will rise from the current $45 a barrel to an average of about $60 for the year. As he sketches out his draft assumptions, Sinitta Khan knocks on his door. Sinitta is one of Alan's brightest analysts, undergraduate from Cambridge and a PhD from Stanford. He looks up and waves her in, "What can I do for you?" Alan asks.

Sinitta sits down. "I've been looking at quite an interesting forecast for next year that if it is even half right could have an enormous impact on our business. I thought we should at least look at it." She pushes the document across Alan's desk. He says, "Okay—what makes it so interesting?'"

"Well," Sinitta starts, "they make a pretty compelling argument that the slowdown in U.S. housing market is going to continue and actually get much worse next year, with prices continuing to fall and foreclosures increasing. At the same time, China's voracious consumption of raw materials is going to drive commodity prices sky high. They talk about oil at $110 a barrel. The combination of these forces will tip the U.S. economy into a mild recession that will ripple across the world causing a slowing of global GDP growth to 1–2 percent."

"Interesting," says Alan, "none of the other forecasts I have looked at comes close to any scenario like that. I'll take a look at the report tonight. Let's talk again in the morning."

The Next Day . . .

Alan walks over to Sinitta's cube, "Very interesting, that report. They make a good case for 2008 being really bleak, but I just don't see it happening. Interest rates are low and credit is plentiful so homeowners can easily refinance; the Dow is at an all-time high; and there's no way I can see oil getting to $100, never mind $110. The consensus of all the other forecasters is for a modest reduction in the rate of growth, so I think we should go with that view."

Sinitta nods and says, "You're probably right. After all, there hasn't been a downturn that matches their prediction since the 1930s. Imagine what would happen if Americans had to pay $4 a gallon for gas and unemployment doubled to 10 percent?" Alan chuckles and heads back to his office.

The Boardroom—March 2008

Steve opens the discussion: "So what about this Bear Stearns thing? How is it going to impact the economy and our business?"

Henry responds: "Well, the housing market is slowing down, but it does not seem to be impacting consumer spending yet. Most forecasters see Bear Stearns as an isolated case that will have some short-term effects due to the shock, but in a few weeks it should blow over. We can expect some initial hesitancy as customers digest the news, but overall it should not alter our forecast for the year. I have spoken to all our bankers and they are quite relaxed at present. They say it was a well-known fact that Bear was taking on excessive risk and gambling with its balance sheet."

June 2008

Brent crude oil hits $147 a barrel. Alan sits at his desk looking at the analysis Sinitta had prepared just nine months earlier and shakes his head—maybe he should think about a career change, the world is just getting too crazy.

September 16, 2008

Steve is shouting: "What is happening? First, Bear Stearns and now Lehman Brothers. The market is in freefall, our stock is down 17 percent."

"Quite remarkable," comments Henry. "These are exceptional times. I have never seen anything like it before and frankly I have no idea where it is going."

September 23, 2008

Henry reports to Steve: "The Royal Bank of Wales (RBW) has been on the phone. They are pulling back the $50 million credit line. We have drawn down about $14 million and will need to refinance in the next seven days."

Steve: "Why are they doing that? We have not broken any of the loan terms have we?"

"No, we haven't," Henry responds. "It seems that all the banks are shutting down credit. The whole system seems to have frozen. I am hearing rumors that RBW had significant exposure to credit default swaps that they can't unwind, and it looks like the British government may have to inject capital to save them. The real problem is that I am not sure we can refinance at the present time, which means we cannot fund the Asian expansion."

September 24, 2008

Steve issues a press release:

"I feel it is important for me to comment on Cruciant's position in light of the unprecedented dislocations occurring in both the financial markets and the broader economy. We are not immune to the effects of the credit crunch, but I want to reassure all our investors, customers, and business partners that Cruciant is well capitalized, has strong cash flow from operations, and is executing exceptionally well despite the current economic turbulence. However, in light of the darkening picture for credit, we feel it is prudent to slow down our planned Asian expansion and conserve cash. We expect that this will reduce our full-year earnings by three cents a share this year and five cents a share next year. Finally, I want to pay tribute to all our outstanding associates for their dedication and focus during these uncertain times."

October 24, 2008

Sarah marches into Steve's office, "Have you seen the latest pipeline report?" she asks.

"No—what's up?" Steve responds.

"At least $20 million of orders in the United States have been cancelled in the last fourteen days and another $5 million in Europe. Everyone has just stopped spending. No one is prepared to make a commitment." Sarah explains.

"How does that affect our forecast?" asks Steve.

"Oh, you mean the forecast we developed two weeks ago? You can forget about that. We will be lucky if we make 70 percent of that number," Sarah responds. "And I think it is going to get worse. We haven't seen any impact on Asia yet but you know it's coming. I cannot see sales getting much above $400 million this quarter compared to the $550 million in the forecast."

Steve looks shocked and punches Henry's number into this phone. "Henry, can you join Sarah and me in my office?"

Henry walks in, but before he can sit down, Steve asks, "Have you seen the latest pipeline numbers?"

"Yes, I have, and it doesn't look good. If the trend continues, we will miss the top line forecast by miles, and without some significant cost cutting there will be no earnings at all," Henry responds.

"Why didn't we anticipate any of this when we were building the plan?" Steve asks.

"I don't think anyone anticipated it," Henry responds, "We based the budget on a consensus economic forecast that projected a very modest slowdown. All our detailed budgets used that scenario and the numbers looked pretty good."

"Why don't we build budgets and forecasts around multiple scenarios so we are better able to respond to situations like this?" asks Sarah.

Henry sighs and says, "That would useful, but it takes us almost six months to build the detailed budgets and about a month to create a forecast under just one scenario. I am not sure there would be much appetite for repeating the process two or three times."

Sarah and Steve nod, although Steve is thinking that perhaps all the time spent creating the enormous amount of detail in Cruciant's budgets and forecasts may be better used understanding how the business will perform under different future scenarios. He makes a mental note to address it with Henry before next year's budget process gets started.

Facts: Forecasts—The Only Certainty Is That They Will Be Wrong

An April 2009 survey by Duke University and *CFO* Magazine reported that the "ability to forecast results" was the number one concern of CFOs, ranking ahead of working capital management, maintaining employee morale, and balance sheet weakness.[1] The same week the survey was published, thirty U.S. companies announced a reduction in forecasted earnings for 2009 including Boeing, DuPont, Eaton, Goodyear, and NCR. Forecasting has become one of the most challenging activities in the new world of business, and it is clear that the traditional approaches and processes no longer work. Frankly, it is embarrassing how often organizations get their forecasts wrong. Between 2000 and 2008, Sony missed its initial performance targets seven times in eight years. During the 2001 recession, the miss on the bottom line was by a factor of ten. Yet investors and analysts hang on every word as management deliver their forecasts for future performance, and despite much evidence to the contrary actually place some faith in these wild guesses.

Just a Little Turbulence

In March 2008, German airline Lufthansa confidently predicted increased revenues and operating profits for 2008 with further growth in 2009. CFO Stephan Gemkow commented that there hadn't been any "significant repercussions of the U.S. financial crisis"[2] on the airline's sales. At the time, the airline touted its relative protection from rising fuel costs through an aggressive hedging program. By year end, things were not quite so rosy, even though Lufthansa was one of the top performing airlines for the year. While revenues grew 10 percent, operating profits declined by 13 percent, and the company did not hesitate to cite record fuel prices, despite its earlier confidence, as a driver of the poor results. At least Chief Executive Wolfgang Mayrhuber acknowledged that the situation would not improve in 2009 and also introduced a dose of rationality to his forecasts by stating that, "it's not possible to forecast the duration or extent of the current economic crisis."[3]

Of course, occasionally someone does get a forecast right. In July 2004 economist Gary Shilling predicted that, "When house prices return to earth—and price declines of 20 percent in the U.S. and 30 percent elsewhere are warranted—the effects on the global economy will be serious. Subprime loans are probably the greatest financial problem facing the nation in the years ahead."[4] He nailed it. Unfortunately, most forecasters do not; even very smart people screw up. In 1932, Thomas Edison commented that, "The radio craze . . . will die out in time." In 1942, IBM Chairman Thomas Watson went out on limb and forecast that, "I think there is a world market for about five computers." In 1981, Bill Gates predicted that, "640K (of memory) ought to be enough for anybody."

Were they stupid? No, they were simply basing their forecasts on what they knew at the time. After all, if past forecasts were to be believed the human race should have starved itself to death, run out of oil, and be happily living on Mars by now. If we get so many forecasts wrong, why are we so obsessed with them?

The advent of 24-hour news and business channels has led to an explosion of forecasters offering their opinion on all manner of subjects. Tune into CNBC any morning and a crowd of talking heads will be delivering projections on everything from whether the market has hit rock bottom to where Warren Buffett, a CNBC favorite, will invest next. I think these so-called experts called the market bottom at least weekly from late September 2008 through March 2009, during which time the Dow Jones Industrial Index fell from 11,400 to 6,500—a decline of 42.5 percent. Credibility and forecasting are words not often mentioned in the same sentence, yet organizations spend countless hours building forecasts of the future. Even great companies struggle in volatile times. In October 2008, as the financial crisis was accelerating, Peter Oppenheimer, the CFO of Apple, commented, "Visibility is low and forecasting is challenging."[5] This was executive code for: We have absolutely no idea what is going to happen tomorrow. So why bother?

Used correctly, forecasting can be one of the most valuable decision support tools available to managers; unfortunately, too many forecasters believe the objective is to get it right, and that is unrealistic. Peter Schwartz in his 1991 book *The Art of the Long View* correctly identified the real purpose: "The end result . . . is not an accurate picture of tomorrow, but better decisions about the future."[6]

For most organizations, forecasting is an exercise in futility. Detailed financial projections are religiously created and then manipulated across the organization to provide some sense of what the future may look like. Senior management reviews the results, challenges the assumptions, and puts its own stamp on proceedings before the results of the exercise are used to adjust tactics and communicate to investors. For all the good it does, management might just as well get out the Ouija board and crystal ball and place a phone call to Mystic Meg. Why is forecasting such a mess? Aside from the most obvious reason, that forecasting the future is by definition an exercise in being wrong or lucky, there is a stunning lack of common sense applied to the forecasting process. For example:

- All time periods are forecasted to the same level of detail; this fails to recognize that the further out you look the less certainty you have.

- Most forecasts provide a single point estimate of the future. Even if ranges are used, they are unrealistically narrow.
- Forecasts focus on financial items with little attention paid to the drivers of financial results.
- Forecasts are often an attempt to rework the numbers to try and get back to the original plan or budget, particularly if bonuses are on the line.
- Forecasts are developed by the finance department, with little or no input from other functions.
- The people developing the forecast try to deliver the result they think management expects rather than the most likely view of future performance based upon the best available information.
- The start point for developing the forecast is past performance, which limits the consideration of new trends or unexpected events. It is a "business as usual" projection.
- Forecasts take too long too develop. This has two effects: Managers are loath to forecast too often as its hard work and takes a long time, and the forecast is based on data that is already out of date.

Mythbuster Wisdom: Mistaking Forecasts for Facts

One of the biggest illusions occurs when forecasts are represented as facts. Politicians, CEOs, and the media are very good at confidently inferring that a forecast, which may be based upon highly suspect data, is actually an incontrovertible fact. Perhaps the most famous was the *Chicago Tribune*'s headline proclaiming that Dewey had defeated Truman in the 1948 Presidential election. My local paper, the *Akron Beacon Journal* along with many other media outlets, repeated this feat on the morning of November 8, 2000, in proclaiming Al Gore's victory. The forecast-as-fact syndrome is rife in corporate public relations as business leaders confidently proclaim success for every new strategy or product while minimizing the negative impact of any uncertainties in the marketplace. Microsoft confidently predicted that its Zune digital music player, launched in late-2006, would secure a 15–20 percent market share in the iPod-dominated market—by February 2009 the Zune had captured an 8 percent share. Renowned venture capitalist John Doerr forecast in 2001 that Segway Inc. would be the fastest company to reach a billion dollars in sales on the back of its Segway Personal Transporter as the company invested in factories capable of producing 480,000 units a year. It still had not happened by 2009 and cumulative sales had barely topped 50,000. Smart people confidently espousing their predictions for the future are downright dangerous.

The Extraordinary Is Now Ordinary

In March 2008 one commentator noted that "Extraordinary events now seem commonplace, and ordinary events get almost no notice."[7]

For years, leaders of all types, political, business, or military, have resorted to the same excuses to explain away failure. The circumstances are extraordinary, unprecedented, or extremely challenging. Be it the Federal Emergency Management Authority's (FEMA) botched response to Hurricane Katrina or the demise of Bear Stearns, the explanations focused on the extraordinary nature of the circumstances. We need to realize that the extraordinary is ordinary and that our fundamental assumptions about stability, predictability, and certainty are fatally flawed. When CEOs and CFOs talk about their company's performance on quarterly earnings calls, any blip in performance is explained away as being the result of extraordinary circumstances, unprecedented times, and unexpected events. It has become so commonplace that it has lost all credibility. How many quarters in a row of explaining performance problems as being the result of extraordinary events does it take before it becomes ordinary?

General Motors went from acknowledging "challenging North America market conditions"[8] in November 2007 to "challenging conditions in important markets"[9] in February 2008 before having to resort to the "rapidly deteriorating market conditions" and "unprecedented economic and credit market turmoil"[10] by November 2008.

Was it really that hard to believe in November 2007 that the collapsing North American market was going to have some global impact? After all, America still accounted for 25 percent of global GDP and 22 percent of global car sales during the economically disastrous 2008.

UK retailer Marks & Spencer, long seen as a bellwether of UK consumer spending, went from expressing some doubts in September 2007, "the short term economic outlook remains uncertain"[11] to acknowledging the rapid pace of the economic decline in September 2008, "the economic environment has changed dramatically and we are now facing the most difficult retail conditions since the early 90s"[12] before projecting a lengthy downturn in January 2009, "we expect challenging economic conditions to continue for at least the next 12 months."[13]

Even very successful companies are sometimes forced to resort to economic hyperbole. Southwest Airlines racked up its 36th consecutive profitable year (yes, this is an airline we are talking about) in 2008. A year earlier it described the market in relatively mild tones acknowledging, "softer demand for air travel."[14] By January 2009 this had morphed into "unprecedented economic challenges."[15]

The extraordinary is now ordinary; just look back at some of the events that have had broad economic impact over the last few years: the Russian economic crisis and the collapse of Long-Term Capital Management in 1998; the launch of the Euro and collapse of WorldCom in 1999; the dot.com bubble bursts in 2000; 9/11 and the Bush tax cuts in 2001; Sarbanes-Oxley in 2002; the SARS outbreak and the start of the Iraq War in 2003; the Asian tsunami in 2004; hurricanes Katrina and Rita in 2005; option backdating, and the Dow topping 12,000 in 2006; the U.S. housing market starts to implode in 2007; and then in 2008 all hell broke loose! In previous eras, the impact of many of these events would have been largely localized, but increasing global interdependency through trade and technology magnifies both the scale and speed with which the effects are felt around the world.

Not only do managers have to navigate these macro events, but they must also deal with a series of potential events that, while not global in impact, can have a dramatic effect on a single company. In 1984 the explosion at Union Carbide's plant in Bhopal, India, is estimated to have killed more than 15,000 people. Union Carbide paid out damages of $470 million (you could argue they got off lightly as this equated to an average of $2,200 for each victim's family). On a much smaller scale in terms of the direct monetary cost was Mattel's $2.3 million settlement in 2009 of charges that it knowingly imported and sold toys with excessive levels of lead paint. Such events occur regularly and while the direct costs may be manageable the impact upon an organization's reputation and the trust of its customers can have damaging long-term effects. Union Carbide was unable to survive as an independent company, becoming a subsidiary of Dow Chemical in 1991, while Mattel struggled to convince parents that its toys were safe with CEO Bob Eckert assuring customers in adverts that "nothing is more important than the safety of our children."

The need to manage the extraordinary is now ordinary. An organizations ability to effectively manage the potential damage from such events and even profit from them distinguishes the great from the merely lucky. Johnson & Johnson was widely praised for its adept handling of the Tylenol poisoning episode that killed seven people in Chicago in 1982. Southwest Airlines was lauded for its clear and unequivocal handling of both customers and employees in the aftermath of 9/11. Both companies actually enhanced their reputations through successfully managing the extraordinary. Conversely, Arthur Andersen's complicity in the Enron debacle killed the company, costing 85,000 people their jobs; Exxon Mobil ended up paying out over $3.5 billion for clean-up and legal settlements that did little to enhance its reputation following the Exxon Valdez incident. Wal-Mart has managed to be on both sides. It has been accused of discrimination against female workers, use of undocumented aliens to clean its stores, and provoking local communities to change zoning regulations to prevent Wal-Mart moving in, and received praise for its ability to serve local markets in Mississippi and Louisiana after hurricanes Katrina and Rita, putting the government response to shame.

Accepting the extraordinary as ordinary is the first step. Many organizations simply refuse to contemplate the impact of seismic shifts, particularly negative ones, on their markets or businesses. Such events are dismissed as being so unlikely that even considering them would be a distraction to management. Yet recent history confirms that such events are all too common. Nassim Taleb describes in his book *The*

Black Swan—which focuses on the nature of rare, high impact and hard to predict events—that "the highly improbable consequential event"[16] is a fact of life that dictates performance. Taleb describes the experience of supposedly knowledgeable people encountering events on a daily basis that "lay completely outside their forecast" during the conflict in his Lebanese homeland. As he explained, "Much of what took place would have been deemed crazy with respect to the past." Much the same could be said for the demise of Lehman Brothers in September 2008 and the global economic crisis that followed.

Failure to contemplate such events or develop contingency plans increases the risk of poorly thought-through or emotional responses that can result in irreparable damage. The cumulative effect of panic reactions can have devastating effects. In his 1936 book, *The General Theory of Employment Interest and Money,* economist John Maynard Keynes described the ability of a human's "animal spirits" to influence economic activity. Keynes' described animal spirits as "a spontaneous urge to action rather than inaction, and not as the outcome of a weighted average of quantitative benefits multiplied by quantitative probabilities."[17] In other words, economic activity can be driven by waves of spontaneous optimism or pessimism that may not necessarily be supported by rational analysis. I think that pretty much explains nearly every boom or bust from railway mania in the UK in the 1840s (272 new railway companies were founded in 1846 alone) through the dot.com and housing bubbles of the early twenty-first century. Writing in November 2008, Robert Shiller, a professor at Yale University, noted, "The erosion of animal spirits feeds on itself. Immense market volatility serves only to reinforce people's sense that something is really wrong. A volatility feedback loop begins: the more volatility, the more people feel they must pay attention to the market, and hence the more erratic their trades."[18] All too often forecasters get caught up in a torrent of exuberance or pessimism that leads organizations to plan for a very narrow range of future scenarios. The illusion of forecast capability that induces us to believe that some people or institutions have unique insights into the future can be very damaging. Look at the table produced by the Federal Reserve in November 2007 (Exhibit 6.1). The ranges contained for the key economic metrics represent the consensus view of the seventeen members of the Federal Reserve Open Markets

Fed's Crystal Ball				
New forecasts center on these ranges; fourth quarter to fourth quarter				
	2007	2008	2009	2010
GDP growth	2.4–2.5%	1.8–2.5%	2.3–2.7%	2.5–2.6%
Jobless rate*	4.7–4.8%	4.8–4.9%	4.8–4.9%	4.7–4.9%
PCE inflation[†]	2.9–3.0%	1.8–2.1%	1.7–2.0%	1.6–1.9%
PCE inflation excl. food and energy[†]	1.8–1.9%	1.7–1.9%	1.7–1.9%	1.6–1.9%

Note: Assumes appropriate monetary policy
*Fourth-quarter average   †Price index for personal-consumption expenditures
Source: Federal Reserve

Exhibit 6.1   Fed's Crystal Ball

Committee (FOMC) with the three most optimistic and pessimistic forecasts removed. The Fed's forecast is one of the most closely watched global economic indicators; it drives numerous decisions and is used as the basis for budgets and forecasts at many organizations. Yet accuracy is not a hallmark. For 2008 the results were way off the mark. GDP growth came it at 1.1 percent compared to the forecast of 1.8 to 2.5 percent, unemployment had reached 7.1 percent (forecast 4.8 to 4.9 percent), and inflation was at 0.8 percent (forecast 1.8 to 2.1 percent). The only metric that the Fed came close to getting right was inflation after stripping out food and energy costs where the actual result was 1.8 percent, slap bang in the middle of the range the Fed forecasted. No doubt the forecast misses would be explained away by the extraordinary, exceptional, and unprecedented events of 2008—but that is exactly my point. It is the regularity with which such events are used as excuses for getting forecasts wrong that makes it even more important that we adapt our forecast processes to the new reality.

I mentioned earlier that the FOMC forecasts discounted the three most optimistic and the three most pessimistic forecasts. I find this very interesting; surely those would be the most interesting forecasts to look at? Rather than following the herd, the most useful insights might be found in the rationale of those that have a contrarian view. At the very least we would be in a position to positively discount the more outlandish forecasts rather than be caught by surprise when the unexpected actually happens.

Mythbuster Wisdom: Sandbagging the Forecast—A 100-Year-Old Problem (At Least)

Sandbagging or padding the forecast is a global pandemic. Managers seek to deliver the forecast that their bosses expect, or they use the forecast to manage expectations so they can appear to be stars when actual results exceed the forecast. Rarely does the forecast represent a rational projection of what is most likely to happen in the future. Forecasting is a game where executives demand ever better numbers and their subordinates seek to ratchet down expectations. Regardless of the motivation, the end result is not a sound basis upon which to make resource allocation decisions. This is not a new phenomenon as I found out a few years ago.

During the mid-1990s I was consulting with General Motors long before it became Government Motors, and no, I don't think I am responsible for their subsequent problems—well, not all of them, anyway. While conducting some research for a project, I came across an old memorandum in the company's archives that brought home to me that issues of forecast credibility have been around for a long time. The memo was dated May 10, 1927, and was from General Motors President Alfred P. Sloan to his general managers. Among other comments, Sloan chastised his direct reports about the quality of the forecast process: "My attention has been called to a tendency which seems to be developing which I do not think is based upon either sound accounting or correct reasoning. I am referring to the fact that some Divisions, after the forecasts have been developed by their Accounting Department . . . arbitrarily alter certain of the figures in order to have a cushion . . . It is always pleasing, of course, to do better than one stated and it is well to be conservative in all these things but the arbitrary changing of figures simply to show a better result than forecast . . . is not sound accounting and serves to invalidate and discredit the whole process that has contributed so much to our welfare."[19]

> Sloan is rightly credited with developing many of the management practices that served American business for more than half a century, yet even he had to wrestle with subordinates padding their forecasts in order to make themselves look better.

If you were to judge our inability to forecast anything with confidence by the words of our business leaders, you would conclude that it is not really their fault. Politicians and business leaders have an arsenal of excuses. In January 2009, Vikram Pandit, the embattled CEO of Citigroup, commented that:

> "For much of the year, we have been dealing with dysfunctional markets, which deteriorated even further after Labor Day, but we kept working through all the dysfunctionalities."[20]

Of course, investing billions in securities that ended up being worthless had nothing to do with the firm's problems.

It is ironic that in uncertain times, when fast, confident decision making is most important, traditional planning and forecasting techniques work least effectively. Instead of increasing confidence, they simply raise doubts in the minds of managers. The old adage about past performance being no indicator of the future has never been truer. History provided few pointers to the near collapse of the global banking industry, the dramatic decline in automotive sales and property values, or the incredible volatility in oil and other commodity prices during 2007–2008.

Gary Kelly, Chief Executive of Southwest Airlines, offered the following advice, "What I have to guard against is using previous downturns as a road map and assuming that: Oh, yeah, things are going to happen just like they did in, say, 1991."[21] He is dead right. We ought to know better, but we continually rely on historical data as an accurate predictor of the future. Be it the weather, the economy, the prospects of our favorite sports team, we look backward in order to look forward. History is a useful crutch; there is comfort in the certainty of what has already happened that reduces our trepidation about what has yet to happen. The left side of our brain knows it makes no sense, but we continue to extrapolate the future based upon the past.

Unfortunately, we rarely make the distinction between things we can forecast and things about which we can only guess. Wild guesses emanating from austere and supposedly credible institutions have the aura of credibility. Economic forecasts issued by both the UK and Australian governments as part of their 2009 budgets were widely ridiculed as being overoptimistic and politically self-serving for the ruling party. Similarly, the construction of San Francisco's Bay Area Rapid Transit (BART) system was justified to voters based upon a 1962 forecast of almost 260,000 daily passengers by 1975; the actual results showed that passenger numbers were only 51 percent of the forecast and that each passenger cost the taxpayer more than the fare paid for the journey. Would voters have approved the $1.6 billion in initial costs (over $18 billion in 2008 dollars) if the forecast had been accurate? At the other end of spectrum, the construction of London's orbital motorway, the M25, illustrates the problems of underestimation. The original projections of traffic volumes for the motorway developed in the 1960s and 1970s woefully underestimated the actual traffic volumes when the full motorway opened in 1986. The M25 was rapidly nicknamed, "The largest car park in Western Europe" and has been under almost constant construction ever since it opened. It is regularly voted Britain's worst road.

Despite these and many other expensive forecast misses, few managers will make investment decisions without some future projection of the likely costs and benefits; therefore we need to develop new approaches to forecasting that explicitly recognize uncertainty and caution decision makers to pay attention to the risks of a forecast being wrong, sometimes materially. How is this accomplished?

Mythbuster Wisdom: The Monte Carlo Myth

For a few years now it has been a very cool to tout one's use of Monte Carlo simulations when discussing forecasting techniques. A casual "Yes, we used to develop a simple extrapolation of past performance to develop our forecast, but we found it so imprecise that we decided to become a little more sophisticated and use Monte Carlo simulations" is sure to impress.

Further embellishment of one's standing is assured if you follow up with, "Monte Carlo allows us to evaluate thousands of different scenarios based upon different sets of assumptions and then tells us how likely different strategies are to be successful. It is a really powerful technique."

While Monte Carlo analysis has advantages over traditional methods and it has been widely used in many industries, it is not a cure-all for the ills of forecasting. One of the most popular applications of Monte Carlo analysis has been for personal financial planning where the technique is used to model the effectiveness of different retirement planning strategies under a vast range of different scenarios. It is a powerful technique, but like all analytical models it is only as good as the assumptions used—and that's the rub. Most users of Monte Carlo simulations discount very low probability events or apply standard bell curve or normal distributions to the range of probabilities. This approach assigns a very small probability to events such as a major stock market decline in a very short time period—say 10 percent or more in a one-month period. By eliminating such "unlikely" events, your finely crafted retirement strategy will be found to be sound in almost all probable scenarios. Unfortunately, the performance of the stock market during the fourth quarter of 2008 and again during the first quarter of 2009 accounted for two scenarios under which almost all such strategies failed, leaving many retirement plans in tatters.

Not One Size Fits All

For decades, everyone developed forecasts according to the same rules. Forecasts were developed through the end of the current financial year: so if your financial year-end was December 31 and you were developing a forecast in April, it would include three months of actual results and a nine-month forecast. By July, there would be six months of actual results and six months of forecast and so on. After many years of building forecasts this way, some companies started to question the logic.

Why are nine months in the future important in April but only three months in October? Had any of the key business cycles such as product development, customer sales, collections, or supply chain shortened, or was the forecast simply being tied to the accounting calendar? The answer was that the accountants did in fact rule the world.

The fix was easy: Simply move to a forecast that always looks out the same distance into the future. The result was the emergence of the rolling forecast, which maintained a consistent time horizon, typically four, five, or six quarters. While the logic of a consistent time horizon is eminently sensible, I could never understand why many organizations that were spectacularly bad at forecasting one, two, or three quarters into the future suddenly thought that by moving to a four-, six-, or eight-quarter rolling forecast they could suddenly develop a better forecast. But this question seemed to pass many by, and the rolling forecast wave took hold. Fortunately, not all organizations charged blindly down this path. A few asked some sensible questions such as:

- How far out can we realistically forecast with any degree of accuracy? Sounds sensible doesn't it, yet I am amazed how many companies forecast everything in the same level of detail for each of the next eighteen months when in reality their predictive ability declines dramatically the further out they look.
- What time horizon do we need for the decisions we are trying to make? Again very sensible. An oil company does not need to forecast the profitability of a new oil well on the same time horizon as the restocking of the chocolate bars in the gas station convenience store.

Asking these commonsense questions results in a much smarter process. For example, Genentech periodically develops a forecast, not in mind-numbing detail, mind you, that looks out 20 years. Why? It's simple really: The patent protection for new drugs is 20 years, and therefore the company needs to understand the likely profitability of a drug before cheaper generic versions flood the market upon expiration of the patent. Conversely, Southwest Airlines updates its revenue forecast on a daily basis but looks out only one month, while it updates its forecast for aircraft maintenance twice a month and looks out six months. Again, Southwest is matching its desire for detail with both its predictive ability and its decision-making cycles. Both companies are linking the time horizon and level of detail to a blend of their decision-making cycle and predicitive ability.

In April 2009, a survey by the National Investor Relations Institute reported that a third of the 600 companies responding had changed their policies about giving forecasts of future financial performance. By far the most common change was to eliminate or limit the guidance given about earnings and revenue. The report commented that, "If you don't know what the future holds and you can't accurately predict it, you don't want to be out there telling somebody something you don't have confidence in."[22] Sound advice, which Toyota might have been well advised to heed after forecasting in December 2007 that it would sell 9.95 million vehicles in 2008. Actual sales came in at only 7.5 million and the company recorded its first ever loss. Back in 2006, long before the recession started, Eric Schmidt, the CEO of Google, explained why the company declined to provide forecasts, "There is a cost to not providing guidance and I understand that. The reason that we don't is our business is so dynamic we'd have to give very broad ranges and I don't think that would be constructive."

Now apply that logic to your own plans, budgets, and forecasts. Are you happy that your organization bases major investments decisions, allocates resources, and sets compensation levels on the very detailed, but likely very wrong, budgets, plans, and forecasts that exist today?

Are Long-Term Forecasts an Oxymoron?

It would be easy to assume from my comments that forecasting is a waste of time—it is not. The key is to take a forecast for what it is—an uncertain projection of what the future might look like. Even things that on the surface appear to be easy to forecast can be problematic. For example, developing a forecast of the number of 25-year-olds there will be in 2020 or the number of ten-year-old cars on the roads in 2015 appear to be pretty straightforward as the people are already alive and the cars are already on the road. However, imagine it is 1913 and you are developing a forecast of the number 18- to 24-year-old men there would be Britain and France in 1918. This should be a pretty straightforward analysis as all the members of the group are already alive and aged between 13 and 19. Simply factor in historic mortality rates for that age group and you have your answer. Yet how many forecasters would have projected that almost two million young men in that age group would die other than from natural causes in those five years? This may be an extreme example, so here is one from more recent times. Imagine you are a large automotive service and repair company doing business in Germany and it is the third quarter of 2008. You are building your 2009 plan by looking at the number of older vehicles on the roads that potentially need your services in order to estimate the size of the market. The future looks rosy, especially as sales of new cars are slumping, driving up demand for maintenance of older vehicles. Would your forecast have projected that new car sales would increase by more than 25 percent in the first four months of 2009 as nearly a million old cars were traded in to take advantage of the German governments €2,500 tax rebate for trading in old cars?

One technique that many organizations successfully employ to anticipate the impact of material but unexpected events is to integrate elements of scenario planning into their forecasts. Instead of developing a single forecast based upon one set of assumptions, the forecast also includes an assessment of the upside and downside impact on key business measures of material events that could dramatically impact performance. Testing the sensitivity of forecasts against changes in key assumptions accomplishes two things. First, it sensitizes managers to the inherently uncertain nature of any forecast, which should be reflected in the degree of reliance they place on the numbers. Second, simply considering the possible uncertainties that can impact future performance prepares managers to act with increased confidence and decisiveness when variances do occur.

Restoring Credibility

Forecasts should be the business equivalent of the global positioning system (GPS) or satellite navigation system in your car. Your GPS tells you the instant you screw up by making a wrong turn, it lays out a corrective action plan to get you back on track, and it updates the forecast of when you can expect to arrive at your destination based upon your rate of progress and the impact of your screw-up. The more sophisticated systems also give you advanced warning of hazards ahead and offer suggestions as to alternative routes. They also tell you where the nearest Starbucks is so you remain adequately "resourced" for your journey. Effective forecasting is the GPS for your business by providing rapid real-time reporting when actual events deviate from the forecast, suggesting alternative courses of action and provide advance warning of the likely future impact of current events.

Mythbuster Wisdom: And You Thought General Motors Had Problems

Over the years I have found that cars are great tools not just for consuming large parts of my discretionary income but also for providing a metaphor for running a business. Planning a journey is akin to strategic planning—you set goals and then work out a way to achieve them. Larry Bossidy, former Chairman and CEO of Honeywell, went so far as to describe a strategy as, "a roadmap lightly filled in."[23] Once you have set your plan, you make sure you have the right resources—fuel, snacks, air in the tires—and begin your journey. Unfortunately, cars work far better than the average management process. Imagine if your car worked like your business:

- Your route map would describe in mind-numbing detail not just the roads to be taken and the major cities you would pass through but also detail the specific locations and times for every restroom break and refueling stop for the whole journey. *Business budgets contain very precise details about a lot of relatively unimportant items long out into the future, practically guaranteeing that numerous variances will be generated.*
- The car's engine will take about 10 seconds to respond after you apply pressure to the accelerator or brake. *In most businesses the time from decision to action can be measured in days rather than seconds.*
- The GPS system will report your position every 10 minutes regardless of whether you are lost. It will also inform you that you missed your exit exactly 20 seconds after you

have passed it. *All actual versus plan reporting is done on a lagging basis and is driven by the passage of time not the occurrence of events. Major performance issues are rarely anticipated with reporting occurring after the damage is done.*

- The rearview mirror will be a hundred times bigger than the windshield. *Businesses have much more data about things that have already happened than about things that may happen in the future.*

- You will spend more time concentrating on things inside your car (changing the CD; stopping sibling wars in the back seat; munching on your burger; and texting your best friend) than what's going on in the outside world. *Relatively little effort is spent trying to anticipate the actions of others such as customers, competitors, and regulators. Crunching numbers about what is going on inside your business will consume 90 percent of professional staff time. This may be one area where driving and business management are almost identical!*

- The windshield will only refresh your view of the road ahead once every 10 seconds, no matter how fast you are traveling. *Key performance measures are reported on a set calendar (daily, weekly, monthly) with little real-time information to monitor progress as you execute. How confident would you be in driving your car at 60 mph if your view of the road ahead was only updated once every 10 seconds?*

- You would set your course and stubbornly stick to it even if the road ahead were closed, the weather deteriorated to the point where it was dangerous to continue, or you were delayed so much that you had already missed the event you set out to attend. *You will not deviate from your strategy, plan, or budget no matter what the real world is telling you about its prospects and no matter how late and over budget you are.*

- The dashboard will have three times as many dials and gauges on it. You will be able to tell precisely how much life is left in the bulb that comes on when you open the trunk but will have no idea how fast you are traveling. *Your management reports will be able tell you exactly how much you spent on office supplies but give you no insight into how much you are investing in keeping your best customers.*

- The fuel warning light will come on 5 minutes after you run out of gas. *The standard reporting will tell you that a number of your biggest customers cancelled their contracts last quarter; there will have been no early warning given of increased customer dissatisfaction prior to the cancellations.*

If we drove our cars like we manage our business, we would never get out the garage in the morning!

As you design your GPS, there are some simple steps you can take that can rapidly improve the quality and accuracy of your forecasts.

- Recognize that your predictive ability declines the further out you look by expressing forecasts as ranges that reflect your confidence level. The broader the range, the less confidence you have in the numbers and the less reliance managers should place on those numbers for making critical decisions.
- Match the level of detail in the forecast to your predictive ability. Develop less detail the further out you are looking.
- Link forecast time horizons to decision-making cycles. If you only need to make the decision three weeks ahead of time, don't bother developing a 90-day forecast.
- Adjust the time horizon of the forecast. If you can only develop an accurate view for the next 90 days, don't try to develop a six-quarter rolling forecast.
- Avoid simply forecasting the future by just looking at the past. Remember Gary Kelly's advice, "What I have to guard against is using previous downturns as a road map and assuming that, 'Oh, yeah, things are going to happen just like they did in, say, 1991.'"
- Use tools such as scenario forecasting to assess how your business will perform under a range of different views of the future. For example, how will your business look if oil averages $40, $100, or $175 a barrel over the next three years?

- Add additional insight to your forecasts by identifying the real drivers of changes in the forecast. Explaining a change in terms of volume, rate, or mix does not identify the underlying cause. A sales volume variance could be caused by competitors undercutting your prices or by a production problem that caused a decline in inventory levels leading to "stock-outs." The action to be taken is different depending upon the driver.

- Communicate the possible upside and downside to your forecast. For example, you maybe aware of a potentially favorable settlement of a lawsuit but have little insight as to the timing or value of the settlement.

- Let the real-time flow of business drive the forecast by decoupling the forecast from the accounting calendar. Don't wait for the quarter to end and the books to close; forecast when you need to, that is, when the market tells you things have materially changed from your previous view.

- Don't be afraid to change forecast frequency in response to changes in the market. In early 2009, fast-food chain McDonald's instructed managers in its UK operation to look at key data tracking customer buying patterns, competitor traffic, and local employment data every two weeks instead of just once or twice a year in response to the prevailing economic uncertainty.

- Be very cynical of any forecast that purports to offer rich and specific insight into an uncertain future.

Don't Believe All Forecasts

Back in 1987 my wife and I decided to move out of London and capitalize on one of the city's periodic property booms by selling the apartment we had lived in for eighteen months at close to a 50 percent profit (still my only really successful real estate investment!). We bought a small house in the market town of Harpenden about 30 miles north of the city. As a young hotshot in the City (hey—it's my story, so humor me), I researched all the most creative mortgage schemes on offer to secure the best deal. Unfortunately, the "no doc/125% loan" where I could inflate my meager income and secure a truly enormous loan had not yet made its debut, so I decided to go with the current flavor of the month—an endowment mortgage. The premise of the endowment mortgage was very simple. I would borrow £72,000 of the £90,000 purchase price and also take out a 25-year "with profits" life insurance policy that guaranteed a payout of exactly £72,000 if Donna or I were to die but also would provide a long-term investment, which, assuming we both survived until 2012 (back in 1987 that seemed an awfully long way off) would provide a lump sum return on our investment to repay the mortgage principle and, according to the very smooth salesman, almost certainly leave quite a bit of spare cash to fund a middle-aged spending spree. It sounded great. We would make interest-only payments on the mortgage and also pay a £97 ($150) a month premium for the life policy. I well remember Kim, our salesman, sorry client executive, as he ran Donna and I through the possible scenarios for our investment—there was no apparent downside. The policy was certain to yield at least £72,000 and probably much more. After all at the time, May 1987, the market was roaring with the FTSE index already up 17 percent in 4.5 months on its way to a 42 percent gain by early October. We eagerly signed up and almost immediately came October 19, 1987, or Black Monday, when markets around the world crashed spectacularly. I was not worried; with 24.5 years still to go, the outlook was all rosy and Kim, my friendly client executive, called to reassure me all was well. It was the last time I ever heard from him.

Just two years later we moved again and the mortgage was repaid and replaced by a new, even bigger one. In the aftermath of Black Monday, my risk tolerance was ratcheted down so we opted for a traditional repayment mortgage, so we no longer really needed the endowment policy; however, I still had high hopes of buying that boat in 2012 so we kept paying our £97 a month. In 1991, we moved to the United States but by now I had already paid over £5,000 in premiums and early redemption would only net a few hundred pounds so the payments continued. As the nineties bull market roared, I fully expected that my nest egg had more than made up for any ground lost back in the crash of 1987. The first warning sign came just after the millennium. Along with our annual statement came a terse letter advising us that we should make sure we had access to alternative sources for possible repayment of the original mortgage as there was a small possibility that the policy would not yield the expected £72,000 upon maturity. I was a little concerned but as the actual mortgage in question had been repaid about ten years earlier, I paid little attention. Then the news stories started to emerge in the British press of homeowners who had heard the same sales spiel as Donna and I and were now finding that their endowment policies came nowhere close to paying off their outstanding mortgages, never mind funding that round-the-world cruise. By this time I felt a little trapped. If I stopped paying the premiums (I had now "invested" more than £17,000) I would only get a fraction back, so the payments continued. Each year along with my statement came a further warning, worded a little more strongly each time, advising me that there was an increasing likelihood that the policy would not pay out as originally expected. Then, in early 2009, the bombshell hit. With global financial markets retreating to levels not seen in a decade, the insurance company finally gave me some numbers to review. The best-case scenario showed that if returns averaged 8 percent over the next three years (a tall order given the red ink being spilled everywhere), the policy would pay out a grand total of £50,206. By this time the insurance company had clearly read one of my articles since it included a couple of other scenarios for my delectation—both showed payouts of well below £50,000. So after 25 years of investing, I would be lucky to get 70 percent of the minimum I had expected, and if I had still had the original mortgage would have faced a £22,000 shortfall. I wondered where Kim was now. I consoled myself a little by working out that the total of my premium investment would be $29,100, so I would be getting an extra $21,000 back. But over a 25-year timeline that works out at an annual return of just 4 percent. Not quite what I expected when we started out.

I will leave the final words on the futility of forecasting to Peter Drucker, who had this say about the traditional approach to forecasting by commenting that, "Uncertainty—in the economy, society, politics—has become so great as to render futile, if not counterproductive, the kind of planning most companies still practice: forecasting based on probabilities." He wrote these words in 1992. I suspect events of the last few years have proven their validity more than ever.

So What?

- It's not about getting a forecast right—it's about how quickly you identify that it's wrong and then doing something about it.
- Time spent creating a forecast is time spent missing the opportunity to act—forecast frequently and act quickly.
- Focus on how your behavior and performance will change under different views of the future.
- It is the decisions that you make that determine the value of your forecast. Having a great forecast and doing nothing about it is one definition of stupidity.
- Match your desire for detail with your predictive ability.
- Don't be a slave to the accounting calendar; use the forecast to reflect the latest and greatest intelligence about the future to support faster and more confident decision making.
- Just as with your budget, the more detailed your forecast, the more wrong it will be.
- Embrace uncertainty through the use of scenarios, ranges, probabilities, and confidence levels.
- Always ask three questions:
  - What if the forecast is wrong?
  - How will I know?
  - What will I do?

Notes

1. Duke University/*CFO* Magazine Global Business Outlook Survey of 1,268 CFOs, April 2009.
2. Aude Legorce, "Lufthansa Expects Growth in 2008," *Marketwatch*, March 12, 2008.

3. Ibid.

4. A. Gary Shilling, *Insight* newsletter, January 2004.

5. Peter Oppenheimer, CFO Apple Inc., *Wall Street Journal*, October 29, 2008.

6. Peter Schwartz, *The Art of the Long View* (New York: Doubleday, 1991).

7. Rex Nutting, "Ordinary Data Overshadowed by Extraordinary." MarketWatch.com, March 16, 2008.

8. GM Third Quarter Earnings Release, November 7, 2007.

9. GM Fourth Quarter Earnings Release, February 12, 2008.

10. GM Third Quarter Earnings Release, November 7, 2008.

11. Marks and Spencer Group plc Interim Results 2007/08, September 29, 2007.

12. Marks and Spencer Group plc, Half Year Results 2008/09, September 27, 2008.

13. Marks and Spencer Group plc, Interim Management Statement, Q3 2008/09, December 27, 2008 .

14. Southwest Airlines, Fourth Quarter Earnings Release, January 23, 2008.

15. Ibid.

16. Nassim Nicholas Taleb, *The Black Swan* (New York: Random House, 2008).

17. John Maynard Keynes, *The General Theory of Employment Interest and Money*, (published by Macmillan 1936, reprinted in 1964 by First Harvest/Harcourt).

18. Robert Shiller, "Reviving the Animal Spirits." *Business Standard*, Delhi, November 22, 2008.

19. Memo from Alfred P. Sloan, President of General Motors Corporation to General Managers, May 10, 1927.

20. Vikram Pandit, CEO Citigroup, Fourth quarter earnings call, January 15, 2009.

21. Gary Kelly "A View from the Top," *Fortune*, March 16, 2009.

22. David Pitt, "Companies Pull Back on Earnings Guidance," *Business Week*, April 20, 2009.

23. Larry Bossidy and Ram Charan, *Execution* (New York: Crown Business, 2002), p. 185.

Chapter 7

Total Quality, Six Sigma, Process Re-Engineering and Other Management Fads

Sometime during the 1980s, American business got very scared. Suddenly, Japanese companies were stealing market share in America's backyard by delivering higher quality products at lower cost. Panic set in and the country was seized by a wave of process-centric fads that promised to restore U.S. hegemony over its own market. It didn't work, but it did usher in a wave of new management crazes—sorry—tools, that promised to improve efficiency, reduce cost, and enhance quality. Total quality management, statistical process control, kaizen, process re-engineering, and Six Sigma entered the lexicon of business. Today, every organization, including Cruciant, must have an insane focus on quality.

Fiction: Quality Is Job 1—April 2006

Stephanie Ekblom has just been hired as Cruciant's Director of Quality. She is a Master Black Belt, which is a sort of Zen master of quality management. Her mandate, direct from Steve, is to make Cruciant, in his words, "A total quality company. If it was good enough for Jack Welch at GE, it is good enough for me."

Over the next twelve months, Stephanie launches a quality program that trains over 300 Cruciant associates in Six Sigma principles; 270 of them attained Six Sigma "green belt" status and thirty make it all the way to "black belt" in this modern management martial art. In addition, Stephanie hired five other Master Black Belts from organizations such as GE and Motorola, the creator of Six Sigma. As she explains in her elevator speech: "Six Sigma will allow Cruciant to deliver the highest quality at the lowest cost consistent with our mission and vision. It is not just a process; it is a culture of excellence that will pervade everything we do. We fully expect to realize savings in excess of $10 million in the first year alone."

Mythbuster Wisdom: Elevator Speech
Jargon, American—a short, pithy marketing pitch for your project, job, or company that allows you to convey complete understanding and secure total commitment from your audience during a 45-second elevator ride.

During the first two years of Cruciant's quality revolution, numerous teams across the company complete thousands of t-tests, benchmarks, and chi-squared tests; first time yields and defect rates are calculated; root causes are analyzed; and confidence levels defined, so that by the end of the year, Stephanie can deliver a report to the management team that shows that over 75 different Six Sigma projects have been launched and that conservatively the savings realized to date total more than $12 million—20 percent ahead of plan. Steve is ecstatic and does not hesitate to add comments about the phenomenal impact of Six Sigma at Cruciant to his standard investor presentation that he will be presenting at a Goldman Sachs conference the following week.

Henry is less impressed. He sits and listens to Stephanie's presentation but is struggling to see where the $12 million actually shows up in the firm's profit and loss account. He bites his tongue, knowing that Six Sigma is one of Steve's pet projects and that Steve personally brought in Stephanie on the recommendation of a fellow CEO he met at the Allen & Company conference in Sun Valley, Idaho, last year.

April 2008

Stephanie proudly reports that cumulative savings from Six Sigma initiatives now total more than $25 million. Henry cannot keep quiet any longer and asks, "Stephanie, these are outstanding results; however, my team is having a hard time isolating the specific areas where costs have been reduced. Can you help me understand how you came up with your numbers?"

Stephanie is not at all fazed: "Certainly. The total reflects the estimated annual value of savings that result from each individual Six Sigma project. We rigorously measure the activity cost at the start of each project and then use the Six Sigma toolkit to estimate the value of improved quality in each area. The approach is the accepted industry-standard, but I do understand that it can create some confusion with the traditional accounting view of the world. Savings from our quality programs are not restricted to absolute cost reductions. We also estimate areas of cost avoidance, where the improvement in quality reduces future costs—this actually makes up about 75 percent of the total. By making our processes and products more efficient, we are reducing our cost structure for years to come and that has real value."

Henry nods but adds, "I understand, but we need to be careful because Steve is always shouting about the $25 million number, yet our financials actually show that are margins are narrowing and our costs are rising faster than our revenues. That can look suspicious to the outside world."

November 2008

Steve walks into Stephanie's office and closes the door. "We need to talk," he states before going on, "Stephanie, I am sure you understand the devastating impact the credit crunch is having on our business.

The whole Asian strategy has been torpedoed as a result, and next year looks really bleak. As you know, I am one of the strongest advocates of Six Sigma and the value it is delivering to the company, but we all need to look carefully at our spending and make sure every cent is directed at efforts that deliver measurable results in the short term. With that in mind, I have decided that we simply cannot afford to maintain the Six Sigma program at its current level. For next year I need you to reduce the total spend by 50 percent. We have made large investments over the last two years and I am convinced we can get some real value from those investments at a lower cost going forward."

Stephanie looks shocked and responds, "But Steve, you know as well as I do that Six Sigma is a process and culture that needs sustained investment if it is to yield results over the long term. We are only just over two years into it, and cutting investment could be devastating. Are you certain this is the right thing to do?"

Steve: "I am. We really have no choice. We can only invest in things that deliver results in the near term. Once the market recovers, we can ramp back up again. I'm sorry but we all need to share the pain." With that he turns and leaves her office. Stephanie sits there for a few minutes in stunned silence. Later in the afternoon she fires off an email to her former boss at the consulting firm TPC (The Process Czars) to see if they would be open to her return. She ends the note by saying that Cruciant is not serious about quality and she cannot work in such an environment.

Facts: The Scourge of Management Communism

In the world of business, standardization, consistency, uniformity, automation, and systemization have long been viewed as good things. Companies strive to standardize processes and systems, deliver consistent, uniform levels of service, and develop common policies and practices, usually in the name of delivering higher quality at lower costs. Minimize variability and maximize conformity is the mantra. Companies are awash in process maps, standard operating procedures, common data definitions, universal metrics, enterprise-wide systems, routinized processes, and corporate policies. The level of dictatorial conformity reminds me of the Soviet economic model—perhaps not the ideal benchmark.

Communism may have failed as an economic model, but it is alive and well in twenty-first-century organizations. Unfortunately, management communism often serves as a straitjacket to entrepreneurial zeal and initiative. Phrases such as "it's not in the budget," "that's out of policy," "it does not conform to our standards," "you need approval for an exception," "that's outside our prescribed service level," or "that's out of tolerance" serve to ensure conformity, and that's not always a good thing. How often do you hear people complain that excessive rules and policies hamper their freedom, flexibility, and creativity? Standardization may not be such a bad thing in some areas of business, but, at its heart, it destroys the essence of what makes a company, product, or manager great in the first place.

Henry Ford was probably the first management communist. In 1909, eight years before the Russian Revolution brought the communists to power in Russia, Henry announced that from that point on his eponymous car company would build only one model, the Model T. He went on to famously say that, "Any customer can have a car painted any color that he wants so long as it is black."[1]

Ford's argument was based on the fact that salesmen "always want to cater to whims instead of acquiring sufficient knowledge of their product to be able to explain to the customer with the whim that what they have will satisfy his every requirement."[2]

Ford was at least clear in his reasoning: "The selling people could not of course see the advantages that a single model would bring about in production." Ford's model ushered in the era of mass production that has characterized most operating models of the last century. The impact upon management practice has been profound. Organizations built up a system of management practice that was cost and volume based rather than value and customer based. Many of the tools upon which managers rely, such as budgeting, cost accounting, volume planning, transfer pricing, and product costing, reinforce the mantra of management communism. Variability is frowned upon and conformity is rewarded. This makes sense up to a point, but in recent years management communism has spread far beyond where it had some merit and simply serves to constrain creativity by reducing services, products, or processes to a uniform one-size-fits-all level.

This is ironic, since nearly every example of dominant market leadership is predicated upon a unique twist or differentiation that distinguishes one provider from another. Of course, some of these winning models embody "communist" attributes: Both Southwest Airlines and Wal-Mart dominate their respective markets by primarily using a low-cost, standardized model; however, the ultimate objective of both companies is to deliver exceptional value to their customers through a potent combination of quality, price, and service. Other companies have established market-leading positions based upon innovation and customization where standardization is valued, but only up to a point. Apple, Nordstrom, Singapore Airlines, Ritz Carlton, Johnson & Johnson, and BMW's Mini division all illustrate the balance of discipline and diversity.

Innovation and communism rarely work together. When large centrally planned and managed (communist?) companies develop breakthroughs, they have often had to circumvent the homogenous model that drives the majority of their business to successfully bring such innovations to market. When IBM developed the IBM PC, it assembled a small team of twelve people operating almost completely outside IBM's traditional research and development organization and processes. General Motors (GM) launched the Saturn brand in 1990, a little more than five years after a group of 99 GM employees comprising United Auto Workers (UAW) members, GM managers, and personnel from 55 plants across 17 divisions were brought together to create "A New Kind of Car Company." Largely built from the ground up, Saturn developed a distinctive brand and loyal customer following. Not for the first time, GM failed to capitalize on its success, and within a few years Saturn had become just another brand among many. It is ironic that, despite initial success, IBM is no longer in the PC business and Saturn is one of many victims of GM's decline.

Other companies have been able to develop a stream of breakthrough inventions but were then unable to translate them into commercial success. Most notable is Xerox, which through its Palo Alto Research Center (PARC) invented a string of important technological innovations including the computer mouse, the graphical user interface, the WYSIWIG (What You See Is What You Get) text editor, Ethernet, and the laser printer. However, none of these innovations "fit" within Xerox's core business. They were outside the rigid constraints under which the business operated, and the opportunity was lost, only for others including Apple, Microsoft, and Epson to profit.

In recent years, the ability to innovate has become a strategic imperative—how's that for jargon? General Electric devotes a whole section of its website to its focus on innovation, and consultants warn their clients that they must "Innovate or Die." Every company touts its innovative capabilities, but all too often innovation is more of a marketing campaign than a core skill. Marketers love to tell us that every product or service is innovative. So with all this innovation going on there should be some really cool things happening out there, yet real innovation is still relatively rare. Yes, I've got my iPhone and I love the utility of the Post-It Note, but there is a lot more talk than actual innovation going on. Managers need to take a hard look at whether their claims of being innovative are real or illusory. Adding a feature or function to a product is not innovative—it is incremental. It can extend the life of a product relative to its direct competitors, but it provides little protection against true innovation. Blockbuster's abolishing of late fees on video and DVD rentals was not going to slow down the rise of video on demand, just as Kodak's offering to put your film-based photographs on a CD was not going to stop the adoption of digital photography.

Many have recognized the risks of excessive uniformity; however, communism remains embedded in today's management practices—the Cold War is alive and well in the corridors of corporate life. The secret is to balance the benefits in terms of cost, quality, and productivity associated with standardization with the value delivered by innovation, customization, and personalization. Unfortunately, all too often companies see the answer as being marketing. The argument is that if we spend enough to promote our brand, we can convince customers to pay much more for our product than for a comparable but less well-advertised alternative. This can work in the short term, but marketing hype without true value-add is not sustainable in the long term. However, it can be very profitable in the short term as the purveyors of various diets, hula hoops, get-rich-quick schemes, and numerous over-hyped pieces of exercise equipment have found.

Cheap Is Not Always Good

Wal-Mart has grown to become one of the largest companies in the world on the back of a long-term commitment to everyday low prices and it has worked. As Tom Peters said, "Never compete with Wal-Mart on price or China on cost." However, low prices are not always a sure-fire path to success. Sometimes customers won't buy even when prices decline dramatically—as many homeowners found during 2008–2009.

Moving down market has become an accepted tactic for businesses. The Marriott hotel chain added the Courtyard and Fairfield Inn brands. Much of Procter and Gamble's response to the 2008–2009 recession was focused on ensuring that the company positioned products at lower price points as consumers cut their spending and traded down to lower-priced options. This was in direct contrast to the company's strategy during the boom years of adding new and improved features at higher price points.

Implemented correctly, moving down market can be very effective; however, make a mistake and customers may simply substitute your cheaper offering for the higher-priced one they used to buy, a problem experienced by Levi-Strauss and by many companies who sacrificed prestige for shelf space at Wal-Mart. An even more dangerous consequence of a failed move down market is that your customers will take their business to one of your competitors. Back in the mid-1990s, Southwest Airlines was turning the traditional U.S. airline business model upside down by delivering low fares, no-frills service, high reliability, and profits—a pretty unique combination in the airline industry at the time. It was no surprise when other industry players tried to copy the Southwest model.

In late 1993, Continental Airlines, then emerging from its second bankruptcy, sought to replicate the successful model of Southwest Airlines by launching a low-fare, no-frills carrier called Continental Lite, or Cal Lite. First-class seats were ripped out and service was pared back to a minimum. Eighteen months later and with losses totaling $120 million, the airline reversed course. Then-CEO Gordon Bethune commented at the time: "If we had let things go for another six months, we could have lost the farm." Continental Lite was clearly a failure, but what is more interesting is how the company responded.

Continental refocused on its most profitable customers—business travelers and other frequent flyers. The company expanded its Business First service, added new international destinations, and offered incentives to staff for improvements in on-time arrivals, baggage handling, and other competitive benchmarks. The effect was almost instantaneous. Profits increased and customer satisfaction improved dramatically. From a low of $6.50 in January 1995 the company's stock price rose to $47.50 by the end of 1995. In January 1997, *Air Transport World* named Continental the World Airline of the Year for 1996. For the next decade the company consistently ranked as one of the top U.S. airlines while many of its competitors failed to learn the lessons of Continental Lite and paid the price with painful bankruptcies. Most notable being Delta Airlines who chose to ignore Continental's failure and embarked upon a similar strategy with the launch of Song in April 2003. Less than three years later, and six weeks after Delta filed for Chapter 11 bankruptcy protection, the airline announced the closure of Song. Like Continental, Delta's strategy failed to dent the low-cost market leader, Southwest, while at the same time alienating many of its best customers.

Mythbuster Wisdom: Adventures in Corporate Communism

Since 1991, I have achieved the highest level of frequent flyer status on Continental Airlines every year except one. In 1994, Cal-Lite communism drove me into the arms of a competitor. Instead of my usual 80 to 100 Continental flights a year, almost all of which were full fare—that is high profit—tickets, my flight total for Continental in 1994 topped out at 18.

In my almost 20 years as a Continental customer, I have accumulated more than 2.5 million frequent flyer miles and traveled more than 1.5 million actual miles, so I consider myself a very loyal customer. Most of the time the service is great but some things just baffle the heck out of me and make me wonder why companies forget about the basics of service. For example, Continental, like most other airlines, has over the last few years been trying to encourage customers to buy tickets online rather than over the phone. This has worked very well. The airlines used a combination of carrot (bonus frequent flyer miles for buying online) and stick (long wait times and extra fees for human contact) to drive you to their website. But overall some of the logic is questionable. For instance, when calling the Continental Airlines Elite Frequent Flyer Desk, a service supposedly for the company's most valuable customers, you are presented with the normal automated menu. Here is where my confusion begins. If I want to actually spend money with Continental, I have to wait to option 4 to buy a domestic plane ticket, after listening to options to check flight times, find out how many frequent flyer miles I have accumulated, and inquire as to where my lost baggage may be. Even more intriguing is that if I want to buy an International ticket, which is typically both the most expensive and most profitable for the airline, I have to wait until option 6. It appears that the company is doing all it can to delay me, one of their best customers, from spending my money with them.

Besides spending much time on planes I also get to sample the beds at numerous different hotels. Every hotel chain seeks to market itself as friendly, customer focused, and offering a "home away from home." The truth belies the hype every time. You would think with all the advances in check-in technology, the process of actually getting your room key would no longer require standing in line for a reception clerk to process your reservation and swipe your credit card, which they already have on file. After all, I can buy thousands of dollars of merchandise on the Internet without having my card swiped. When I do finally get a key, it is usually a magnetic key card that supposedly enhances my security. Of course, the key frequently fails to work, so I have to traipse back to the reception desk and queue up all over again. But it gets better. After standing in line for what seems like an eternity, I finally reach the front of the line and begin to introduce myself to the receptionist. At that moment I can guarantee that the phone on the reception desk will start to ring. Suddenly I become invisible, and answering the phone within the stipulated two rings becomes the sole focus of the receptionist's attention. I am left standing there while the receptionist offers a critique of fifteen local restaurants in order for someone to make a dining decision, solicitously asks if he or she would like a wake-up call, and inquires as to his or her newspaper preference. After 5 minutes or so, the call ends and I suddenly move back into focus and receive a very insincere apology along the lines of "sorry to keep you waiting, sir." Why are phone calls more important than the customer standing right in front of the person? This is mad, stupid, and ridiculous. It's symptomatic of blanket customer service maxims (or should it be communist dictates?) such as answer "all phone calls in two rings or less." Management communism strikes again.

The 1990s probably marked the zenith for management fads. In addition to the total quality revolution and its siblings of Six Sigma, statistical process control, and ISO 9000, we were treated to activity-based management, the balanced scorecard, benchmarking, best practices, core competencies, key performance measures, knowledge management, lean manufacturing, outsourcing, the re-engineering revolution, self-directed work teams, shared services, and shareholder value analysis, among others.

Choosing the right tools became so confusing that consultants were even able to sell their clients on a project to help them select the right tools, which they were only too happy to help implement often at considerable expense. Consultants Bain & Company even produced a handy guide entitled *Management Tools and Techniques—An Executive's Guide* to help bewildered managers sift through the competing offerings. In the introduction to the 1997 edition, author Darrell Rigby succinctly encapsulated the sad state of affairs with his commentary: "In the absence of objective data, groundless hype makes choosing and using management tools a dangerous game of chance."[3] All too often the results of such programs proved the validity of Rigby's assertion. Even the proponents of the techniques themselves were not afraid to cite the risks. Michael Hammer and James Champy came to define the re-engineering wave through their 1993 book, *Reengineering the Corporation,* yet they asserted that "Our unscientific estimate is that as many as 50 percent to 70 percent of organizations that undertake a re-engineering effort do not achieve the dramatic results they intended."[4] Luckily, their caution had little effect on the corporate world's appetite to re-engineer, since it did not appear until the final chapter of the book and no one ever reads a business book right to the end, right?

There was a more serious effect of the explosion of new management fads. When all the projects that were initiated to capitalize on these new tools were combined with the numerous systems projects such as enterprise resource planning (ERP), customer relationship management (CRM), and web enabling everything, many organizations suffered from project overload. This was particularly true when companies attempted complex enterprise-wide implementations. Over time the lessons were learned but not before many millions of dollars were poured into projects that promised a lot and delivered little. One large financial institution was infected by more than 10,000 scorecards that measured absolutely everything except what was important; another developed a list of more than fifty key performance measures, surely an oxymoron, don't you think? Despite investing billions to implement common systems during the 1990s, the average large company found itself with two or more ERP systems—yet another oxymoron. The downturn following the dot.com collapse introduced some sanity as managers began to pay close attention to the scale and scope of projects. Many adopted a more commonsense approach that embraced smaller projects with clearly defined outcomes, establishment of clear coordination between projects, increased use of piloting or prototyping to validate the expected outcomes before beginning full implementation, and the addition of more effective oversight by senior management to ensure the continued relevance to the overall business strategy. Amazingly, some organizations began to understand that one size fits all was not necessarily the answer and that flexible, adaptable, and cheap could work very nicely, thank you. Management communism was under attack, but the wall hasn't yet come tumbling down.

Mythbuster Wisdom: Great Customer Service from AT&T—Surely Not?

The words "great customer service" and "AT&T" have rarely appeared in the same sentence. I have been a customer of AT&T (on and off) since first arriving in the United States in 1991. Over that time, no organization has managed to consistently irritate me as much, although there are a couple of credit card companies that have come very close. On four separate occasions I have defected to the opposition, only to return meekly to the fold as some compelling economic ($100 checks to switch my $7 a month long distance account back to them) or monopolistic ploy such as being the only company to offer the iPhone, breaks down my resistance. So you can imagine my shock as I type these words describing one the greatest examples of customer service excellence I have ever experienced that the provider of such service was none other than AT&T. Let me explain. In September 2008 I embarked on a two-week trip to Europe. Armed with my iPhone, I was fully equipped with telephone, email, and Internet access, which I used extensively on the trip. I knew I had an international calling plan that offered reasonable rates on voice calls, but I neglected to check the status of my data plan. During the trip, most of the financial world collapsed with alarming rapidity and the U.S. investment banking industry evaporated overnight, so news updates and emails were my lifeline from deepest Prague as details of Lehman Brothers bankruptcy reached me on the morning of September 15—my birthday, no less!

A couple of weeks after returning home the bad news hit home as my AT&T bill whistled through cyberspace and informed me that my data roaming charges for September were a little over $800. Unlike the precipitous fall in the value of my retirement accounts, I could not blame this on dodgy mortgage brokers, collateralized debt obligations, Alan Greenspan, or even George Bush; I had screwed up and would have to pay the not insignificant price. Then a very strange thing happened.

I was sitting at my desk one day when the phone rang. I normally ignore most calls as constant demands to solve world hunger or take out yet another home equity line can get a bit wearing, but for some reason I answered this call. A very polite lady introduced herself as calling from AT&T, and I braced myself to reject whatever offer she would make that would provide unbeatable value but also increase the size of my bills. However, she started off by asking me if I was aware I had downloaded a lot of data on my recent European trip. I explained that I was and that I understood that it was just a little expensive in a rather resigned voice. And then a strange thing happened. She went on to explain that AT&T had a roaming data plan for which I was eligible, that could reduce my international data roaming charges by over 90 percent, and would I be interested? As a frequent traveler, I agreed in the hope that future trips would be less financially damaging. At this point she thanked me and commented that the activation would be backdated to September 1 and would therefore apply to my September usage. As a result, my $800 of roaming charges would be reduced to $50 and my account would be credited next month. I was speechless. Here was a company with decades of experience in the art of poor customer service so completely exceeding my expectations that I had to ask her to repeat what she just said. I hung up a happy man; AT&T had just proven that loyalty can be bought!

Too Much Process, Not Enough Product

A major factor in the rise of new management fads over the last 30 years is that we have become obsessed with processes. Ever since Ford's introduction of the production line, process has been king. The results have been impressive as waste has been minimized, processes streamlined, and error rates cut. Much of the productivity improvement realized in recent years has come from process simplification, redesign, and automation, but as with many other fads some have overdosed. During the 1980s something approaching paranoia gripped America as concerns mounted that Japan was destroying the U.S. economy. In 1980, NBC ran a documentary entitled *If Japan Can, Why Can't We?* This was a strange irony in that Japan learned about quality from the Americans during the post-war reconstruction period. One American in particular, W. Edwards Deming, is widely credited with teaching quality to the Japanese. In 1981, Deming was hired by the Ford Motor Company to help them close the quality gap, both perceived and real, between Ford and its Japanese competitors, particularly Toyota and Honda. As part of its quality campaign, Ford adopted the slogan, "Quality Is Job One." The program delivered, and in 1986, Ford launched the Taurus line, which rapidly became the best selling car in America, a position it held until being displaced by the Toyota Camry in 1997. However, while the "Quality Is Job One" slogan lasted for seventeen years before being replaced by what the company suggested was the more inspirational "Better Ideas, Driven By You," quality (and process) alone was not the answer for Ford or its U.S. rivals. Despite dramatic improvements in quality, market share for General Motors, Ford, and Chrysler kept declining, reaching a historic low of 44 percent in early 2009. Maybe one reason was that the facts got in the way of a good story. In 1999, Ford issued recall notices affecting more than 250,000 vehicles across its Ford, Lincoln, Mercury, and Volvo brands. By 2009, there were more than 5,700 outstanding recall notices affecting millions of Ford vehicles. So much for quality being job one.

Such was the paranoia about America's quality problem that in 1987 the government stepped in and created the Malcolm Baldrige National Quality Award to stimulate companies to focus on process and quality improvement. Early winners of the award included AT&T, Cadillac, Merrill Lynch, Motorola, Texas Instruments, Westinghouse, and Xerox—proving that quality is no defense against future performance challenges or even irrelevance.

After being dominated by large corporations, quality seems to have fallen off the radar. Since the late 1990s the public sector has come to dominate the Baldrige awards with school and health systems taking the prize. Recent winners include the Poudre Valley Health System, Colorado (2008); Mercy Health System, Wisconsin (2007); City of Coral

Springs, Florida (2007); North Mississippi Medical Center, Tupelo, MS (2006); Richland College, Dallas, Texas (2005); Jenks Public Schools, Jenks, OK (2005); Bronson Methodist Hospital, Kalamazoo, MI (2005); and Robert Wood Johnson University Hospital, Hamilton, NJ (2004). There is some irony that the highest quality organizations in the United States apparently reside in the healthcare and education sectors. I wonder if a poll of average citizens would identify these two sectors as the most efficient or effective. The only Fortune 500 companies to win the award in the twenty-first century are Motorola in 2002 and Boeing in 2003. By 2008, Motorola's once-famed cell phone business was for sale, and Boeing was repeatedly delaying delivery of its new 787 aircraft due to production problems—neither of which are great advertisements for the quality of their processes. There can only be two possible explanations for the dearth of big companies in the winner's circle: Either they cannot be bothered to enter or their quality sucks.

Like everything, a focus on quality is about balance. Some Baldrige winners such as 3M, FedEx, and Ritz-Carlton have successfully combined high quality with outstanding products and services. Achieving a balance between process quality and product or service value is at the heart of an organization that can sustain top tier performance over the long term such as Apple, Costco, Federal Express, Southwest Airlines, Tesco, and Toyota.

So What?

- Management tools are just that—tools. They are not silver bullets but specialized tools that have specialized applications. One of management's primary tasks is to select the right tool for the job.
- Standardization, uniformity, and consistency have their place—but be careful what you ask for. You may kill creativity, flexibility, and innovation.
- Exceptional quality that people don't value is pointless.
- Standardization can be expensive. Forcing all your operations to use the same systems sounds logical, but can a single system support both your largest business or market and your smallest business or market?

- Large enterprise-wide programs are fraught with risk. Companies, markets, and technologies change so fast that any project that takes more than a year or so is likely to be fixing yesterday's problems with yesterday's solutions.
- Improvements in quality can have an adverse effect on customer service and satisfaction, as with airport security post 9/11.
- Innovation is not a marketing campaign—it is a function of talent, culture, process, behavior, and leadership.

Notes

1. Henry Ford, Samuel Crowther, *My Life and Work* (New York: Doubleday, 1922).
2. Ibid.
3. Darrell K. Rigby, *Management Tools and Techniques—An Executive's Guide* Boston (Bain & Company, 1997).
4. Michael Hammer and James Champy, *Reengineering the Corporation* (New York: HarperCollins, 2003), p. 200.

Chapter 8

New Risks for a New World

C redit risk, interest rate risk, foreign exchange risk—these are all risks that are familiar to managers. Most organizations have sophisticated mechanisms for measuring and managing such risks. Of course, sometimes these procedures break down as was spectacularly demonstrated by the absence of effective credit risk assessment in the U.S. mortgage market between 2003 and 2007. However, as the world becomes increasingly interconnected, and communications are near instantaneous, a whole new class of risk has emerged that requires close attention by managers. Broadly speaking, this can be termed reputational risk or perhaps more pointedly—trust and credibility. One of Warren Buffett's many insightful quotes was, "It takes 20 years to build a reputation and 5 minutes to ruin it." The truth of his assertion was proven in September 2008 when the rapid loss of confidence among Lehman Brothers' trading partners consigned the company to oblivion.

Similarly, Bob Nardelli's dismissive treatment of shareholders at Home Depot's 2007 annual meeting tarnished the company and hastened Nardelli's departure. Naturally, Cruciant values its reputation but does not foresee too many risks.

Fiction: The Boardroom—April 2007

Rich is pumped. He is presenting the new marketing program to the rest of the management team. "I think our ad agency, Cool, Hip and Trendy (CHT), has nailed it. They have developed a whole branding, marketing, and advertising strategy around the tag line "Innovation You Can Trust." The message is that Cruciant can be relied upon to bring the most innovative new products and services to market at a price and quality that you as the customer never have to worry about. We are the most trusted provider in the marketplace. I think it's brilliant and as you can see the message carries through to our packaging, advertising, online presence, and even through to our redesigned business cards."

Sarah adds, "I love it, and my team is really excited about the positioning. It gives us permission to immediately engage prospects and customers in a discussion of our new products and also emphasize our quality and outstanding customer service. We can draw a direct comparison with our competitors and show where we differentiate ourselves."

Steve smiles, "I like it, too. The $80 million investment is huge, but I think now is the time to do it as we start to expand into new markets. It should also further distance us from the old United Integrated legacy and set Cruciant apart in the marketplace. Let's go for it!"

Five Months Later . . .

It seems like you can't walk through an airport or watch television without hearing the line "Cruciant—Innovation You Can Trust." The reaction has been largely positive; *Advertising Age* is tipping the campaign to win a number of awards at the year-end ad industry ceremony. The *Wall Street Journal* commented in its Marketplace section that the Cruciant campaign was a landmark in rebranding for the new world. CHT picked up a couple of awards for its work, and even investors seemed to like the program, as the stock had moved up 9 percent since the campaign was launched.

Of course, there were the usual cynics who pointed to every slight misstep that Cruciant made as yet another example of marketing hype triumphing over reality, but on balance it was clear the strategy was working.

At the September management meeting, VP of Operations Martin Campbell is discussing plans for the launch of a major new product: "I am concerned that the initial test batch shows far greater variance in quality than we expected. It seems there may need to be a couple of design changes to improve the consistency."

"What will that mean to the launch date?" asks Steve.

"Modifying the designs and rerunning the tests to get to production-ready will take about 90 days."

"We can't wait that long," Phil exclaims. "The advertising campaign is already rolling. We have 15,000 prospective customers signed up on the website for the "First Look" promotion, and retailers are already taking orders. Ninety days will kill us. How bad are the variances?"

"Well, about 95 percent of the test run were within tolerance; the other 5 percent were outside, and we are not quite sure what's causing it. My guys expect to have an answer in a day or so."

"95 percent is pretty good for a test run, and those that are out of tolerance still work, don't they? So why can't we launch on time and run the modifications in parallel?" Phil asks.

"We could do that," says Martin "I am just a little concerned that there may be a surprise we haven't found out about."

"I know it is your job to worry about these things," says Steve, "but I think the risks are manageable. Given the upfront investment we have already made, let's go with Phil's plan."

Martin nods his agreement. He is not completely happy but understands the need to get into the market fast.

Six Weeks Later . . .

Sarah is updating the management team on the rollout of the new product: "Sales are ahead of plan and the backlog is building nicely. Almost all the reviews have been positive. The *Straits Times* in Singapore described it as a new product for a new age, which is brilliant. The only downside is that we are seeing some returns due to an apparent defect in the casing. This seems to be the same problem we had in the test batch that Martin described a few weeks ago. The good news is that we have identified the problem and a second release should be in the market within three weeks, which is ahead of schedule."

One Week Later . . .

Phil reports that a couple of blogs are reporting that the product is defective and that the failure rate is much higher than the company has been reporting. It appears that failure rates are approaching 10 percent, but the company has offered full refunds or guaranteed delivery from the new batch. Phil thinks the issue is manageable.

Two Days Later . . .

"What is this?" screams Steve. "CNBC is showing a video that is apparently on YouTube of some guy taking a hammer to our product while ranting about how our tagline really stands for 'Innovation you can trust to rip you off and deliver a product that's so crappy it drives you to seek violent retribution for being conned.' In the background they are playing a modified version of 'I Can't Get No Satisfaction' with the words 'from Cruciant' added. Apparently, it's already been seen by over two million people and is the most watched video on the whole Internet!"

Phil: "It's a disaster. How can one idiot be allowed to get away with this? Yes, we have seen a much higher failure rate, but it will all be fixed in a few days when the new batch comes online."

"Maybe we should have delayed the launch until the problem had been fixed" shyly comments Martin.

"Well, it's done now. What's happening to sales, Sarah?" Steve asks.

"Not good," she responds. "We are seeing a 40 percent order cancellation rate. It's going to take months to restore our credibility."

The Next Day . . .

"Cruciant counts the cost of failed launch," reads the headline in The Wall Street Journal. By day's end, Cruciant's stock is down 17 percent, and Steve has to issue a statement apologizing for the breach of customer trust and vowing to never make the same mistake again.

Nine Months Later . . .

Sales have slowly started recovering, but Steve has asked CHT to start working on a new branding program that emphasizes the innovation component but plays down the trust element.

Facts: Risk Is a Four-Letter Word

"The capacity to manage risk, and with it the appetite to take risk and make forward-looking choices, are key elements of the energy that drives the economic system forward."[1]

Peter L. Bernstein

Why is the phrase, "that's risky" seen as a negative, while "risk-free" is seen as positive? Without risk-taking there would be no innovation—no iPod, no jet engine, no heart transplant—yet as human beings we are trained to shy away from anything that is described as risky. Of course, this does not stop us from doing risky things; we simply attempt to rationalize the risk to ourselves:

"I'm not too drunk to drive."

"Everyone is getting rich from Internet stocks, so why not me?"

"Gas will never get to $4 a gallon."

"Real estate is a safe bet."

"All the other players use steroids, so why shouldn't I?"

Unfortunately, our rationalization process is anything but rational—it is rarely supported by facts, driven by emotion as opposed to logic, and simply serving to justify the decision we really want to make. In the examples above, we want to drive home, make money, buy that big SUV, use our home as an ATM, and make it to the major leagues.

In business, we make many of the same mistakes with the added cushion of being able to find data to support just about any decision we want to make. In 1992, Iridium, the ill-fated satellite phone venture backed by Motorola, spoke excitedly of "bringing dial-tone to places no dial-tone has gone before." The company cited the fact that "Half the people in the world today live more than two hours from a telephone." Lost in the justification were the challenges of enticing those same people, typically not the most affluent in the world, to spend $3,000 for a handset and then pay $3 a minute to make a call. After years of development and billions of investment, the service became operational in November 1998; nine months later, Iridium defaulted on $1.5 billion in debt and filed for bankruptcy.

In recent years, the tools and techniques for assessing and managing risk have advanced significantly. Massive amounts of both brain and computing power are now dedicated to the task as ever more complex and nuanced models seek to measure risk and condition human responses to it. Yet despite all the investment, it appears that our ability to effectively navigate through an uncertain world is no better than back in 1492 when Columbus was convinced that he had found the East Indies when in fact he was in the Bahamas.

Peter Bernstein cautioned against an overreliance on computer-based models, "Nothing is more persuasive than the computer screen, with its imposing array of numbers, glowing colors, and elegantly structured graphics. As we stare at the passing show, we become so absorbed that we tend to forget that the computer only answers questions; it does not ask them. Whenever we ignore the truth, the computer supports us in our conceptual errors."[2] How many ignored this wisdom in recent years?

In the aftermath of the global credit crisis, financial engineers and their models were derided for their failure to provide an effective mechanism for valuing the collateralized debt obligations (CDOs) that contributed so much to the near-collapse of the banking system. One finance expert commented that using many of the models upon which the banks relied was "essentially just making up numbers."[3] Unfortunately, those made-up numbers included house prices, reported incomes, corporate profits, asset valuations, share prices, and executive management compensation payouts. The whole housing market in the United States became a virtual Ponzi scheme that dwarfed the antics of Bernard Madoff. New loans were made to borrowers who couldn't afford them on the back of old loans to borrowers that could not afford them, fueling demand for housing, which in turn drove prices ever higher until the music stopped—and then the whole house of cards came tumbling down.

The failure both to understand and to manage risk is at the heart of all major economic debacles. René Stulz, a professor at The Ohio State University, identified six ways in which companies mismanage risk:[4]

1. Rely on historical data.
2. Focus on narrow measures.
3. Overlook knowable risks.
4. Overlook concealed risks.
5. Fail to communicate.
6. Do not manage in real time.

I wonder if Stulz knew that he was describing the way most organizations have been planning and forecasting for the last fifty years! Last year's results are the basis for next year's plan; revenue and earnings are the only metrics that matter; risk is only given cursory consideration and often discounted by stating that it won't happen to us; hidden risks such as reputational damage are ignored; plans and forecasts are created by a small group with little input from the people who will be asked to execute against them; and reporting progress will be done only once a month while forecasts will be only be updated once a quarter. Not exactly a recipe for effective management—but still very popular.

Stulz probably could have added greed, stupidity, and naïveté to the list but otherwise his analysis is pretty much spot on. All six mistakes were made at the same time in the collapse of the housing market in the United States:

1. Rely on historical data: House prices rose consistently starting in 1996; the Case-Shiller house price index rose from 75.71 in January 1994 to a peak of 226 in June 2006.
2. Focus on narrow measures: Rising home values became the sole measure of personal wealth, income mattered less and less, as everyone tapped the ever-increasing value of his or her home to engage in a decade-long spending spree.

3. Overlook knowable risks: Credit standards were progressively relaxed as lenders bet on the inexorable rise in home prices as security for ever more exotic (i.e., risky) loans.

4. Overlook concealed risks: Banks invested billions in supposedly safe securities, often rated AAA by the credit rating agencies, such as collateralized debt obligations and credit default swaps that were incapable of being efficiently priced in the marketplace.

5. Fail to communicate: Borrowers failed to communicate the true state of their finances, lenders failed to accurately report the true risk in their loan portfolios, and mortgage brokers were incented to drive volume regardless of the credit quality.

6. Do not manage in real time: House prices peaked in mid-2006, but subprime lending continued at record levels for at least another year.

It is easy to get caught up in all the hype when times are good. More disturbing is when supposedly professional advisors fall victim. In 2003, in a report entitled *The Housing Boom: Another 20 Years of Growth,* Al Ehrbar, a partner at consulting firm Stern Stewart & Co., described a radical new role for housing:

> "Instead of adding to the severity of the recession, it helped sustain employment and consumption, and softened the economic landing. Housing went from being a safety valve at the inflationary peak of the cycle to acting as a safety net on the downside.

> "So why is all this important? It could mean we've seen the end of the boom-bust cycle in real estate. The smooth, steady rise in the value of homes—and therefore the value of home builders—should mean we'll see increased access to the capital and financing that could be used to reduce the shortage of housing in the United States."[5]

Well, he nailed that one, didn't he?

In late 2008 the Conference Board conducted one of those surveys (there seem to be millions conducted each week, which makes my life really easy because I can usually find at least one, albeit obscure, survey that supports my point of view) that sought to identify the top five

Table 8.1   CEO Challenge 2008: Top five Challenges?

Rank July 2008	Rank October 2008	Concern	Increase in Those Ranking It as of "Greatest Concern"
1	1	Excellence in execution	+ 9.4%
3	2	Consistent execution of strategy	+ 6.9%
7	3	Speed, flexibility, adaptability to change	+ 22.1%
16	4	Global economic performance	+ 27.4%
11	5	Financial risk, including liquidity, credit, and volatility	+ 23.0%

Source: The Conference Board

concerns among global business executives. Table 8.1 shows the results for July 2008 and again for October 2008.

Not surprisingly, global economic performance (up from #16 to #4) and managing financial risk and volatility (up from #11 to #5) shot up in the rankings, but what I found interesting was that in July 2008 (after Bear Stearns and with oil at $147 a barrel) financial risk only ranked number 11 and the global economy ranked number 16. I am sorry, but I cannot think of another ten or fifteen things respectively that could have been of more concern to business leaders. Yet another example of the illusion of competence or is it the delusion of competence?

Learn from Tiger, Phil, and the Rest

I have been trying to play golf for nearly forty years. In the early years I held out hope of being competent. That soon evaporated and now I just try not to embarrass myself too often. I am addicted, as much to the mental side of the game as to the physical execution. Golf is a very humbling game. Tiger Woods, probably the best golfer ever, averages only three or four shots under par for each round he plays. He fails to hit the fairway almost 43 percent of the time and misses one in three greens. Do you think his plan before the round is to miss six fairways and six greens? In my forty years of watching professional golf, I have attended 22 major championships and over 50 tournaments in all. My conclusion is that while the best players hit the ball further than the average amateur, the real difference is how they deal with adversity. When Tiger misses a green, he still makes a par or better two-thirds of the time. I have been a single figure handicap golfer since 1976, and I get "up and down" in golf parlance maybe 20 percent of the time, and of course I miss more greens than Tiger does. The same is true in business: The best companies are defined by how they respond to adversity.

When I watch top golfers practice, they spend more time working on short chips than big drives; for us amateurs, it is the exact opposite, we go to the range and blast away with the driver, which we will use at most fourteen times during our 100 or so shots. If we have a few seconds before teeing off, we may drop a couple a balls and hit a chip or a putt before rushing to the tee. We would be better served by walking over to the trees at the side of the range to practice chipping the ball back onto the fairway than thrashing around with our drivers. Success in golf, like business, is more about how you deal with the unplanned, adverse events than how you execute when everything is going smoothly. We will learn a lot about which companies are really great in the next few years.

Mythbuster Wisdom: Tracking the Mac—Managing Uncertainty at McDonalds

Sustaining profitability during a recession is challenging, yet one of the relative winners during 2008 was fast-food chain McDonald's. The company operates more than 30,000 restaurants in over 100 countries. As the recession began to bite, McDonald's benefited from a couple of trends: First, customers traded down from more expensive restaurant offerings; second, the weak dollar during the first half of 2008 increased the dollar value of McDonald's overseas business. For 2008, U.S. earnings rose by 8 percent, earnings in Europe rose 23 percent, and in Asia/Pacific, the Middle East, and Africa they rose 33 percent. But it was not just favorable external events that helped McDonald's thrive. The company also took a much more active approach to its planning and forecasting activities.

Less than two months after completing a new three-year strategic plan in October 2008, managers understood that the rapidly changing global economic outlook necessitated that they revisit the plan. All too often, organizations stubbornly stick to a plan that has been made obsolete by rapidly changing market events. Just because it is not planning season does not mean that plans cannot be revisited if the world changes around you.

One aspect of McDonald's strategy that required careful management in light of the changing economic outlook was plans for nearly 1,000 new outlets. Managers looked closely at the housing, employment, and retail market data in the specific locations where new openings were planned to fine-tune plans using the latest and greatest data. Paying attention to changes in very localized markets can greatly aid management decision making. In the UK market, one of McDonald's most profitable and fastest growing, managers typically reviewed a broad set of market indicators such as consumer spending patterns, competitor traffic, and projected unemployment rates once or twice a year. By early 2009, managers were reviewing the same data every two weeks and fine-tuning advertising and promotional campaigns in response.[6] Adjusting planning and management processes to reflect increased volatility and uncertainty just makes sense. Successfully navigating through an uncertain world requires flexibility to adjust tactics and sometimes strategies in response to trends in the marketplace.

They Were Going to Change the World

Remember back in 1999? Amazon was the most boring dot.com while Webvan and Kozmo were cool. The late 1990s was a time when the world was supposed to be redefined by the Internet. You name it and it was on the Internet, from pet food to tax forms, and the world would never be the same again. And yes, everything did change. Ten years on most of us file our taxes online, are reunited with school friends we could not be bothered to keep in touch with for the last thirty years, and post intimate details of our lives online for the entire world to see. However, few of the providers of these services were the hyped stars of 1999.

Prominent members of the dot.com graveyard include Webvan (1999–2001), which burned through $800 million in less than two years; Pets.com (2000) proved that shipping dog food via UPS was uneconomical; Kozmo (1998–2001) promised to deliver a pound of Starbucks coffee direct to your door for free in less than an hour; Flooz.com (1998–2001) tried to reinvent Green Shield Stamps online with help from pitchwoman Whoopi Goldberg; eToys.com (1997–2001) was going to put Toys 'R Us out of business; while Boo.com (1998–2000) would become the Harvey Nichols of the Internet; and MVP.com (1999–2000) had John Elway, Michael Jordan, and Wayne Gretzky at the helm so it surely couldn't fail, could it?

Despite the bloodbath, the five-year survival rate of dot.com firms was about 48 percent, which was on a par or slightly better than previous booms in other emerging industries such as automobiles, tires, and television; however, a very small number have emerged as dominant players with a long-term future. Of the first wave, probably only Amazon, Yahoo, and e-Bay can be defined as superstars, and both e-Bay and Yahoo have struggled in recent years. The second wave has given us Google, YouTube, Facebook, and Twitter, yet only Google demonstrates a clearly profitable business model.

I can confidently predict (safe in the knowledge that I will never be held accountable) that the next bubble will be environmental sustainability. Green is big, and the flood of investment in thousands of ideas is already underway, with $7.7 billion of venture capital investment in 2008, more than double the amount in 2007. Established companies are rushing to establish their green credentials. BP is going "Beyond Petroleum," IBM is building the "Smarter Planet," and General Electric touts "Ecoimagination" as one of its core strategies. The next few years will see numerous ideas for recycling, reuse, conservation, and renewal. Many will soar to lofty heights (and absurd valuations) for brief periods only to crash and burn. So invest with caution or sell early!

Beware Irrelevance

Managers agonize over the threat from competitors, analyzing every piece of new intelligence for insight into a competitor's intentions. The big competitive rivalries are like heavyweight boxing matches used to be when Ali fought a continuous war of words, and the occasional actual fight, with Frazier and Foreman: overhyped, vitriolic, but great spectacles. Think of Coke and Pepsi, Bud and Miller, Apple and Microsoft, BBC and ITV, and the Beatles and Stones. In each case the players are partly defined by their rivals.

Rivalry is a powerful motivating force, driving each player to push harder for an edge; but it can also be distracting. Did Coke and Pepsi spend so much time watching each other that they were slow to see the redefinition of the soft drink market as bottled waters, iced teas, and other non-carbonated beverages took hold? For decades, U.S. car companies fought each other for market share and largely ignored the growing threat of import models, and major airlines disparaged upstart Southwest for years before recognizing that it was their own model that was broken.

Being vanquished by a rival is not the primary risk an organization faces. Far more dangerous is becoming irrelevant in the eyes of your customers. Direct competitors largely play in the same space, making similar products that they market and sell in much the same manner as each other. True disruption occurs when a new product or approach hits the market that offers your customers a very different proposition. For example, the soda drinker might gravitate to the more social pursuit of sitting in Starbucks with a no-fat, triple-shot latte; the beer drinker might switch to a glass or two of Pinot Noir as part of a (misguided?) weight-loss/healthy-heart program; and the Barnes and Noble customer might not defect to Borders but might buy an Amazon Kindle and download books on the road.

Keeping an eye on competitors is common sense, but it is much more important to understand why customers value your company and its products or services. Becoming irrelevant to your customers is

Table 8.2   Indirect Threats to Market Dominance

Market	Threats
Soda wars	Bottled water, non-carbonated drinks, coffee
Bud–Miller	Imports, craft beers, wine, diets
Apple–Microsoft	Google, Facebook, Linux
BBC–ITV	Sky, Hulu, XBox
Beatles–Stones	Jack Daniels, Yoko Ono, Pink Floyd . . .

far more damaging in the long run than ceding a few points of market share to a competitor. There are many different reasons for a business to be relevant to its customers; understanding the connection is vital.

Convenience: People don't drive through McDonald's for the ambience or gourmet cuisine; it is about convenience. Similarly, the corner shop in a London suburb is not competing with a Tesco superstore on price or selection; it is all about being able to buy a pint of milk at 1 AM in the morning.

Speed: Originally, I was going to write about the drive-through as a time-saver, but that obviously is a fallacy as demonstrated by the number of people who park their car, go into the fast-food restaurant and order their food "to go" demonstrates. However, one-hour photo processing, overnight delivery, and 20-minute oil changes all sell on speed. At the time of writing, October 2009, I can ship a four-ounce (113 gram) envelope from my home in Ohio to San Diego by first class U.S. mail for 96 cents and expect it to arrive at its destination in a couple of days; alternatively, I can send it by FedEx and have it arrive at 8 AM tomorrow morning for $56.79. So assuming the post office takes a full three days I am paying $1.16 for every hour that FedEx saves me.

Price: Perhaps the most well understood competitive tool—low prices do work as Wal-Mart's everyday low-price strategy and Ryanair's no frills airline service at low cost prove; but having the lowest price for a product people do not want or need will do little for your bottom line. Try selling yesterday's newspaper or a video cassette player; they have ceased to be relevant, so no price is low enough—not even free.

Trust: Building a relationship with your customers that is based upon trust is one of the most powerful connections any organization can develop. Many customers will happily pay a higher price for the peace of mind that trust engenders. It is also very fragile. The deep crisis in the banking sector during 2008 severely weakened customers' traditional trust in financial institutions. Customers of Northern Rock, Washington Mutual, and many other financial institutions saw supposedly trusted providers disappear and had to rely on government guarantees to safeguard their money. A survey by the UK consumer magazine *Which* reported in February 2009 that 37 percent of consumers thought that banks could not be trusted to act in the best interests of the UK economy, while 21 percent did not trust banks with their money.

On May 11, 1996, ValuJet flight 592 crashed in the Florida Everglades after an onboard fire caused oxygen generators stored in the hold to explode. All 110 people onboard were killed. Subsequent investigations revealed numerous lapses in the airline's maintenance procedures. Not surprisingly, customer confidence in the airline disappeared. In 1997 the company was forced to merge with the much smaller AirTran Airways and the ValuJet name and tarnished reputation were history.

Choice: Providing customers with choices has long been a driving force for business. The first department stores emerged in the 1830s and before long became the dominant retail model. In more recent times, the Internet has greatly expanded customer choices. A few clicks and any consumer can find all manner of different choices for a particular product from life insurance to a plane ticket or a car. The abundance of choice that the Internet provides has actually served to reduce the perceived customer value of choice in the physical retail environment. Today, many customers use the Web to research a product, and even if they do not buy on the Web, they locate the nearest retail outlet with the best price and make their purchase there. In such situations, choice in the retail outlet is of much less importance.

Reliability/Quality: For decades Maytag stood for quality; the Maytag repairman, who first appeared in an advertising campaign in 1967, has become a common metaphor for an individual whose services are rarely needed, a tribute to the reliability and quality of the company's products. Similarly, Toyota led the way in establishing quality as an attribute in its vehicles, particularly in the 1960s and 1970s as U.S. manufacturers struggled to match the quality of imported vehicles. Even today, as many American cars deliver equivalent or even superior quality to imports, the perception of the customer is still colored by thirty years of quality shortfalls.

Technology Leadership: Companies have long used technical leadership as a means to appeal to customers. Audi's long running *Vorsprung durch Technik* (advancement through technology) campaign clearly defined the company's positioning. Numerous companies tout their products as being "leading edge" or "technologically advanced." Yet technology leadership is fragile and very susceptible to obsolescence through innovation. Sony led the market for portable music players for over twenty years through both the cassette tape and CD eras but lost its position as the technology moved on to digital music. Polaroid was an innovation powerhouse but was unable to adapt to the world of digital photography and, after struggling for years, went bankrupt in October 2001.

Compliant: U.S. car insurance company SafeAuto markets itself as "keeping you legal for less" by offering policies that meet the minimum legal requirements in each state in which it does business. Numerous lawyers, accountants, and consultants offer audit services for everything from employment contracts to environmental protection to provide companies with the assurance that they are in compliance with laws and regulations. The pace of regulatory change ensures a steady stream of business for providers in this space.

Compatibility: Want to buy accessories for your iPhone? How about games for your Xbox or tires for your BMW? Positioning products as being compatible with products made by another company drives revenue at thousands of businesses. In this case, relevance requires that the customer choose another company's products in order for your business to succeed. Your success depends upon another company remaining relevant to your customers. Get it right and it can be very lucrative; get it wrong, as software developers who backed IBM's OS/2 PC operating system or toy makers who invested in products tied to the *Incredible Hulk* movie in 2008 as opposed to *Iron Man,* and you are rapidly on the road to irrelevance.

Aura/Hipness: Perhaps the most fickle foundation of relevance is to be fashionable, trendy, cool, hip, or wicked. The litany of once-hot products that enjoyed brief moments of popularity is long: Remember Clackers, Rubik's cube, leg warmers, the Osmonds, Cabbage Patch dolls, Beanie Babies, Fresca, the PT Cruiser, and Crocs? The key is to capitalize quickly and if possible carve out a position beyond a single product or time period as Nike and Apple have done. Lately, there has been a booming business in resuscitating once-hot brands that had fallen on hard times. Procter & Gamble's Old Spice grew sales faster than its overall category from 1997 to 2001 on the back of a refreshed product line and new advertising.[7] BMW reintroduced the Mini in 2001 and enjoyed great success with a vehicle that called to mind the iconic original that was one of the symbols of the "Swinging Sixties" in London.

While difficult, it is possible to regain lost relevance. On his return to Apple, Steve Jobs redefined the company and triggered a second epoch for a fading brand. Jobs transformed Apple from a niche computer company to a global consumer products company. He recognized that the connection between the company and its customers was through cutting-edge products that were superbly designed and seamlessly integrated. In short, it was cool to be an Apple customer. Once the connection was understood, it was a logical step to the iPod, iTunes, and iPhone. Reinforcing the redefinition of the company on the day the iPhone was launched, the word "Computer" was dropped from Apple's name.

Different Customers, Different Connections

It is easy for managers to describe their company's positioning in terms of price, quality, or convenience; however, the connection between a company and its customers can vary across different markets or segments. For example, Yum Brands, the parent company of Kentucky Fried Chicken, Pizza Hut, and Taco Bell, benefited in the U.S. market during late 2008 as consumers traded down from more expensive dining options to the company's lower-priced offerings. However, in China, where consumers were doing exactly the same, Yum was not a beneficiary. In China, Yum's brands were not the lower-priced option. Eating Western fast food was more expensive than the local fare offered from carts and stands in the street, so as the recession bit, Chinese consumers returned to the cheaper alternative. Understanding that your products may be low-cost essentials in one market and higher-cost luxury items in another market can lead to key differences in the way you plan, market, and invest in different products or services. As the world globalizes at an increasing pace, these localized differences will become increasingly important sources of profit.

Beware the Noncompetitive Threat

Sure, VHS vanquished Betamax and iTunes rode roughshod over Musicmatch, but often the seeds of a company's challenges are not competitive. In recent years, the biggest threat to Wal-Mart has certainly not been Kmart.

Some of Wal-Mart's biggest challenges have come from groups that have sought to paint the company as a poor employer and a less than desirable corporate citizen. Class action lawsuits accused the company of discriminating against 1.6 million women in pay and promotion. Another lawsuit alleged that the company forced employees to work unpaid overtime, which the company settled in December 2008 for over $350 million. There have been numerous allegations of anti-union activity to prevent the organization of its workforce, and some local communities have changed their zoning regulations with the express purpose of preventing Wal-Mart from building new stores in an attempt to protect local retailers.

There is ongoing debate about the company's provision of adequate healthcare coverage for its employees, and there have been news stories claiming that the cleaning crews in Wal-Mart stores are made up of large numbers of illegal immigrants. It has been quite an onslaught, but the company has fought back, and its growth has hardly been impaired—sales grew from $322 billion in 2006 to over $400 billion in for the year ended January 31, 2009.

Wal-Mart is not the only target of noncompetitive actions. The financial crisis triggered violent protests outside the Royal Bank of Scotland's London offices, and companies as diverse as Nike, Exxon, and Google have been subjected to protests from well-organized special interest groups.

Managers must pay close attention to trends or events that could materially alter their prospects that do no result from the actions of competitors. Consider the impact of the introduction of a flat rate income tax on accountants and companies like H.R. Block and Intuit's TurboTax business; or the introduction of universal government funded healthcare in the United States on the medical insurance industry. How about a successful "alcohol kills" movement, similar to that which reshaped the tobacco industry? Of course, such moves would ignite a fire under well-funded lobbying groups that populate Washington, Brussels, and, increasingly, Beijing.

No one likes to plan for his or her own demise, yet many people buy life insurance, write wills, and take statins just in case. But how many companies have contemplated the possible causes of their own demise? The corporate graveyard is full of once "great" businesses and even whole industries. Assessing the likely demise of one or more of your products or services and acting to mitigate the effect and develop new sources of growth is one of management's most important jobs. Microsoft has seen at least three cycles with DOS, Windows, and Office. General Electric has moved from being a product company to one that combines products with services and financing that can yield three different revenue streams from a single transaction.

Obsolescence and irrelevance go hand in hand; the Pony Express ceased to be relevant to its target customers once the Transcontinental Railroad was completed, and Kodak's withdrawal of its iconic Kodachrome film in 2009 came after a 70-year run but ended with sales totaling a fraction of one percent of the company's sales. Table 8.3 illustrates the transitory nature of many once-hot markets.

Table 8.3   Once Hot, Now Not

Gone	Going?
Moonshiners when prohibition ended	Local newspapers
Canals upon arrival of the railways	CDs and DVDs
English seaside resorts when the package holiday to Spain arrived	All things gasoline-driven
Pay phones	The English pub
Dial-up Internet access	Photographic prints
LP records	Fax machines
Film-based photography	Wired telephone service
Pagers/Beepers	Paper-based mail services
Floppy disks (both 5-inch and 3-inch)	Saturated fats
Video cassettes	Network news shows
Manually operated car windows	Reality television (I can dream, can't I?)

Remember—Stuff Happens

I so desperately wanted to use another word in the title of this section but if my dear, late mother looked down from above she would utter the two words that have echoed through my life: "Now David." So we are left with stuff happening. Simplistic I know, but we keep forgetting that stuff does happen and things do change.

As I approach 50, I can relate to my parents' inability to truly comprehend the VCR, punk rock, jeans, long hair, and premarital sex. I struggle with Tweeting, jeans worn around the knees, rap music, and the desire to text rather than talk. Failing to adapt to change is not just a personal challenge; it is a challenge for all organizations. There is a long list of businesses that failed to adapt to new realities; in some cases the results can be terminal: Wang was unwilling to develop a PC while dominating the market for word processors; Kodak was slow to invest in digital photography; America Online failed to adapt to the demise of dial-up Internet access; and GM never developed a successful minivan.

Sometimes the end can come quickly. In the late 1990s, 48 million pagers were in use in America, and the industry was big business. In 1995, Mobile Media bought Bell South's paging operation for $930 million, but the peak had already passed. Low-priced mobile phones and the introduction of "push to talk" features by Nextel signaled the decline of the pager. Only two years later, Mobile Media filed for bankruptcy, and by 2007, pager use had declined by 85 percent to less than 7 million.

Change happens fast. In 2003 management guru Tom Peters offered up two lists (Table 8.4) developed by Ferrari's former North American CEO, Gian Luigi Longinotti-Buitoni.[8] The first was of common products (i.e., dull and boring) and the second described dream products (i.e., sexy and exciting). Back in those heady days, conspicuous consumption, luxury, and ostentation were in. Brands like Starbucks and Victoria's Secret offered the promise of "affordable luxury," allowing even the less well off the opportunity to sample the good life. Peters described these dream products as going, "far beyond the realm of mere fulfillment."[9] Five years later, boring was back. The only bright spots on the retail horizon were Wal-Mart and McDonald's, neither of which could ever be accused of being luxury brands. Starbucks was closing stores all over the world, and California

Table 8.4 Tragedy of the Common Product?

"Common" Products	"Dream" Products
Maxwell House	Starbucks
BVD	Victoria's Secret
Payless	Ferragamo
Hyundai	Ferrari
Suzuki	Harley-Davidson
Atlantic City	Acapulco
New Jersey	California
Carter	Kennedy
Connors	Pele
CNN	*Who Wants to Be a Millionaire?*

SOURCE: *Re-imagine,* Tom Peters, 2003

was on the verge of bankruptcy. My aim is not to disparage companies that appeal to customer's aspirations but simply to point out that the best will be able to deliver in both good and bad times.

Perhaps most scary for the average manager is Clayton Christensen's assertion in his book *The Innovator's Dilemma* that ". . . managing better, working harder and not making so many dumb mistakes is not the answer to the innovator's dilemma."[10] Innovation is about changing the rules and creating something new. One definition I like is: "Innovation is the embodiment, combination, or synthesis of knowledge in original, relevant, valued new products, processes, or services."[11]

The key words are "original" and "relevant." This has important implications for planning and forecasting. True innovation cannot reasonably be forecast in advance because it represents things that have not been thought of before, therefore, traditional planning processes that are based upon future projections of current and past trends will be of no use in predicting innovations that could potentially destroy your business.

Even companies that are dominant in their markets can miss innovations that you would think should be obvious to them. In the 1990s, Gillette, a company with a strong record of innovation, had significant presence in three markets, toothbrushes (Oral-B), small appliances (Braun), and batteries (Duracell), but it failed to see the potential of combining the three elements into a battery-powered toothbrush. Encyclopedia Britannica had dominated its market for decades and had done all the hard work of developing and maintaining the content that was the essence of its product, but it was slow to move the content online and now lags behind search engines such as Google and free online encyclopedias such as Wikipedia. Both Gillette and Encyclopedia Britannica had the advantage and should have been at the forefront of innovation. How many companies take the time to systematically ask the question: What are we missing?

Mythbuster Wisdom: Caveat Emptor

Superior past performance is very seductive. A cursory glance at any literature advertising a mutual fund makes that clear. Headlines promote a fund's superior past performance. Rankings are offered for numerous time periods, year to date, last quarter, year, three years, five years, and ten years. Comparisons to external benchmarks are offered all in the hope of persuading you to place your hard-earned cash into one fund or another. The irony was that even as markets tanked in 2008–2009, adverts still cheerfully touted funds that performed better than the overall market even though they still lost your money. Strangely, none of the benchmark comparisons showed a comparison to how well your money would have performed if you had stuffed it under your mattress.

By law, mutual fund operators must provide you with a copy of a fund's prospectus. A mutual fund prospectus is a document that is so exciting that it makes doing your taxes seem enjoyable by comparison. Next time you receive a prospectus, break the habit of a lifetime and read it. In particular, look for a priceless phrase that is usually to be found in a very small font somewhere in a section entitled "Performance/Risk Information." It typically reads: "Keep in mind that the Fund's past performance does not indicate how the Fund will perform in the future."[12]

In essence, these words are warning you not to believe any of the marketing hype surrounding past performance since its gives you no insight whatsoever as to what may happen in the future—this is the only sound piece of advice to be found in an investment prospectus.

The iPhone Phenomenon

It took years for CDs to usurp vinyl records and for DVD to surpass video, but it is not safe to assume you will have time to react. In just twelve months, Apple's iPhone went from no presence in the Smartphone market to number 2 behind Blackberry maker Research In Motion, with a 13 percent share, largely at the expense of Palm (down 8 percent) and Motorola (down 4 percent).

Smartphone Market Share 2007/2008

	Jan 2007 – July 2007	Rank	Jan 2008 – July 2008	Rank	Change in Share
RIM	50%	1	50%	1	–
Palm	20%	2	12%	3	−8%
Motorola	10%	3	6%	5	−4%
Samsung	9%	4	9%	4	–
Apple	0%	–	13%	2	+13%

SOURCE: IDC

Revenue Volatility Means Down as Well as Up

Have you ever seen a business plan that projected a decline in sales? It does not happen very often. Yet for many companies declining sales are not just possible but likely in today's volatile world. However, walking into your boss's office and telling him that you think the business will shrink next year can be a career-limiting move, so there is a tendency to ignore it and hope it never happens. Recent evidence shows this to be foolish. No industry or company is immune.

Table 8.5 lists some of the companies that have experienced rapid declines in revenue in recent years. Some of the declines were the result of conscious decisions to sell parts of the business, but most of the companies in the table experienced declines simply because customers chose to buy less of their stuff. For companies like Lucent and Circuit City, the declines marked the beginning of the end. Alcatel acquired Lucent for €S18 billion ($US24 million) in 2006 and the merged company has

Mythbuster Wisdom: The Perils of Fixing Costs in a Variable Revenue World

Both the automotive and the airline industries have suffered mightily due to the volatile nature of customer demand. There have been wild swings in demand in very short time periods as customers react to events like 9/11, $147 oil, global recession, and increasing unemployment. Much of the pain, particularly for U.S.-based industry participants, has stemmed from the fact that both industries have succeeded in converting labor, which was traditionally a variable cost, into a largely fixed cost. As demand for cars and air travel exploded in the 1950s and 1960s, both car companies and airlines traded labor cost flexibility for dispute-free relations through successive rounds of contract negotiation with increasingly powerful unions. This was fine when demand was growing rapidly and markets were less global and therefore less competitive. However, with the entry of import car brands into the U.S. market and deregulation of the airline industry, steady predictable growth was replaced by increasing uncertainty. Companies found that they were locked into inflexible labor agreements that placed them at a significant cost disadvantage with new competitors. They also found that a small decline in sales triggered massive losses due to the high fixed-cost structures that underpinned both industries. Almost all the major U.S. participants in both industries have taken a detour through bankruptcy court since 1990.

struggled ever since. Circuit City held on for a few more years before going bankrupt in 2008. Others, such as Sun Microsystems and DuPont, have struggled despite various restructurings and cost reductions. Sun posted revenues of $13.8 billion in 2008 and eked out an operating profit of $372,000 before being acquired by Oracle, while DuPont's revenues have risen to $31 billion with earnings of $2 billion, still far below their highs a decade earlier. At the other end of the spectrum, both Apple and Hewlett Packard have recovered all of their lost ground and more and have become powerhouses in their respective segments. Apple's revenues for

2008 topped $32 billion, a more than six-fold increase in only eight years. Hewlett Packard posted revenues of $118 billion in 2008, more than 2.8 times greater than a decade earlier. Each took a different path to prosperity. Apple recaptured its reputation for innovative and cool products as successive generations of the iPod and iPhone captured the consumer's imagination. Hewlett Packard focused on excellent execution after its acquisition of Compaq and a big investment in higher-margin service businesses with the acquisition of EDS in 2008.

The recession of 2008 exposed many companies to severe revenue declines. General Motors saw revenue decline by almost $33 billion (18 percent) during 2008 and by $58 billion (29 percent) from 2007. Revenue at Goldman Sachs declined by 43 percent between the third quarter of 2007 and the third quarter of 2008, and homebuilder D.R. Horton saw revenues decline by 54 percent over the same period.

Real revenue declines were not restricted to the obvious sectors such as financial services, automotive, and construction. When *Fortune* magazine's list of the 500 largest U.S. companies was published in May 2009, 151 companies (31 percent) had seen revenues decline between

Table 8.5   Major Revenue Declines 1997–2009

Company		Revenue in $ million			% Change
Altria	2001	$89,924	2002	$80,408	−11%
Apple	2000	$7,983	2001	$5,363	−33%
Boeing	2007	$66,387	2008	$60,909	−8%
British Airways	2007	$17,565	2008	$15,156	−14%
Circuit City	2002	$12,791	2003	$9,954	−22%
Citigroup	2007	$159,229	2008	$130,005	−18%
DuPont	1997	$45,079	1998	$24,767	−45%
Ford	2007	$172,455	2008	$146,277	−15%
Hewlett Packard	1998	$47,061	1999	$42,370	−10%
Intel	2000	$33,726	2001	$26,539	−21%
Lucent	2000	$33,813	2001	$21,294	−37%
Mattel	1999	$5,515	2000	$4,670	−15%
Motorola	2007	$36,622	2008	$30,146	−18%
Sony	2005	$66,912	2006	$54,170	−19%
Sun Microsystems	2001	$18,250	2002	$12,496	−32%
Toyota	2008	$262,394	2009	$208,995	−20%

2007 and 2008, including Berkshire Hathaway, Dell, Home Depot, Motorola, Merck, CBS, Texas Instruments, MGM, and Mattel. Profits were also decimated, with 121 companies (24 percent) losing money.

Evidence that few managers consider the possibility that sales may actually go down can be found in their normal reaction. As soon as sales slump, managers adopt a slash-and-burn approach of cutting headcount and expenses. Any project without an immediate payback is cancelled, travel, training, and marketing budgets are slashed, and suppliers are pressured to cut prices. These knee-jerk reactions offer some temporary relief but often at the expense of long-term vitality as investments in future sources of growth are curtailed, service levels slip as budgets are cut, top talent heads for the exits, and suppliers limit flexibility to meet cost targets.

Managers need a more thoughtful contingency plan for adjusting an organization's cost structure as revenues decline. Perhaps even more sensible would be not to let costs get out of control in the first place. Unfortunately, the new corporate jet, commissioning a designer architect for the new headquarters campus, and adding an in-house spa are, of course, no more than successful executives deserve for their consummate skill in delivering stellar profits (along with everyone else) when the good times roll.

Understanding an organization's cost elasticity, which is the sensitivity of costs to changes in revenue, is an important component of managing in volatile times. The optimal balance between fixed and

---

Mythbuster Wisdom: That's What I Call a Decline in Sales!
During 2007 and 2008, General Motor's revenues declined by more than $58 billion. That's:

- Equivalent to losing $8 million in sales every day for two years.
- Equivalent to selling 270,000 Chevy Malibus, GM's best-selling car in 2008.
- More than the total revenues of Microsoft, Sears, UPS, or Pfizer.
- More than the combined revenues of Disney and Coca-Cola.

variable costs changes depending upon the performance of both the organization and its markets. It can be very attractive to have a high fixed-cost structure with low variable costs if demand for your products and services keeps growing. A successful drug or software product has very large development costs that are incurred before a penny of revenue is realized, but the marginal cost of producing additional units is minimal, leading to enormous profit margins over the long term. However, if demand stagnates or falls, the fixed costs can be punishing. A deeper understanding of the likely volatility of future revenues can give managers valuable insight that can help them make better decisions. Specifically, choices about whether to lease or buy equipment or facilities, how to effectively utilize outsourcing, and whether to implement software as a service (SaaS) systems solutions will be influenced by the business's ability to cover fixed costs in uncertain revenue environments. Opting to lease, outsource, or use SaaS solutions allows an organization to more closely match costs to revenue in times of uncertainty. The key is flexibility.

Reputation Is Everything

Henry Ford once commented that, "You can't build up a reputation on what you are going to do."

In April 2009, Domino's Pizza got to experience the negative impact of a tarnished reputation in the social networking age. Two employees at one of the company's facilities in North Carolina made a video showing one of them preparing sandwiches for delivery while stuffing cheese up his nose and putting certain bodily secretions on the sandwiches while the other provided commentary. These two talented associates then decided to post the video on YouTube. In a matter of days, it had been viewed more than a million times, and Domino's faced a public relations disaster. The two employees assured managers that the sandwiches were never delivered but both were fired and taken into custody by the police; however, the damage had been done. Domino's spokesman commented that "We got blindsided by two idiots with a video camera."[13] He went on to say that "Even people who've been loyal customers for 10, 15, 20 years are second-guessing their relationship with Domino's." The speed with which a prank could escalate into a major public relations disaster caught management by surprise: "What we missed was the perpetual mushroom effect of viral sensations." The company spokesman ended his comments with a forlorn cry of, "and that's not fair."

It may not be fair, but it is reality. We live in a world where both success and failure are instantly acknowledged, reported, and analyzed. A disgruntled hotel guest posts a scathing review on tripadvisor.com, an angry customer who feels wronged by the phone company "tweets" to the world using Twitter, while a passerby films a postman dumping mail in a rubbish bin. Marketing experts have warned for years that a satisfied customer may tell two people about his or her experience while a dissatisfied customer will tell ten people. In today's networked world, ten people can rapidly become ten million. So how effective is your reputational risk management process? Do you even know where the risks lie?

During 2004 I was working for Bank of America as head of Corporate Planning and got first-hand experience of the impact of reputational risk. At the time, Bank of America's advertising tagline was "Higher Standards." However, a series of events served to undermine the considerable branding investment the bank had made. First, it emerged that certain clients of the bank's asset management business had been allowed to "late-trade" mutual funds. These investors were apparently allowed to buy and sell mutual funds at the closing price the prior day thereby allowing them to profit from new news as it emerged; not a facility made available to the average investor. As if that wasn't enough, a scandal erupted at an Italian dairy company named Parmalat in which a former Bank of America executive was implicated and to which the bank had a $647 million exposure, of which $462 million was unsecured. The scandal turned out to be Europe's largest-ever corporate bankruptcy. Neither incident did much to enhance the firm's reputation or burnish the "Higher Standards" branding. I can vouch for the concern these events caused in the Charlotte headquarters. While there was significant risk of real financial losses and fines from each incident, the long-term impact on the bank's reputation was potentially much more damaging. I was impressed that the bank's risk management function already actively managed reputational risk and had policies and procedures in place for just such an eventuality. The Bank's skills were further tested by the fallout from its acquisition of Merrill Lynch in 2008. No organization can afford to ignore the potential impact of such incidents.

The first step toward managing new risks is to identify them. While many organizations are now aware of the existence and impact of reputational risk, there are other risk categories that are emerging. For example, does your organization have an explicit environmental risk management strategy? This is not just the traditional environmental, health, and safety function; it embraces all aspects of environmental sustainability. We are already seeing investors and customers make choices based upon an organization's "greenness." The basics of such a strategy include understanding the organization's total carbon footprint, being able to demonstrate the extent to which waste is recycled, and communicating the environmental impact of all products and services. The impact of new environmental risks was brought home in July 2009 when Wal-Mart announced that all its suppliers would have to provide an eco-rating, at their own expense, for all products sold through Wal-Mart. Risk management is continuously evolving, yet most organizations are stuck in the dark ages.

So What?

- Effective risk management must encompass more than traditional financial risks such as credit, foreign exchange and interest rate to include nontraditional risk categories such as reputation, innovation, environmental impact, and cost elasticity.
- Success is as much about quickly identifying bad decisions as it is about making good decisions.
- Having the courage to admit mistakes and quickly take corrective action is a hallmark of good managers.
- Understand why your organization is relevant to your customers and other constituents and then identify what can cause irrelevance.
- Risk management is more about preparation than it is about reaction. In today's world that means expecting the unexpected. Any sane company should consider the possibility, no matter how uncomfortable, of one or more of the following events occurring and have thought through its response:

- A 20 percent decline in revenues in 90 days.
- The bankruptcy of your biggest customer.
- The bankruptcy of your biggest supplier.
- A tripling in the price of your most important raw material.
- The merger of your two biggest competitors.
- A four-week disruption to your global supply chain.
- The loss of 20 percent of your sales force over a six-month period.
- Your biggest competitor calls you and suggests a merger, giving you seven days of exclusivity to do a deal.
- A major innovation is likely to make your best-selling product obsolete in less than five years.
- All your lenders freeze credit and demand repayment of at least 50 percent of outstanding current debt.

Notes

1. Peter L. Bernstein, *Against the Gods—The Remarkable Story of Risk* (New York: John Wiley & Sons, 1996), p. 3.
2. Ibid., p. 336.
3. Scott Paterson, "Math Wizards Working on Spells to Cure," *Wall Street Journal,* February 23, 2009.
4. René M. Stulz, "Why Companies Mismanage Risk," *Harvard Business Review,* March 2009.
5. Susanne Trimbath, "No More Boom-Bust Blues," *Los Angeles Times,* July 20, 2003.
6. Janet Adamy, "McDonald's Seeks Ways to Keep Sizzling," *Wall Street Journal,* March 10, 2009.
7. John Blasberg and Vijay Vishwanath, "Making Cool Brands Hot," *Harvard Business Review,* June 2003.
8. Tom Peters, *Re-imagine* (London: Dorling Kindersley, 2003), p. 126.
9. Ibid.
10. Clayton M. Christensen, *The Innovator's Dilemma* (Cambridge, MA: Harvard Business School Press, 1997).
11. R. Luecke and R. Katz, *Managing Creativity and Innovation* (Cambridge, MA: Harvard Business School Press, 2003).
12. Vanguard U.S. Stock Index Small-Capitalization Funds prospectus, The Vanguard Group, April 29, 2008.
13. Stephanie Clifford, "A Video Prank at Domino's Taints Its Brand,"*New York Times,* April 16, 2009.

Chapter 9

Pay for Performance? Failure Pays Very Well These Days

Incentive compensation has become one of the most emotive subjects in the business world. The gap between the compensation of top executives and the average employee has widened dramatically, but it is not just the size of executive pay packages that causes public and political anger—it is the perception that much of the money paid out is not really earned. The furor over bonuses paid to AIG executives after the company received more than $160 billion (or $1,400 from every U.S. taxpayer) from the U.S. government became an all-consuming political issue for Barack Obama in 2009. How could executives at a company seen as one of the primary instigators of the global financial crisis be so richly rewarded? In the UK, anger over former Royal Bank of Scotland chairman Sir Fred Goodwin's £700,000 annual pension, after the bank had to be rescued by the government, was front-page news for weeks. The apparent rewarding of failure points to serious flaws in the whole approach to the "pay for performance" compensation philosophy. Undoubtedly, increased scrutiny of pay will be one of the lasting legacies of the Crash of 2008. Naturally, Cruciant follows many of the "best practices" regarding compensation.

Fiction: January 2010

In late 2006, Steve Borden presented a new incentive compensation plan to the Board. The aim of the plan was to focus incentives for the top management team on growth—specifically revenue growth. Cruciant had been growing its top line (sales) in the low single digits, so maintaining double-digit earnings growth was being achieved solely through cost reductions. Steve rightly saw that this could not continue. If Cruciant was to grow profits in the years to come, it needed top line sales growth in the 8 to 10 percent range. The new compensation plan tied incentives to achieving minimum annual sales growth of 8 percent. Below that level no bonuses would be paid. The Board loved it and quickly approved the new plan. Management was equally happy, because their internal projections based upon growth in the economy, the launch of some new products, and a couple of acquisitions virtually assured the target would be met.

Sure enough, come the end of the year, Cruciant posted an 11 percent sales gain, and managers were rewarded with rich bonuses. Strangely, the stock price did not increase by anywhere near the same amount. Analysts covering Cruciant commented that while the company had increased sales, it still lagged behind all of its major competitors, which had logged gains in the 13 to 17 percent range.

The Board was a little perturbed that rich incentives had been paid out even though the company had lost market share; however, they also could not argue that the bonus targets had clearly been met. Despite their concerns, the Board agreed to stay with the plan for one more year, because they liked the new growth culture that the plan had triggered. After years of low single-digit growth, the 11 percent increase was a big step forward. Unfortunately, the next year, 2008, proved to be very challenging as the economy softened dramatically. After a solid first half, Cruciant ran into problems, and at year-end overall sales were down by 1 percent compared to the previous year. Under terms of the plan, no one received any bonuses. Ironically, not long after Borden left to "pursue new opportunities," the Cruciant stock price moved up around 15 percent and analysts were praising the company for its exceptional performance in a terrible economy. All of Cruciant's major competitors saw sales decline by more than 5 percent, and none came close to making a profit.

Not surprisingly, the announcement that no bonuses would be paid for 2008 was not met with much joy among the ranks. Within six weeks, seven of Cruciant's top ten sales people had left to join competitors. New CEO Chuck Williams had to scramble to provide coverage of key accounts during the first half of 2009. The inevitable loss of momentum as a new sales team was assembled led to the company' being unable to capitalize on the effects of the government stimulus package, and a number of opportunities to ensure the company gained a piece of the government pie were lost. Meanwhile the broader economy continued to worsen. Sarah, the VP of Sales, was working feverishly to hire new salespeople and get them trained. By the middle of 2009, Cruciant was forced to report that sales were down 7 percent even as their competitors reported flat or slightly improving sales.

By September, Sarah had managed to persuade three of the defectors to return, albeit for higher base salaries and guaranteed bonuses for the next two years. Around the same time, two of Cruciant's customers approached Sarah to question some transactions that had occurred during the third quarter of 2008. Apparently, their auditors had highlighted a series of purchase orders that had been issued to Cruciant during the last two weeks of the third quarter of 2008. Upon further investigation it appeared that no actual goods had been shipped relating to the purchase orders and no payments were subsequently made. The POs in question had all been booked by one of the departed sales stars. As Sarah and Cruciant's internal audit team probed further, it appeared that the saleswoman in question had persuaded the two customers to provide her with phantom purchase orders in order to boost her quarterly sales numbers. At the time, she was very close to making her target for the quarter and with the economy in freefall following the collapse of Lehman Brothers, she was desperate to stay on plan.

As the investigation continued, the story became murkier. Apparently, the saleswoman had paid purchasing officers at the two companies to generate the purchase orders; six months earlier she had purchased a high-priced condo in downtown Miami that was now worth only about 60 percent of what she had paid for it and considerably less than her outstanding mortgage; her monthly lease on the silver Mercedes 500 SLK was $1,200 per month, and her American Express Platinum card had a balance of $63,000. In 2007 she had been a star, netting a bonus of $250,000; apparently 2008's bonus had already been spent, hence the desperate need to make the numbers. Cruciant's new CFO, James Morrison, pushed for an early settlement and managed to negotiate the fine down to $600,000. The saleswoman is now serving a 19-month sentence in a low security prison in Kansas—her book chronicling the "culture of greed" that apparently pervaded Cruciant's sales organization is scheduled for publication upon her release.

Facts: The Great Incentive Scam

An article in the *Harvard Business Review* commented, "The value that many superpaid CEO superstars supposedly created has largely disappeared, and the likelihood of it being recovered anytime soon seems remote." The article went on to comment, "a good number of senior executives treated their companies like ATMs, awarding themselves millions of dollars in company loans and corporate perks. It's hard to dispute the idea that executives were somehow corrupted by the dazzling sums of money dangled in front of them."[1] A pretty accurate commentary on executive compensation in 2009, except that the article was published in January 2003 and referred to the fallout from the dot.com bust, the meltdown in the telecommunications sector, and the raft of corporate accounting scandals that dominated the business news that year. Despite political outrage and public scorn, nothing much changed in the next five years.

So What Is the Problem?

Describing the mess that is pay for performance could fill a very thick, and very boring, book. Suffice to say that the key elements of the story are greed, conflict of interest, and naïveté.

Mythbuster Wisdom: Oh, the Beauty of Hindsight!
A March 2009 study by the UK consultancy Oliver Wyman for the Institute of International Finance came up with two stunning statistics:

1. 98 percent of survey respondents believe that compensation structures were a factor underlying the crisis.
2. 95 percent of respondents have plans to increase the alignment of compensation delivery with risk.

I wonder how many would have agreed with the following statement from the report if it had appeared in March 2007?

"Our compensation practices encourage our people to take on excessive risk which is likely to lead to a global economic meltdown in the next 18 months."[2]

The principle of paying for performance is elegant and simple. Sport has done it for years. However, in the corporate world, the problems start with the most basic element. Most organizations still insist on setting goals, targets, or budgets that determine rewards. If performance meets or exceeds the standard, bounteous rewards will be paid out. Once this principle is adopted, the rot has already set in. It is both naïve and stupid to believe that a fixed performance target set months, or sometimes years, in advance of the measurement period will remain relevant given the uncertainty and volatility that are inherent in today's world. However, this is not the only problem. The setting of fixed incentive targets destroys what should be one of the most valuable of all management processes—planning.

Planning is supposed to be an exercise in developing tactics, allocating resources, and optimizing performance to meet strategic goals. As soon as people understand that their personal rewards will be tied to the outcome, it immediately becomes a game to negotiate a set of performance targets that set the lowest bar possible for maximizing compensation. As Jeremy Hope and Robin Fraser commented in their book *Beyond Budgeting*, "The extent of gaming the numbers has risen to unacceptable levels."[3] Again, they wrote this in 2003.

The fatal flaw is that payouts are tied to meeting some fixed target that is the result of a negotiation process that is completed long before the end of the measurement period. As all participants in the process are fully aware that the agreed-upon numbers will set the threshold for their individual payouts, there is no incentive whatsoever to develop a plan that optimizes performance. Hence the games begin. Using tactics that resemble a Cold War negotiation, participants bring the full array of tools to bear including, but not limited to, bluffing, lying, cheating, blackmail, and extortion to ensure that the chances of being richly rewarded for mediocre performance are maximized—and it's not even a fair fight. The board of directors, which is theoretically charged with safeguarding shareholder interests, is usually made up of friends of the CEO; the consultants they engage to advise them are seeking to sell large amounts of additional work to the company and therefore wish to keep management sweet; and the management team clearly wants to ensure they are richly rewarded for their effort if not their performance. The result is a system that in today's over-hyped incentive culture frequently rewards failure.

Many recent ex-CEOs were fired, or left to "pursue other opportunities," and found that rather than being punished, they had won the lottery. Bob Nardelli walked away from Home Depot with $240 million, Stan O'Neal left Merrill Lynch with $150 million, and Chuck Prince got $30 million from Citigroup. The relationship between pay and performance is not broken, it is inverted—the bigger the screw-up, the bigger the pay-off.

Unfortunately, this phenomenon is not restricted to the most senior executives, although they do get the biggest payoffs—funny how that works, isn't it? All across the corporate world there are managers and employees being rewarded for below average performance and being punished for exceptional performance—the exact opposite of what a rational compensation system should be doing.

Basing incentive payouts on whether an individual or organization meets a predetermined target or budget is not just daft—it is dangerous. There is the very real risk that tying incentives to meeting fixed targets or budgets achieves the exact opposite of what was intended by rewarding poor performance and punishing outstanding performance.

Yet most companies tie management incentives to some type of fixed performance target set months or even years in advance. There are three big problems with this approach. First, conservatism or sandbagging becomes pervasive as all participants engage in seeking to negotiate the most easily achievable target thereby maximizing the chances of earning all the available incentives. Jack Welch, former CEO of General Electric described the impact this way: "It sucks the energy, time, fun and big dreams out of an organization. It hides opportunity and stunts growth. It brings out the most unproductive behaviors in an organization, from sandbagging to settling for mediocrity."[4] But this is not the biggest problem! Consider the following two scenarios.

A. If the overall market assumptions built into the plan are overly pessimistic and actual performance greatly exceeds planned performance due to a booming market, incentives may be be paid that were not really earned. For example, if the plan for next year calls for 10 percent growth, incentive payouts will be tied to meeting or exceeding that number. If at the end of the year, actual results show a 15 percent gain, everyone is a hero and gets a big bonus, right? But what if the market grew 20 percent? Did they really perform so well or just have a bad plan?

B. Consider the reverse situation in which many companies found themselves in 2008. Again, assume the plan called for 10 percent growth, but this time the economy soured dramatically after the plan was developed. By the end of the year, the organization was barely able to eke out any gain at all. Obviously, everyone failed miserably and no bonuses will be paid. But what if all the organization's competitors reported negative growth? Did they really do such a poor job? After all, isn't one of the hallmarks of a great company the ability to outperform in the toughest of markets?

So there we have it; most incentive systems motivate people to promise little, reward them when they deliver on those promises, and punish them when they perform like heroes. As my American friends would say, "That's oh for three, baby."

But wait—it gets worse.

Mythbuster Wisdom from Al Dunlap

Al Dunlap, former CEO of Sunbeam, a company he destroyed, was for a brief time one of America's highest profile CEOs. Al was not shy about giving his opinions. In his book *Mean Business* (Random House, 1998) he described his philosophy on executive compensation: "The best bargain is an expensive CEO. . . . You cannot overpay a good CEO and you can't underpay a bad one. The bargain CEO is one who is unbelievably well compensated because he's creating wealth for the shareholders. If his compensation is not tied to the shareholders' returns, everyone's playing a fool's game." Al did not comment on whether CEO pay should also be tied to the destruction of shareholder wealth.

Not only are reward systems skewed toward mediocrity, some companies go even further. If managers fail to meet even mediocre targets, they will then change the rules to ensure managers can still be handsomely rewarded. Usually, this is explained away as being essential to retain talent, but how talented are they if the rules have to be changed in order to make sure they can afford the new Porsche? The late 1990s were a great time for reevaluating performance awards—some companies, including well-regarded companies such as Apple, Dell, and United Health went so far as to back-date the issue date of stock options to ensure a favorable, that is profitable, transaction for recipients.

During the 1990s, the stock option became the must-have element of compensation. Stock options were issued to employees at no cost to them. The options gave the employee the right to buy shares in the company at a fixed price over a certain period of time, typically ten years. So if you were granted 20,000 options at $30 a share, you could buy 20,000 shares of stock for $30 any time between the date of issue and the expiration of the option. Obviously, if your company's shares never made it to $30, the options were worthless. However, as soon as the share price moved above $30, you were "in the money." If the price went to $45, you could buy 20,000 shares at $30 for a total cost of $600,000 and immediately sell them for $45 each or $900,000 and pocket a nice little profit of $300,000. Many people made millions during the bull market that ran until the dot.com crash in 2000. Unfortunately, in the aftermath of the crash many others were left with options that were not just "underwater" (i.e., where the share price was below the price to exercise the option), they were drowning. No problem. Companies simply cancelled the old options and issued new ones with a more favorable exercise price. After all, we don't want our wonderful team to be punished because the market crashed, do we?

A Personal Story—My Path to (Almost) Affluence

During the dot.com boom years, a lot of people got very rich by exercising richly valued stock options—I was so nearly one of them. In 1991, I moved to the United States to help set up a consulting firm called The Hackett Group. We started with three people and managed to grow the business very successfully over the next six years. Over 90 of the Fortune 100 companies were our clients. In 1997, we sold the business to a venture capital–backed outfit called Answerthink. Answerthink's strategy was to buy up a bunch of consulting firms, roll them up into one entity, and then take the company public and make a lot of money. It all sounded very simple and was a popular approach across many industries at the time. I well remember sitting through presentations that confidently predicted a run-up in the share price to over $100 in the first two years as a public company.

At first things went very well. Answerthink went public in May 1998 with the shares priced at $13 each. By the end of the first day they were up to $15.44; not bad, but not great in those early dot.com-fueled days. I was fortunate enough to have received both shares in the new company and options to buy shares as a result of the sale of The Hackett Group. By the end of that first day I was already sitting on a nice paper profit. Unfortunately, that was all it was, as I was not allowed to sell any of the shares or exercise any of the options for at least a year. Both the shares and the options vested at the rate of 25 percent a year for the next four years, meaning that while I sort of owned them already, I could not sell until they vested.

Over the next few months the share price steadily increased, and by January 26, 2000, the price had reached $39.38 a share. By now 75 percent of my shares and options had vested, but I didn't sell any. That $100 a share story was still rattling around my brain. Along the way I had accumulated more options, some were priced at $28 a share and others at $32 a share, yielding yet more paper profits. My personal balance sheet looked pretty good. Then came the collapse. One month later the shares were down to $20.35; I did manage to sell a few shares on the way down but kept over 95 percent of my holdings. By May the price was down to $14, barely above the offering price three years earlier. But surely this was only a temporary blip so I sat tight. By August 2002, the price was at $1.57, and I was feeling pretty sick by now. As the price plummeted, I managed to sell most of my shares and at least get some cash out of the deal; as for the options, forget it, they were not just underwater they were swimming in the Puerto Rico Trench in the Atlantic Ocean.

I left Answerthink in late 2002, as my four-year "handcuffs" after the IPO expired; the share price was $2.30. I left behind more than 50,000 stock options that had exercise prices somewhere between $20 and $40. Answerthink still exists, although in a move that was hugely ironic to me, the company was renamed The Hackett Group in 2007. This apparently recognized that Hackett was the only one of the many acquisitions that had any lasting value, which may explain the anemic stock performance. The name change did little to improve the stock price. In April 2009, the price was $2.27, a loss of 3 cents of in six years.

Executive pay is a bit like politics. It is riddled with conflicts of interest, half-truths, and alliances of convenience as numerous interest groups vie for their piece of the pie. A good example is the role of compensation consultants who theoretically act as independent advisors to a company's board of directors. Unfortunately, all too often the relationship is more akin to that of a lobbyist for a special interest group and a politician seeking to ensure that enough "pork" is directed toward their constituents. As one observer noted, "Compensation consultants know that if they win big pay packages for their CEO clients, they'll be rewarded with lucrative contracts to administer employee-benefits plans and the like."[5] Not exactly a recipe for objective advice.

As mentioned earlier, at the heart of the Great Incentive Scam is the process of rewarding people based upon meeting some mutually agreed performance target in the form of a plan, budget, or quota. As a result, planning is not an exercise in optimally allocating resources in order to achieve superior performance, but rather it is a warped and twisted negotiation of targets that subsequently govern incentive payments and performance reviews. This is how it plays out. The most desirable outcome for shareholders is a stretch target set to drive the optimal balance between risk and return.

Management's goal is to negotiate the lowest possible target in order to maximize the likelihood of earning the biggest possible bonus. The negotiation follows a predictable pattern. The CEO argues for growth using the time-worn phrases such as the need to maintain last year's momentum, leverage the value of past marketing and new product investments, exploit weaknesses in key competitors, add some great new products to the portfolio, and expand into a few new markets. Managers caution the CEO that last year's success has heightened the awareness and focus of competitors, the new products and markets will have a "ramp-up" period before they reach full potential, existing customers have limited capacity to increase order volumes, and economic uncertainty clouds the overall demand picture. After a few weeks of this horse-trading, the result is a compromise that satisfies no one and is almost certain to bear little relation to what will actually happen as the few reliable facts that were available at the outset will have been manipulated, framed, and massaged in such a way as to be almost unrecognizable. The CEO is convinced that managers can do better, but he or she also wants them to "own" the target and be "committed" to its achievement so they compromise; management feels they have been pushed to agree to a "stretch" target a little beyond their comfort zone, but at least they were able to negotiate the CEO down from the original target.

Defending the indefensible is one of the core skills for any budding chief executive. We will discuss the art of spin in business in chapter 16, but for the time being all you need to know about defending excessive pay packages is to use one or more of the following phrases: "Pay is in line with the industry" or "Compensation is determined independently by the board of directors" or arguing that the total package "represents the cumulative reward for many years of outstanding service" and that it is "essential if we are to retain the best talent."

Most of the time these empty platitudes work, but beware of coming up against a curmudgeon such as Warren Buffett who perhaps said it best: "Too often, executive compensation in the U.S. is ridiculously out of line with performance. The upshot is that a mediocre-or-worse CEO—aided by his handpicked vice president of human relations and a consultant from the ever-accommodating firm of Ratchet, Ratchet & Bingo—all too often receives gobs of money from an ill-designed compensation arrangement."[6]

Some pay packages do not require spinning. In 2000, after returning to Apple in heroic style, Steve Jobs accepted no compensation but did get $90 million to cover the cost of a nice, new jet. Unlike many CEOs, Jobs clearly earned his wings based upon Apple's stellar performance in the years since his return. Apple shares stood at just over $5 when he returned in 1997. By December 2007, they were at $198, and even the crash of 2008 only brought them back to $85 a year later, still seventeen times higher than upon his return. Jobs' annual salary during that time was $1. Not every CEO can claim the same return.

So What's the Fix?

Fixing executive compensation is not difficult—in theory. After all, it simply requires common sense, rational calculations, honesty, and trust. In reality, it will always be an imperfect system. Any time you define performance over a fixed time period, there is a risk that actions will be tailored to maximize results within the time period, often at the expense of future periods. This happens with quarterly earnings, annual results, and economic statistics, so it should be no surprise that results that drive rewards are "managed." But there is another factor that is not always the result of conscious manipulation. Performance will vary over time, and there is a strong possibility that current performance will not be sustained. Sport offers a good model for this. Players and teams are largely valued on their past success. A championship season typically leads to higher attendance (and ticket prices) the next season. A player who performs exceptionally well is likely to be rewarded with a much richer contract for the future. But as we know, past success is no guarantee of future success so there are many instances of teams and players reaping rich rewards that are not supported by their subsequent performance. The reality is that the past is all we have so we must make the best of it.

In well-run sports there is a balance between rewards for past performance in terms of guaranteed money and incentives for future performance. However in America it seems that the trend is to more and more guaranteed money and less and less risk for the athlete—this is somewhat akin to paying for failure in the corporate world where rich payouts follow an executive's termination. I may be biased, but golf, and tennis to a degree, seems to offer the best model. Professional golfers are independent contractors whose pay is determined almost solely by their performance. If you don't show up or don't play well, you don't get paid. Even the rich endorsement contracts or appearance fees that the top players can command rapidly evaporate if their performance dips. There are one or two exceptions—attractive female golfers and box office stars like John Daly can command premium rewards not necessarily tied directly to their performance, but even that won't last long if they fail to make it to the weekend in tournaments.

After the stock option scandals of recent years there has been a half-hearted attempt to redress the balance and actually introduce some measure of real performance into the equation, but old habits die hard, and very rich payouts for failure came to the fore again during the crash of 2008. Even some companies that tried to do the right thing then screwed it up. Shell, one of the largest oil companies in the world, had developed a measure that rewarded senior management if the company's total shareholder return for the period 2006–2008 ranked in the top three in the industry—a sensible relative performance measure.

However, when the results were added up in early 2009, the French company, Total, had pipped Shell for the number three spot. Not to worry, said the company's compensation committee, management had worked really hard, and it was such a shame that they missed out by such a small margin, so we will give them half their bonus anyway. What's next, awarding half a bronze medal for finishing fourth at the Olympics?

The good news is that a growing number of organizations recognize the flaws, or are being forced to by their shareholders. The bad news is that if companies don't address the issues, then government will. The fix is not that complicated. The first step is to base incentives on performance-based metrics rather than plan-based metrics. For example, tying incentives to measures such as absolute performance improvement relative to prior periods or relative performance to a credible market benchmark or peer group can all but eliminate the motivation for games playing. General Electric talks about seeking out businesses that have the potential to grow at twice the rate of Gross Domestic Product (GDP)—an external benchmark that is difficult to sandbag. Using market benchmarks also allows for rewards to be structured in such a way that excelling in poor markets can be rewarded.

A number of companies are now including benchmark comparisons in their incentive process; others are introducing mechanisms to ensure that payouts reward sustained performance over an extended period of time rather than exceptional one-off performance. For example, starting in 2009, Swiss Bank, UBS will pay out rewards over a three-year period, and if it becomes apparent that the company's profits were unsustainable or an individual's performance was short-lived, payouts could be cut or even reduced to zero. Other forms of clawback will become more prevalent as companies seek to balance short- and long-term performance. Another important step that the collapse in the financial markets during 2008 brought home is that many companies were making significant profits, and therefore paying out huge bonuses, by taking on excessive risk. In most companies the management of risk and the setting of performance targets are poorly linked. Targets emphasize growth in sales and earnings, but how often do companies then analyze the likely risks associated with meeting the targets? Part of the stress testing of performance targets demands that management ask questions such as:

- Can the targets be met without relaxing our credit risk standards?
- Is there a risk that our sales team will be motivated to ignore policies regarding promotions, pricing, and other incentives in order to make their quota?
- Can our suppliers or manufacturing operations meet the implied cost targets while still meeting quality standards?
- Are the growth targets consistent with our resource levels, or is there a risk that meeting the targets will negatively impact service levels?

Of course, these are exactly the questions that an effective planning process should be answering anyway, but as we have seen when pay is tied to plan, the words effective and planning can no longer co-exist.

The era of setting fixed performance targets for a year or more into the future is over—unfortunately, many organizations don't realize it yet. No one's crystal ball is clear enough to tie a significant portion of incentives to a fixed target or budget. While budget myopia persists, expect failure to continue to be richly rewarded for sometime to come.

So What?

- Base incentive compensation on metrics that cannot be negotiated or sandbagged.
- Keep the rules consistent over an extended period of time.
- Balance short- and long-term performance.
- Always ask the question "are the risks associated with meeting the targets acceptable?"
- Ensure complete transparency of the calculation of rewards.
- Balance measures of absolute performance with measures of relative performance.
- Don't pay out rewards in one lump sum; stagger the payments.

Notes

1. Charles M. Elson "What's Wrong with Executive Compensation?" *Harvard Business Review,* January 2003.

2. Institute of International Finance, "Compensation In Financial Services: Industry Progress and the Agenda for Change" (Washington DC: IIF, March 2009).

3. Jeremy Hope and Robin Fraser, *Beyond Budgeting* (Cambridge, MA: Harvard Business School Press, 2003), p. 8.

4. Jack Welch with Suzy Welch, *Winning* (New York: Harper Business, 2005), p. 189.

5. Harris Collingwood, "Do CEO's Matter?" *Atlantic Monthly*, May 2009.

6. Chairman's letter, Berkshire Hathaway annual report, 2005.

Chapter 10

Lies, Damn Lies, and Performance Metrics

We are drowning in metrics. The last few years have seen a measurement revolution. Actually, it has been more like a tsunami, as wave upon wave of new measures have been defined. We have numerous measures of quality, economic value, customer delight, earnings, first time yields, employee satisfaction, on-time arrivals, miles per gallon, carbon footprints, net promoter indexes, innovation, brand equity, and just about everything else. But is all this measurement making things better? Obesity is a growing problem (sorry about that one), economic cycles seem more volatile, quality still varies dramatically, and service is often lamentable—but at least we can now measure it. The logic of the measurement mania appears to be that if we measure it and tell you about it, it must mean that we care about it. For example, while wandering through London's Heathrow airport in early-2009 I was confronted with a scorecard tracking such metrics as departure lounge seat availability, something called wayfinding, which apparently measures the ease of finding your way around the airport, cleanliness, flight information and security waiting time. Our lives are now dominated by measurement. Unfortunately our ability to measure things greatly outstrips our ability to manage things.

For most organizations the plethora of metrics creates an optimization problem that cannot be solved. After all, how do you deliver great products at really low costs with outstanding service all the time? There have to be trade-offs somewhere—you don't find personal shoppers at Wal-Mart, Four Seasons doesn't offer rooms for $69 a night with the option to rent by the hour, and Southwest Airlines does not provide a warm towel to mop your fevered brow. At Cruciant, Steve and his team are well versed in all the fads—balanced scorecards, dashboards, key performance indicators, and critical success factors are religiously tracked, reported, and analyzed.

Fiction: Strategic Alignment—May 2007

The Cruciant annual report begins, as does every other annual report, with the Chairman's letter. In the 2006 report, Steve Borden describes the two major elements of Cruciant's strategy—a focus on innovation and establishing a strong presence in fast-growing, emerging markets. He goes on to describe the key attributes that are essential to Cruciant's being able to successfully execute against the strategy. Top of the list is the ability to attract, develop, and retain talented associates. Borden emphasizes that Cruciant's most valuable assets, by far, are its associates. He comments, "Without our exceptionally talented workforce we could not consider pursuing this aggressive and exciting strategy." He goes on to praise the value created by "the critical strategic partnerships that Cruciant has developed with both key customers and suppliers."

Following the Chairman's letter is a 70-page section devoted solely to Cruciant's financial results for the past year. There is an income statement complete with comparisons to past years, a balance sheet, and cash flow statement together with page after page of footnotes that address numerous different accounting rules and seek to explain some but not all the numbers in the main financial statements. However, anyone reading the report would not be able to find any information about the total investment Cruciant has made in innovation for this or any other year; the cost of Cruciant's establishing a presence in any of the emerging markets that it is targeting; the investment Cruciant makes in attracting, retaining, and developing its associates; or even the value of what Steve insists are Cruciant's most valuable assets—people. No line item exists in any of the financial statements that puts a value on those strategic partnerships or provides information as to the amount being invested in maintaining such partnerships that are apparently so critical to the company's strategy.

The report does contain such vital information as the expected Medicare Part D subsidy that will be part of the company's post-retirement benefits plans and the value of intangible assets subject to amortization—clearly items of vital importance to the average investor. Despite Steve's assertions that innovation, talent, and supplier partner-ships are key elements of Cruciant's strategy, they are nowhere to be found in the financial statements contained in the annual report. Even more surprising, they do not exist on any other financial report at the company. CFO Henry Pritchett knows exactly how much Cruciant is spending on travel or rent but can only guess at the cost of all the innovation that Cruciant is engaged in.

Searching for Truth—An Executive Management Meeting —February 2008

Each member of the management team is sitting in the Board Room staring at the latest corporate performance scorecard while waiting for Steve to show up. There are twelve measures, each of which has been deemed to be "key" or "critical" to Cruciant's performance. It looks like this could be a short meeting. Nine of the measures glow green, signifying that Cruciant's performance is at or ahead of plan; three are orange indicating some concerns, but they are all known quantities where action plans are already in place. Beside each "traffic light" is a directional arrow that indicates whether the metric is trending better (⇑), worse (⇓), or remains constant (⇔). All three oranges are showing a ⇑ so everything looks good.

Steve glides into the room and takes his customary position at the head of the table; however, he is frowning. All members of the management team immediately reset their facial expression from contentment to one of earnest concentration as they wait for Steve. He picks up the scorecard report, glances at it, and tosses it aside.

"The scorecard looks great: Revenues are up; margins are improving; so earnings look great. Quality is at an all-time high, as is customer satisfaction. Associate satisfaction and customer delight are moving in the right direction, and inventory levels and cash are both fine. So tell me, why has Transoceanic beaten us to market in both India and Russia with their rip-off of our digital sequencer? We have lost first-mover advantage and will be forced into a price war if we are to get any sort of market presence."

For the next hour, debate focuses on both the causes of the problem and possible strategies to blunt Transoceanic's offensive. There is no discussion of the supposedly key performance measures on the scorecard. Why? Well, every measure is backward looking (describing what has already happened), inwardly focused (reflecting solely on what Cruciant is doing), and an absolute value giving no sense of Cruciant's performance relative to the market or key competitors. In short, the scorecard is useless for managing in a competitive market.

Facts: Measurement Mania

There are only three problems with performance measurement today: the number of things that are measured, how they are measured, and how the measures are used. Aside from that everything is hunky-dory in Metricland.

Drowning in data? How about drowning in metrics? As we automate more and more aspects of our lives, we are creating a digital record of almost everything that happens. Metrics dominate our lives. The Dow Jones Index measures our wealth (or lack thereof); cholesterol, triglycerides, and body mass index, among many others, measure our health; odometers measure our speed; and the number of followers we have on Twitter measures our popularity. No self-respecting organization can survive without its balanced scorecards, key performance indicators, and performance dashboards. If it moves, measure it. Unfortunately, all too often measurement has become a substitute for action. We forget that measurement by itself changes nothing. I have been getting on the scales for years and can verify that the simple act of measurement does not induce weight loss. We need to get back to basics and make sense of the measurement mess. Management is getting a little like baseball where there's a statistic for everything but only one stat really matters: In baseball it is wins and losses, and in business it is profit and loss.

Mythbuster Wisdom: The Mirage of Measurement
In today's world the phrase, "You can't manage what you can't measure" must be replaced with "You can't manage what you can measure."

When I was growing up in England, I used to watch a lot of football (soccer) matches. There was only one statistic or metric that was ever reported and that was the score. Now I can get precise statistics on the time of possession, tackles made, the cumulative distance covered by every player on the field, the number of passes that connected with the intended target, as well numerous other data points. Soon there will be a graphic showing the blood pressure, heart rate, and level of neural activity (if any) of the player in possession. The instrumentation of life has many positives, but it can become a bit overwhelming. No matter how many good scores I get when I have a medical, there are always a few pesky problems that inevitably trigger my doctor to offer the same prescription—eat better, drink less, and get more exercise. The impact of metrics on business has also been a double-edged sword. The ability to understand infinite details about business operations can drive rapid improvements in performance, but it can also cause confusion and distract managers from the big issues as they seek to manage the miniscule. The impact of technology has been profound, allowing for closer inspection and much more granular detail than previously believed possible. We have the power to know more about the inner workings of our companies than ever before. However, new advances on the technological front have also contributed to a morass of data, statistics, and empirical measures that have left even the most astute managers searching for clarity.

Mythbuster Wisdom: The One Calculation Every Public Company CEO Can Do in His or Her Head

The mathematical ability of CEOs varies widely, but there is one calculation every CEO can do almost instantaneously in his or her head. No matter what the circumstance, CEOs can translate any monetary amount into the earnings per share impact in about one nanosecond. A project that costs $50 million really costs six cents a share. Increased earnings of $12 million equal a cent a share. It is the lingua franca of the executive suite.

I used to think that such a focus on earnings per share was a great example of the alignment of the CEO's interests with those of the shareholder, but sometimes I am not so sure. In the last few years, the focus of executive compensation has shifted to where the most significant portion of pay is in the form of ordinary shares, restricted shares, or options in the company, the theory being that the executive's wealth is tied to that of the shareholder. Unfortunately, an executive's motives may be colored by things like option grant and expiration dates, annual performance reviews, and negotiation of new employment contracts. But that's just me being cynical again, isn't it?

Lost in the fog of measurement are those metrics that allow managers to make better decisions faster. Perhaps we should add a new metric that measures the mean time to make a decision. Getting from measurement to decision is a simple process that all too often takes an age. The process is simple. The first question to ask is: Is this material? If the answer is yes, then the next question is: What are the implications? Once the implications are understood, ask: What should we do? Then comes the hard part—executing. Fast, confident decision making demands that the focus is on volatile and material information critical to an organization's performance. We don't need more metrics; we need better and more focused metrics.

Easier said than done, right? Maybe not, especially if you focus on simplicity and clarity. The ability to spot mistakes (or opportunities)—and thus save time and money—earlier in the game is the hallmark of high-performing organizations in turbulent times. Early identification and action provides a competitive advantage in a marketplace.

> **Mythbuster Wisdom: Separate the frequency of measurement from the frequency of reporting.**

Think of effective performance measurement in this way: When driving a car, the dashboard provides access to just the right amount of information to make informed decisions, without getting bogged down in extraneous data. Some metrics, like speed, amount of fuel, and oil pressure are important to be apprised of continuously. At the same time, sensors are monitoring myriad other facets of performance, but alert you only if there's a problem—a perfect example of just-in-time reporting. For instance, a warning light alerts you when the engine is overheating—and hopefully provides you with enough time to make adjustments to correct the problem. The dashboard gives you the *right* information at the right time, but doesn't inundate you with *all* the information.

Performance measurement should follow a similar model. By identifying those elements critical to both the long- and short-term performance of your organization, while also keeping an eye on those areas that can cause problems or affect other links in the management chain, performance measurement can shorten reaction time, allowing you to align resources and energies with strategy.

Part of the problem is that demand for information is changing radically. The traditional approach to management reporting has been, "If it is in the general ledger, we'll print it out and give it to you every month, so you better have a strong desk." Unfortunately, what often isn't obvious is that a key variance is buried on page 55 of the report. It could be critical information, but senior management may be looking for the proverbial needle in a haystack—with severe consequences if it is missed.

The goal is to make better decisions faster. The corollary for this is that no one gets every decision right, and it is equally important to know when you have made a bad decision. In both instances, speed is of the essence.

Metric of the Month

Today we have metrics for everything, and if we can't really measure it, we will make something up. Metrics and statistics are one area where America's world domination remains unchallenged; after all in baseball there are at least 37 statistical categories for batting and more than 40 for pitching—and Americans tell me cricket is difficult to understand! Everything is ranked: *Fortune* magazine started out in 1955 with a humble ranking of America's 500 biggest companies that has now mushroomed to ten different lists. Cable channel VH1 ranks everything from Hair Metal Bands to One Hit Wonders. Yet despite the burgeoning business of metrics, many areas of life are dominated by a single measure. U.S. economic health is reflected by the "Dow"; in the UK it's the "Footsie." Retailers salivate over sales per square foot; airlines fixate over on-time arrivals. Quality gurus want to know your sigma, and car geeks your cars' BHP. Sometimes measures change over time; I used to worry about my weight, now it is my cholesterol; and crossing the Atlantic forced me to reacquaint myself with Fahrenheit after having just got used to Centigrade.

The sheer volume of metrics can be overwhelming. This can lead to the exact opposite of what was intended when the metrics were defined. Instead of a balanced view of performance, managers become fixated on a single metric, which becomes an all-consuming focus—sometimes it is sales, sometimes it is quality. Frequently, an executive becomes so locked in on a particular measure that the whole organization focuses its attention on it since we all know that everyone watches what the boss watches. Business cases start to isolate the specific impact on the metric in question; departmental managers introduce their own tracking and reporting mechanisms so they can stay one step ahead of the boss; and campaigns, slogans, and pithy catchphrases are launched to ensure everyone gets the message. Ford had "Quality Is Job One;" credit card company MBNA had the phrase "Think of Yourself as a Customer" written above every door in its Delaware headquarters; and Zappos, the online shoe store bought by Amazon in July 2009, doesn't care about price or quality. As its website screams, "Customer Service Is Everything. In Fact, It's the Entire Company." Such myopic focus can be effective in uniting employees and ensuring a common

purpose; however, there is a risk that an overarching focus on one metric can have unintended consequences.

A few years ago, a waste disposal company introduced an incentive
for its drivers to reduce overtime costs. Crews would be paid a bonus
if they completed their routes by a certain time. The incentive worked
better than anyone expected; crews finished their routes on time and
overtime costs were cut in half. Unfortunately, in their zeal to meet
the time target, some crews decided they did not really need to make
all the stops on their route, while others decided that speed limits and
red lights did not apply to them as they rushed to make it back to the
depot. The situation became so bad that there were a number of fatal
accidents involving the company's trucks as crews sought to make it
back to the depot in time.

Another company embarked upon a customer service drive that
emphasized the importance of answering all phone calls no later than
the second ring. The target was easily met but only by hanging up on
existing callers in order to answer new calls. While call answering statistics improved dramatically, customer satisfaction numbers plummeted.
Performance measurement is like dieting—balance is everything.

Single Version of the Truth

Over the last few years, consultants, software salesman, and financial
managers have all rhapsodized about the attractions of a single version
of the truth with respect to financial reporting. What they mean is that
for any particular question there is only one answer or version that is
correct. If everyone uses the same version, ambiguity or confusion can
be eliminated. It sounds attractive and has its place right up there with
such well-worn management aphorisms as "singing from the same song
sheet" and "being on the same page."

The desire for a single version of the truth is born from frustration
at having to reconcile different points of view based upon different
answers to the same question. All too often a group of executives will
gather for a meeting armed with numerous pieces of paper that document their understanding of the current position. The boss starts the
meeting by asking, "How are we doing in terms of sales?" The VP of

Marketing pipes up and comments, "We are about 6 percent ahead of plan so far." At this point the VP of Sales says, "In terms of actual orders booked we are just a shade over 5 percent ahead of plan." Then the CFO chimes in, "Actually when compared to the plan approved by the Board and looking at sales that have been billed, we are 2 percent behind plan." At this point uproar ensues as competing versions of the truth are placed before the group. Much time is wasted as earnest arguments are put forward for each different view; as a result very little time is spent discussing how to improve sales going forward. Multiple versions of the same metric are clearly confusing, but aiming for a single version of the truth is pretty daft as well.

For any organization there will be at least three versions of the truth. There will be a version that reflects the way management views the business; there will be a version that reflects the accountants' view (we will see in Chapter 12 that this bears no relation to reality!), and there will be a version that reflects the view of the tax authorities—which will be even more of an abstraction. All three views are legitimate.

Mythbuster Wisdom: Multiple Versions of the Truth?

- The Bible offers numerous interpretations of the same event and leaves it up to the reader to interpret the true meaning.
- The Supreme Court frequently offers a dissenting view when judges can't agree, which happens more than 30 percent of the time.
- Lee Harvey Oswald acted alone when he assassinated President Kennedy.
- Elvis is really dead.

The quest for a single version of the truth can be very expensive and ultimately fruitless. It often starts in the IT department with an argument for collecting all the data in an organization and putting it into a single database or data warehouse. Proponents argue that this would eliminate duplication and redundancy and hence the risk of different views of the same data. Then the finance people get involved, and teams are established to develop common data definitions or standards that will be applied across the organization. Developing such standards is one of the most obvious forms of management communism discussed in Chapter 7. Once finance and IT are on board, it will not be long before everyone is seduced by the need for a single version of the truth. Unfortunately, even if you discount the management, accounting, and tax views, it is a fatally flawed concept. For all but a very few items of data, there is more than one legitimate view. For example, take the seemingly simple question of, "How many customers do we have?" Surely you can answer that by just adding up the number of records in your customer database? Not so fast. The right answer depends on answering one crucial question: Why are you asking?

For example, if you are asking the question to try and find out how many customers you have so you can roll out a direct marketing campaign, you may define a customer as anyone with whom you have done business in the last two years. However, if you are asking the question to better understand the proportion of your total customer base whose accounts are past due, the correct definition of customer is probably only those customers who have invoices outstanding. Both are valid definitions of customer. My humble attempt to bring clarity to this expensive debate is to offer a simple modification to the flawed phrase. Simply define the objective as being to define *a single version of the truth for a single use*. If we want to have a conversation about the same subject, it clearly makes sense to have a common understanding or definition; but it is perfectly legitimate to have different definitions for different uses.

Mythbuster Wisdom: A Single Version of the Truth— A Personal View

Take a very simple question such as "How much did you earn last year?" Pretty straightforward really, but there are at least three legitimate answers to the question:

- The easiest answer to the question is simply to add up the total of all the paychecks I received during the year.

- However, my accountant takes a slightly different view. She believes that what I earned is different than what I was paid, as there were a few days at the end of the year where I worked but for which I had not yet been paid. Accountants use the accrual method and therefore the driver of my earnings is the days I worked, not just the days for which I happen to have been paid come December 31st.
- The tax authorities take another view: They take my total earned income and then add in all the interest from my bank accounts and dividends from the shares I own in order to calculate something called my gross income. In the United States, this is then modified to reach a number called my adjusted gross income (AGI) which is calculated by deducting certain items such as contributions to health savings accounts and alimony paid from your gross income. As far as the IRS is concerned, AGI is what it is all about.

From my point of view, all these are irrelevant; the only amount that matters is the actual sum that hits my bank account.

The Balanced Scorecard—Yet Another Illusion

The Balanced Scorecard, as defined by Robert Kaplan and David Norton in their book *Translating Strategy into Action—The Balanced Scorecard* (Harvard Business Press, 1996), has become the runaway train of performance reporting over the last few years. There is even a Balanced Scorecard Hall of Fame to which such diverse organizations as the University of Leeds in England (my alma mater), the French Ministry of Defence, Korea Telecom, Tata Motors, and Best Buy have been elected.[1] A whole industry comprising consultants, software applications, and training programs has grown up around the concept to ensure that you develop just the right scorecard for your organization.

Don't get me wrong—the Balanced Scorecard can be a very useful tool—but I think many users have lost the plot. In Kaplan and Norton's original description, the use of the term *balance* was meant to emphasize the need for balanced measurement across four dimensions: short- and long-term objectives, financial and nonfinancial measures, lagging and leading indicators, and external and internal performance. This is an eminently sensible concept.

Unfortunately, something has been lost over time, and despite organizations having designed tens of thousands of scorecards, the overwhelming majority of management reporting is still focused on information that is short term, financial, lagging, and internal. Forget balance; we are still biased. For example, less than one in eight companies routinely tracks and reports measures of competitor performance.[2] To me this means that 87.5% percent of companies are either incredibly arrogant or incredibly stupid.

Despite investing billions of dollars in information technology, not much has changed in the information we use. Too much reporting is driven by the information we have, rather than the information we need. Our systems are chock full of data about the minutiae of events inside our own organization that have already happened. How do you think a CEO would respond to the following question? "Which would you prefer, lots of detail about what we did last month, or a range of estimates as to what our customers and competitors might do next month?" Now consider where most management reporting and analysis time is spent. That's right, it is spent pulling financial data out of internal systems about things that have already happened.

Despite the commonsense logic of the four dimensions of balance that Kaplan and Norton defined, most organizations are a long way from realizing the goal. But wait—there's more. I am not sure you really want balance in everything. Balanced scorecards often embrace many different metrics addressing everything from strategy, operations, financial results, quality, customer satisfaction, innovation, environmental stewardship, and corporate citizenship. Are these all equally important? I sense another intrusion of management communism.

Measurement does not have to be perfectly balanced; in fact, it probably shouldn't be. It should be tailored to what is important to you. Metrics should be dictated by the strategic objectives of your organization and should focus on the main challenges and the key differentiators of your products and services. Scorecards need to be biased to what makes your organization distinctive.

192 LIES, DAMN LIES, AND PERFORMANCE METRICS

Understanding the direction of the bias depends on the priorities of a particular industry or organization. For example, 3M is clearly biased toward innovation; Dell toward inventory management; Ford and Motorola toward quality; and Ritz/Carlton and Zappos toward customer service. The same rules and the same scorecard cannot be applied to everyone.

By focusing on what is important for your organization, you can dramatically simplify the management reporting process. Instead of getting lost in meaningless measurements that don't materially impact productivity or performance, you can deliver focused, insightful metrics that drive better understanding and decision making.

Reporting What or Why

Do you know how much of your organization's travel spending is good or bad? You are probably wondering what the heck I am talking about—so let me explain. Traditional management reporting tends to focus on ever-more-detailed decomposition of what was earned or spent. Rarely is information provided as to why revenue was earned or expenses were incurred. So in my travel example, a typical management report would look something like Table 10.1.

This type of report is the backbone of management reporting the world over. There is nothing wrong with the report: All the data is accurate; there is a logical organization showing aggregate travel spending and then a breakdown of the type of expense incurred such as airfare or

Table 10.1   Department: Northwest Sales
Period: Second Quarter

Travel Spending	Actual	Budget	Variance
Airfare	12,725	9,225	(3,500)
Hotel	4,750	4,000	(750)
Ground Transportation	1,500	1,250	(250)
Entertainment	2,150	2,000	(150)
Meals	600	700	100
Other	275	275	0
Total Travel	22,000	17,450	(4,550)

hotel, and there is a comparison of actual spending to the agreed budget. The report offers a fairly complete picture of what has been spent. A user of this report could ask for further detail showing how much each individual in the Northwest sales team had spent and could also get detail of the specific transactions that make up each expense type. However, look again at the report. Does it give you any insight as to why the travel expenses were incurred? Can you see the sales that were generated as a result of incurring these travel expenses? Do you know how travel spending has changed over time? Do you have any idea whether these travel expenses were an efficient use of the organization's resources?

The report does make it clear that the Northwest Sales Team has exceeded its budget for travel and that the problems are with spending on airfare and hotels. Based upon these insights, a manager reviewing this report would conclude that this sales team has allowed travel spending to spiral out of control; after all they are 26 percent over budget for the quarter. Based upon the information in the report, the manager may demand that the sales team dramatically reduce its travel spending over the next two quarters to ensure that they hit the annual budget.

Now let's look at the same data but presented in a different way in Table 10.2.

Table 10.2   Department: Northwest Sales

Period: Second Quarter

Travel Spending

Actual	Q2	Q1	Q4	Q3
Selling new business	5,700	7,000	8,400	10,500
Selling to current customers	4,600	6,000	7,800	8,000
Education and training	1,000	600	800	1,000
Total "Good" Travel	11,300	13,600	17,000	19,500
Mitigating client service issues	9,700	8,500	5,500	3,500
Administration	1,000	500	300	400
Total "Bad" Travel	10,700	9,000	5,800	3,900
TOTAL TRAVEL	22,000	22,600	22,800	23,400
New Orders	195,000	240,000	235,000	233,000
Good Travel to Orders	5.8%	5.7%	7.2%	8.3%
Ratio: Good to Bad Travel	51%	60%	75%	83%

This report shows the same total travel spending of $22,000 for the quarter but presents the data in a very different manner. First, instead of comparisons to the budget, the trend in actual travel spending over the last four quarters is shown. Second, travel expenses are divided into two main categories: good travel, which represents the sales team's developing new business with either new or existing customers and travel incurred because the team was seeking to improve their skills and capabilities; and bad travel that results from the sales team having to visit customers who have complaints or problems or that is incurred for purely administrative reasons. Third, additional information on new orders received has been provided, as well as a couple of statistical comparisons that show the ratio of travel spending to orders received and the ratio of good to bad travel.

This report has exactly the same number of base data elements, six, as the first report but offers a much richer set of information. The subtotals provide immediate visibility into the proportion of good versus bad travel. The comparison to prior quarters provides a clear view of the trends in travel spending over time. The first statistical measure relates travel expenses to the goal of the sales team, namely securing new orders, and the second measure gives an indication of the effectiveness of the organization's travel spending by showing the percentage of the sales generated that were spent on travel to secure those sales. So what can we discern from this report?

- Total travel spending is trending down slightly (GOOD).
- However, bad travel has increased significantly in the last two quarters while good travel has declined (BAD).
- Orders increased nicely for the first three quarters but suffered a sharp decline in the most recent quarter. This is not surprising given the sharp decline in good travel the previous quarter as there is almost certainly a time lag between a sales visit and an order being placed so the effects were felt in the next quarter. This does not augur well for the next quarter as good travel has declined still further (VERY BAD).
- One possible ray of sunshine is that the ratio of good travel spending to orders has been declining, indicating that the sales team was able to secure orders while incurring less expense. If the

organization can address the root causes of the client service issues that are driving the bad travel, there is hope. (GOOD)

The report in Table 10.1 is a great example of an accounting report. It gives hard facts about what was actually spent but no insight as to why the spending was incurred. The report in Table 10.2 is a true management report that organizes the information in a way that is meaningful for a business manager; unfortunately, the world is still largely managed with accounting reports. The problem is not just the lack of insight offered by this type of reporting but the impact it has upon decision making. There is a real risk that the actions taken will actually exacerbate the problem. In our example, an edict to get travel spending back in line with the budget is going to force deep cuts in travel by the sales team. Such action will result in one of two things: Sales will decline even further as the sales team cuts back even further on good travel, and/or existing customers will become increasingly frustrated at the level of service offered and the sales team will no longer be able to assist in mitigating the impact of such problems, again resulting in lower future sales.

Windshield or Rear View Mirror

In today's world, do you have more time to make decisions? Is your business becoming more predictable and less competitive? Are customers less demanding? I thought not. So why do organizations persist in trying to manage dynamic volatile businesses while using static, out-of-date information? As already discussed, the digitization of business does not leave us short of data—even if it is not always the right data. There is a reason the windshield is about a hundred times larger than the rear view mirror in your car. Looking where you are going is of significantly greater value than looking where you have been. Unfortunately, if we look at the size of the metaphorical windshield relative to the rear view mirror in most organizations you would see that the exact opposite must be true. The view of things that have already happened is detailed and exhaustive, but the view of the road ahead is murky at best. The rear view mirror is thousands of times larger than the windshield. Not only do we spend all our time looking backward, we also only get an update on what is happening once a month, or if we are very lucky, once a week, when the systems spit out the latest set of management reports. Imagine you are hurtling down the road at 70 mph (112 kph). How confident would you feel if the windshield only refreshed your view of the road ahead once every 30 seconds?

How much of the data contained in all the expensive new systems implemented in recent years relates to things that may happen in the future versus things that have already happened? We need to manage more like we drive (see Table 10.3).

Crucial business information is only available on a weekly, monthly, or quarterly basis, yet businesses increasingly operate 24 × 7 × 365. Actually, it is worse than that. Virtually all the information delivered is financial, and the financial result of any business event is the last thing that happens. It is too late to identify the customer service problem after you issue the refund!

Planning and reporting has always been a calendar-driven activity. Typically, planning is annual, forecasting is quarterly, and reporting is monthly. From an accounting standpoint, it is convenient to divide activities into logical time blocks. However, this completely misses the reality that most organizations operate on a continuous basis—work

Table 10.3 Driving Versus Managing

Driving	Managing
Continuously updated view of the road ahead	Monthly or quarterly forecasts
Window on the future many times larger than window to past	Window on the past many times larger than window to future
Satnav or GPS tells you immediately when you deviate from planned route	Variance reporting tells you sometime after the month or quarter end
Most of your time spent looking forward	Most of your time spent looking backward
Dashboard offers a select few critical measures with exception-based early warnings (e.g., fuel warning light)	Management reports deliver great detail on events that have already happened with vague forecasts of future impact

does not conveniently stop according to the calendar. Factories operate three-shift systems; many stores are open 24 hours a day, and almost all now open 7 days a week; supply chains hum 24/7; securities are traded globally around the clock; Amazon.com sells books continuously; and CNN reports the news nonstop. Even computers have moved from batch processing to always-on, real-time processing. Perhaps most shockingly, the archaic licensing laws in my homeland, England, were finally changed in 2005 to allow pubs to be open 24 hours a day if they so desire! While the use of discrete time periods will continue to support the needs of the accountant, it does not meet the needs of the business manager (or the beer drinker). There is no such thing as "Closed" in today's world.

Decoupling internal management processes from the calendar by implementing a set of processes that utilize continuous processing and monitoring of activity not only recognizes today's reality but also equips managers with vital information, allowing them to react to opportunities and threats in a timely fashion. In today's volatile world, the passage of time becomes just one of many criteria for triggering reporting, forecasting, or decision making.

Reports are dominated by information about things that have already happened and, as we saw in Chapters 5 and 6, the information we do have about the future in our budgets and forecasts is often of questionable value. So what should we do?

The first step is to ensure that we at least pay adequate attention to the future. I do not mean the mind-numbing but ultimately useless detail that populates most budgets. What is needed is to ensure that managers spend enough time trying to understand possible future scenarios both externally and internally and develop an understanding of the opportunities and threats posed in each case. The second step is to leverage the tremendous amount of historical data now available in most organizations to develop a deeper understanding of the cause-and-effect relationships that impact an organization's performance. A little rational focus on these two areas might have provided some inkling that most dot.coms were doomed to fail and that giving $400,000 mortgages to people with little or no documented income dramatically increases the risk of default.

198 LIES, DAMN LIES, AND PERFORMANCE METRICS

Mythbuster Wisdom: The More Things Change . . .
The following headlines appeared in the national press, but when?

- Major investment bank collapses.
- End of the "'leveraged'" era.
- Middle East investor buys major stake in a U.S. bank.
- Dow declines more than 20 percent.

Answer: 1990—*Plus ça change, plus c'est la meme chose*

Beware EBITDA

Over the last twenty years businesses have latched onto EBITDA (earnings before interest, taxes, depreciation, and amortization) as a headline measure of corporate health. The acronym itself should be a warning: Danger—Manipulated Numbers Ahead! Proponents argue that EBITDA is a better measure of performance than accounting profit since it focuses more on actual operating performance by excluding certain "non-cash" items such as depreciation and amortization that can vary dramatically between companies, interest expenses that are driven more by funding choices (debt versus equity) than actual performance, and taxes that can be distorted by capital gains and losses in prior years. Not surprisingly, the love affair with EBITDA blossomed during the leveraged buyout boom in the 1980s. Private equity firms bought companies and then loaded them up with debt, often paying themselves a rich dividend with the borrowed money. The combination of high interest payments on the debt and the need to amortize any goodwill associated with the acquisition would tank accounting profits, so EBITDA rode to the rescue. The argument went something like this: Using EBITDA gives us a better sense of the cash-generating ability of the business and can quickly turn an accounting loss into an EBITDA gain. If you then use EBITDA to value a business or calculate a price/earnings ratio, this produces a much nicer result. However, the last time I looked, companies still had to make interest payments on their debt, pay their taxes, and at some point replace the assets that are being depreciated. So beware EBITDA.

Mythbuster Wisdom: Don't Like the Metric?
Well Then—Fudge It

- Sales per square foot—cram more merchandise into the same amount of space or build smaller stores.
- On-time arrival—change the timetable so that a 19-minute flight from Cleveland to Detroit is scheduled to take one hour and seventeen minutes.[3]
- Inflation/consumer prices—exclude fuel and housing costs and call the resulting measure "Core CPI" to avoid the unpalatable.

Traffic Light Syndrome—Should I Stop or Should I Go?

A few years ago I was sitting in on a sales team meeting for a large manufacturer. They were conducting their normal monthly review, and the regional sales director was reviewing performance with each of his area sales managers. The company had recently developed performance scorecards for each function, and the sales team was using them for the review. The scorecard contained ten different measures covering everything from sales booked through to customer satisfaction. As the meeting progressed, the sales director started to review the scorecard of one area manager. As with many other scorecards, this one used a traffic light metaphor to provide a quick status on each metric. For this area, nine of the ten measures showed a green light indicating no problems. One metric, the level of sales force spending on travel relative to budget, was glowing red. The sales director passed over all the green metrics and started quizzing the area sales manager as to why his team's travel spending was 15 percent over budget for the last quarter. The manager looked a little confused and started to try and explain away the variance with vague comments on the need for more visits to close deals, the rising cost of airfares, and other rather unconvincing explanations. He was a salesman after all; finance was not his strong suit. His boss was having none of it. He ordered that for the next few months' sales travel must be contained to only 90 percent of the budget in order to make up the overrun by the end of the year. At this point I could contain myself no longer (I know, I need to get a life), so I made a gentle suggestion that the team look at the first metric on the scorecard. The sales director immediately commented, "Why do we need to bother with that? It is green." Not unreasonable, you may think. The metric in question was sales relative to budget and was glowing bright green—the team was 20 percent better than the budget, so clearly there was no problem. I went on to comment that to me it did not seem unreasonable for the sales team to be 15 percent over the budget for travel when its sales were 20 percent better than the budget; in fact, I could go as far as to say that the area manager deserved a pat on the back for delivering incremental sales at lower cost. After some discussion, it was agreed that I was right and that the scorecard was wrong. So what was the problem?

A little further investigation quickly uncovered what is an all-too-common flaw in many measurement systems. When the budget had been set, late the prior year, everyone had agreed on the sales budget for each month of the year and the travel budget had been set as a fixed percentage of sales based upon the past years' results with some minor adjustments to take account of increasing airfares and other travel costs. The result was that the travel budget was set at 10 percent of sales. Nothing amiss so far; however, when the budget was loaded into the financial reporting system, all the numbers were input as fixed monetary amounts not as a percentage of sales. The records looked something like Table 10.4.

The data accurately reflected the plan, and the finance team then added the triggers for determining whether the indicator would be green, yellow, or red for the travel metric on the scorecard. Green indicated that spending was at or below the budget; yellow indicated that

Table 10.4 Sales and Expense Plan for Area 12: 2007

	Sales	Travel
Jan	10,000	1,000
Feb	10,000	1,000
Mar	11,000	1,100
Apr	11,000	1,100
May	11,000	1,100
Jun	12,000	1,200
Jul	10,000	1,000
Aug	10,000	1,000
Sep	11,000	1,100
Oct	12,000	1,200
Nov	14,000	1,400
Dec	17,000	1,700

spending was less than 5 percent over budget; and red indicated that spending was more than 5 percent over budget.

The problem arose as the year progressed and sales turned out to be better than plan. Table 10.5 shows the sales trend for team 12.

April's sales came 20 percent over plan, warranting the green light on the scorecard. However, the picture for sales expenses was not so bright (see Table 10.6).

April's travel expenses were 15 percent over budget (1,265 versus 1,100), triggering a red light on the scorecard. The problem was that by translating the travel budget to a fixed monetary amount, the relationship between travel expenses and sales that had been built into the plan (that travel was expected to be 10 percent of sales) had been broken. Consequently, the scorecard was reporting the exact

Table 10.5 Area 12: Sales—Actual Versus Budget

	Budget	Actual	Variance
Jan	10,000	10,500	+ 500
Feb	10,000	11,000	+1,000
Mar	11,000	12,100	+1,100
Apr	11,000	13,200	+2,200

Table 10.6   Area 12: Travel Expenses—Actual Versus Budget

	Budget	Actual	Variance
Jan	1,000	1,025	**(25)**
Feb	1,000	1,050	**(50)**
Mar	1,100	1,200	**(100)**
Apr	1,100	1,265	**(165)**

opposite of what it should have been. This simple but real example illustrates a very common problem for many reporting systems in use today. Assumptions and relationships that are developed during the planning process are completely lost when the results of the planning process are input into the financial reporting systems, leading to incorrect reporting and perhaps more important, a loss of trust by the very people who are supposed to use such information to make better decisions.

Mythbuster Wisdom: Massaging the Measure

Manipulation and measurement go hand in hand, so beware of the following behaviors that should arouse suspicion.

- Frequently changing the metrics used.
- Changing the calculation or comparison basis to "better reflect reality."
- Reporting hundreds of different metrics, thereby making it difficult to identify those that really matter.
- Reporting only those metrics that look good.
- Developing complicated composite metrics that combine many different elements in the hope that no one will look at the underlying components.
- And finally, arguing that a poor result for a metric is the result of calculation bias or inaccurate source data—no one ever uses this excuse when the numbers look great.

So What?

- There is no such thing as a single version of the truth.
- The best you can hope for is a single version for a single use.
- Deliver information that managers need, not that accountants produce.
- Understanding why something happened is much more useful than knowing in precise detail what happened.
- Scorecards need to be biased toward the metrics that matter most in executing your chosen strategy. Measure what makes you distinctive.
- Place a high value on external, leading, predictive, and non-financial measures.
- Avoid looking at a single metric in isolation—relationships matter more.
- Consistency, clarity, and simplicity rule.
- Beware a metric you don't understand. Does anyone really know how the Dow, CPI, or body mass index is calculated?
- Make sure you balance the size of your windshield with that of your rear view mirror.

Notes

1. The Palladium Group, *Balanced Scorecard Hall of Fame Report Collection 2004–2009* (Cambridge MA: Harvard Business School Publishing, 2009).
2. Sonax Group Research, 2008.
3. Continental Airlines timetable for February 19, 2009, www.continental.com.

Chapter 11

Leveraging Technology for Competitive Advantage

Technology has transformed the world over the last half-century. For the most part the effects have been positive—but not always. Many executives feel blackmailed into green-lighting investments in each new wave of technology for fear of being left behind without fully understanding the rationale or the economics. As the first generation of CEOs who have spent their whole lives in the computer age settles into corner offices around the world, it is time to take a long, hard look at how technology invest-ments are made and managed. Naturally, Cruciant prides itself on being at the forefront of technology adoption and utilization and sees its systems as a unique source of competitive advantage—just like everyone else.

Fiction: On Time, On Budget—But Irrelevant —February 2008

Candice Molten, Cruciant's Chief Information Officer, is reviewing the status of all major IT projects with her management team.
Cruciant recently implemented a sophisticated project tracking and
management system that integrated all the key elements of the project
management process, giving Candice and her team extremely detailed
information on the status of every project. Employees' and contractors'
time is directly recorded against the specific tasks in each project plan,
and purchase orders for outside materials and equipment are also maintained in the system with direct updates from the procurement and
accounts payable systems so that project managers can see the status of
their projects relative to the total budget and the intermediate mile-
stones. One feature that Candice particularly likes is a metric called
value delivered. This is a measure of the percentage of the total value
of the project that has already been realized. Candice is a big believer
in delivering value fast, and she loves to report the value delivered
at executive management meetings to show her colleagues that IT is
meeting its mission statement of delivering "real value, every day."

Today's review is going well. There are no major problems or delays.
She is aware that the direct sales team has been struggling because two
projects, the upgrade of the order entry system and the introduction of
new PCs, were delayed during the budget process. However, her team was
able to put a workaround in place and the sales team managed to free up
some of its own budget for the new PCs, so that problem should be fixed.

As she scans the report in front of her, she takes particular note
of the status of the emerging market infrastructure build-out project.
This is a critical project that is designed to ensure that all the systems
are in place to support Cruciant's emerging market expansion that is
such a key part of this year's plans. It is ahead of schedule and under
budget. Candace makes a note to mention that at the next executive meeting. As they discuss the project, one of her managers asks a
question, "Candice, how do you see Steve's announcement last month
that we are slowing down our emerging market strategy in light of
the economic slowdown impacting this project?" Candice thinks for
a moment and replies, "I don't think it does. The emerging market

strategy is a cornerstone of our overall strategy—the fact that we are ahead of plan is good. It simply means we will be better positioned when we do ramp up over there." The project manager nods and adds one final comment, "I agree the business case was compelling. It is why we put it ahead of the direct sales order entry system and PC upgrades when we prioritized them last August."

A few weeks later, Cruciant announces the suspension of its emerging market strategy in light of the severe economic downturn. Candice has to halt the project—it is still ahead of plan but is no longer relevant to Cruciant's business.

The IT Sting—May 2008

In late 2005, Candice presented a proposal to the management team for a major project to implement a single computer system to support all Cruciant's manufacturing, distribution, finance, and human resources operations worldwide. At the time this was how she justified the project:

"As you know, since the acquisition of FTE we have been struggling to integrate all their disparate systems onto our own platforms. The root of the problem is that in areas like order entry, billing, accounts receivable, and accounts payable we have more than twenty different platforms around the company. This makes it impossible for us to quickly get a consolidated view of our business at any point in time. I have had BTI (Big Tech Integrators) studying how we can streamline our systems portfolio. They have put together a pretty compelling business case. If we move to the GMS (Global Mega System) platform, we can, within three years, get all of our operations on a single system worldwide. We will have real-time visibility to all aspects of our business on a global basis. It will also allow us to consolidate our back-office operations into three shared services centers: one serving North America, one in Europe, and one in Asia. The investment is significant—$150 million over three years, but the savings are very attractive: $25 million in year one, $40 million in year two, and $50 million a year thereafter. The overall payback is just over 3.1 years, but that does not include the enormous benefits from better information and improved risk management, which as we all know are difficult to quantify. We chose GMS because more than 60 percent of the Fortune

500 use it, and BTI has already completed three similar implementations. They have quoted around $80 million for the implementation, which was the lowest of the three bids we sought. The other costs reflect hardware, software, other infrastructure, and also the severance costs associated with the 4,000 staff reductions we will be able to realize."

Today, three years later, Candice is discussing the project with Steve Borden.

Steve: "Candice, where do we stand on GMS implementation? I seem to remember that we were supposed to be done in three years, but everywhere I go people tell me the migration is not complete and that everything seems to be behind schedule and over budget."

Candice: "We have had quite a few problems. As you will remember, we had to replace BTI. The project started well, but after about six months they started to switch out some their key staff. We also found out that a lot of the supposed consultants they were putting on the project and charging us $1,500 a day for were really new hires who had no experience. As a result, we lost a lot of momentum. The net result was that bringing in Synergistic Excellence to replace BTI cost us about three months. We also found that GMS would not work exactly as we expected, so we had to do some customization work for the European operations. They are all live now, albeit about nine months behind schedule. Despite all these challenges, we were close to getting most of the company on GMS by late this year, but then came the divestiture of the electronics division. It had just gone live, and we had to unwind much of the work in order to split it off. We also had to back those operations out of the three service centers. This has cost us about $25 million and is likely to delay the overall implementation until late next year. With hindsight, we might have been better taking a more incremental approach, but all the advice and due diligence suggested that we took the right course of action."

Steve looked up from notes he had been making and said, "I understand the challenges we have had, but I am very disappointed. The project will be almost two years late and $50 million over budget. Candice, I value your commitment to Cruciant, and you have given the company a tremendous amount over the years, but I think it is time for a change. I want this to be amicable, and we will of course accelerate the vesting of your options. I think your employment agreement calls for one year's severance, which we will of course honor. Work with Jean on the details."

Two Days Later

Press Release: New York: Cruciant today announced that Candice Molten, Chief Information Officer, will be leaving the company with immediate effect. CEO Steve Borden commented, "Candice has been a key member of my management team for many years. I am sorry to see her leave and wish her all the best in the future." Ms. Molten said, "Cruciant has been an enormous part of my life for fifteen years; I just feel the time is right for me to seek out new challenges."

One Week Later

Press Release: Dallas, TX: Big Tech Integrators (BTI) is delighted to announce that Candice Molten, former CIO of Cruciant Inc. is joining BTI as a principal in its IT Management practice. BTI President Greg Hitchens commented that, "Candice has an unparalleled track record as one of the most dynamic and successful IT executives, and adding her to our senior advisory team offers our clients access to one of the great talents in IT today."

Facts: Automating Inefficiency Just Gets You Bad Data Faster

Got a bad process? Then just automate it. No, this is not the accepted wisdom, but it is common practice. Changing processes and perhaps more important, behavior, is a lot harder than throwing some technology at the problem. Of course, no one ever admits to simply automating inefficiency. The politically correct expressions include leveraging technology for competitive advantage, customizing applications to our unique business requirements, or implementing a flexible architecture that can adapt to the complexities of our business. In a few cases this is actually true; however, I have heard such rationales applied to processes such as payroll, accounts payable, employee time-keeping, purchase order processing, and even travel expense reporting—not exactly sources of competitive advantage. After all, how often has a customer explained its supplier preference with the words, "They have a really cool accounts payable system"?

In most situations it is a lot easier, though rarely cheaper, to automate the existing twelve-step process rather than eliminate the seven unnecessary steps and automate what is left. Not surprisingly, software vendors are anxious to get their products implemented as quickly as possible since most of the purchase payment and the incredibly profitable maintenance charges do not kick in until the system is operational. They blithely argue that simple implementation of their solution all but guarantees that your processes will be best-practice compliant without any need to delay the rollout while actually making your processes simpler. After all, we all know that SAP stands for Solves All Problems and that Oracle is the font of all knowledge, don't we?

Unfortunately, it's not that simple. Systems today are so flexible that they will easily allow you to automate inefficiency (or even stupidity). Every vendor touts its ability to support best practices; what vendors do not broadcast is that their products are equally adept at supporting worst or even dumb practices. The choice is yours. If you want to automate your 10,000-line-item budget, the good news is that today's software will allow you to do so and offer a multitude of different automated tools for analyzing each line item. The bad news is that you will still have a terrible budget.

Jim Stent, a client of mine while he was VP of Finance at the Bank of Thailand in the late 1980s, once said to me, "Our ability to create cool new technology greatly outstrips our ability to use it effectively." He was right then, and he is even more right now. Too often we assume that simply upgrading our technology guarantees better performance. Many is the time when I click through my sixteenth screen while making an online purchase of an airline ticket only to have my Internet connection wobble and that is when I fondly remember calling up my friendly travel agent, Anne, and telling her of all my travel requirements for the week. Not just plane tickets, but hotels, and rental cars as well, all in a 3-minute phone call. Anne was brilliant, she knew all my travel quirks, like aisle seats on short flights and window seats on long flights, and I could be comfortable in the knowledge that all would be handled with efficiency. I even got a friendly, "Have a safe trip" every time I spoke to her.

Mythbuster Wisdom: Beware the Multimillion-Dollar Data Collection Tool

A large, well-respected company decided to invest in a new set of systems to support its planning, budgeting, and forecasting processes. The business case was rock solid. Managers and analysts were spending hundreds of hours creating and maintaining individual spreadsheets on which they dutifully developed very detailed budgets and forecasts that were then sent as email attachments to the corporate office, where another cadre of finance professionals worked long hours to consolidate all the inputs. This process was repeated five or six times as the budget was developed and then two or three more times each quarter as the forecast was created. The new systems promised to eliminate all the manual effort, providing everyone with a common system that pre-populated much of the data, allowed for collaboration across functional and organizational boundaries, and then automatically consolidated the results. The project was quickly approved and implementation went surprisingly well, coming in on time and slightly under budget— yes, this is a true story. Everyone was ecstatic.

After a few months the corporate team began to notice that despite all the new systems, people were still leaving it to the very last minute to build their budgets and forecasts, and while there were clearly benefits in the consolidation process, few of the other expected benefits had been realized. A small team was commissioned to investigate. Their findings were shocking. Hardly anyone was using the new system despite its powerful analytical tools, its ability to share data, and automatically extract data from the organization's transaction systems. Employees were still using their own spreadsheets for the bulk of the work and then simply keying the data from their spreadsheet into the new system at the last minute. Why was this happening? Further investigation revealed two reasons. First, people had been developing and using their spreadsheets for many years; they trusted them and felt comfortable using them. Second, the expected users of the new system were wary that if they started using the tool for all their planning activities, then "corporate" would be able to take a sneak peek at their work before they were ready. Such fears were stoked on the budget grapevine when soon after implementation an analyst in the corporate planning department fired off an email to one of the business unit teams questioning an early set of numbers that had been entered into the system but not finalized. Managers quickly found that by sticking with their spreadsheets they could prevent any snooping until they were ready. After spending a few million dollars and many months implementing a state-of-the-art system, the company had effectively created the world's most expensive data collection tool!

Death by Spreadsheet

On a damp September day in 1983, I arrived at Lloyds Bank in London, fresh out of university, armed with a degree in accounting and computer science and ready to start work. After a few weeks of high-powered training, which seemed to involve sorting cancelled checks (or cheques as we say in England) into alphabetical order, I was given a very cool IBM PC and a couple of five-inch floppy disks containing the Lotus 1–2–3 spreadsheet program. My job was to build budgets. For months I happily created gloriously complex spreadsheets that budgeted and forecasted all manner of things. Even then I suspected that the detail I developed would bear little relation to what actually happened but by becoming the office's "spreadsheet jockey," I gained a certain cachet, so I kept quiet.

Fast forward more than 25 years and wander through any finance, marketing, or sales department today and what will you see? The computers will be smaller but more powerful; instead of green text on black screens, there will be nice, big, color flat panel displays; the software will be Excel and the floppy disks will have been replaced by network applications, but what else has changed? Analysts are still slaves to their spreadsheets, tethered to their cubes as they create another pivot table or develop yet another iteration of the budget.

Was this really the promise of technology? I think not. Technology has largely failed the business analyst. Instead of offering clarity, simplicity, and creativity, the technology allows for the development of ever more meaningless detail. In a world where you can Google local Chinese artifacts and instant message your cousin in Botswana, it is a little disappointing, don't you think? Is there another area of life, let alone business, where technology has had less of an impact over the last quarter of a century? Actually, it is much worse than that; it is inefficient and dangerous. Many highly paid professionals in offices across the world spend their time on the caring and feeding of the spreadsheet monster. Their work week can be divided into four parts: collecting data to put in spreadsheets, inputting data into spreadsheets, manipulating data in spreadsheets, and trying to print out the spreadsheet in a readable format. That's it—no analysis, just number crunching. A former colleague of mine put it very succinctly when he described the problem of having too many people collecting data and too few analyzing it: "We have too many people stacking data and not enough staring at it."

When the spreadsheet first appeared in the office, it was a wonderful thing. For the first time people could quickly and easily develop ad hoc reports and analyses on the fly. Pretty soon the spreadsheet became the tool of choice in the world of business as users became evermore creative in its application. Build a budget—no problem; create an expense report—easy; consolidate sales reports from different departments—a snap. By the turn of the century many companies were run by spreadsheets. Every major decision was predicated upon the results spewed out by one or more spreadsheets. Combining the spreadsheet with that other wondrous tool, email, allowed people to collaborate and share. The attached spreadsheet became the financial communication vehicle of choice. Then we hit a wall.

Spreadsheets had become so numerous and cumbersome that simply keeping them functional became a full-time job; the spreadsheet jockey became the most important person in the department. Errors started to creep in and the corporate IT department became concerned about security and integrity, yet the thirst for yet another worksheet continued unabated. The spreadsheet ceased to be a productivity tool,

> **Mythbuster Wisdom: The Biggest Drains on Personal Productivity in the Twenty-First Century**
>
> - Email
> - Spreadsheets
> - Instant messaging
> - Facebook, Twitter, and the rest of the social networking crowd

at least in the positive sense. Spreadsheets became the heroin of the workplace—with Microsoft as the dealer! This addiction needs eradicating; the spreadsheet needs to return to its niche, and we must liberate the analyst from its tyranny.

> **Mythbuster Wisdom: If in Doubt, Cut It Out**
>
> In October 2008, as the credit crisis morphed into a full-blown recession around the world, companies resorted to the usual simplistic tactics for managing when times are tough. If in doubt, cut travel and training, slash IT budgets, and freeze all hiring. You would think in these days of sophisticated modeling tools and rocket science management practices we would have come up with something a little more thoughtful—but no.
>
> One of the more interesting responses came from SAP, the German software behemoth that, together with Oracle, has pretty much cornered the enterprise software market. Naturally, SAP thrives when organizations spend millions on technology. In fact, SAP is one of the biggest beneficiaries of management communism as companies implement standardized global systems that force everyone to operate in precisely the same manner. As the recession hit, the company's co-CEOs Henning Kagermann and Leo Apotheker followed the standard operating procedure in a directive to staff by

announcing a headcount and hiring freeze: "There is a complete headcount and hiring freeze, and all existing job vacancies will be cancelled."[1] Third-party expenses were slashed: "Since we are not hiring, all engagement with external recruiters must cease immediately. We will discontinue engagement with management consultants and evaluate the impact this has on ongoing projects. Until further notice, all external training is to be canceled. Internal meetings must be held within SAP buildings, and you cannot rent external conference facilities for this purpose."[2] Travel was curtailed: "Cease ALL internal non-customer-facing travel in October . . . Any non-customer-facing travel already booked should be cancelled immediately, even if this incurs penalties."[3] No surprises here—this is typical knee-jerk expense management. But most interesting of all was the order to halt all new IT spending. "We will review all planned investments in IT equipment, hardware, software, facilities, and company cars, as well as internal IT projects. Do not order any new equipment at this time."[4] I bet SAP hoped its customers did not take the same course of action. This would be akin to Honda saying that it was eliminating the use of cars and demanding that everyone use cheaper public transport instead.

The price of our collective addition to spreadsheets is high. During 2007 and 2008, I conducted a research study, jointly with IBM's Cognos unit, of more than 100 organizations around the world. One of the questions we asked was: How do finance professionals spend their time? The results were illuminating to say the least (Figure 11.1).

More than 80 percent of every finance professional's time was spent collecting data, maintaining spreadsheets, or preparing reports and presentations, while only 11 percent of time was spent actually performing analysis. Pretty shocking, isn't it? Especially after more than twenty-five years of investment in business systems. Looking at the data in a slightly different way brings home the chronic waste of time and talent (Figure 11.2). In effect, the average finance professional does not

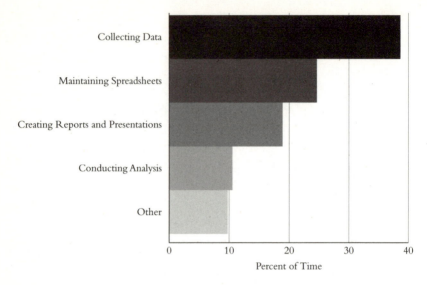

Figure 11.1   Professional Staff Time Utilization

start working on value-added analysis tasks until late-Friday morning. With fully loaded labor costs for experienced finance professionals approaching $100,000 a year, this is akin to setting fire to a large stack of hundred dollar bills every week.

For most organizations the prerequisites for fixing this problem are in place. The progressive application of technology to nearly all aspects of business by implementing enterprise resource planning, customer relationship management, data warehousing, e-commerce, and web enablement has digitized much of the internal and external data available to

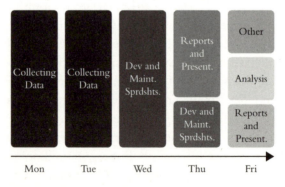

Figure 11.2   A Typical Finance Professional's Work Week

an organization. Access to critical information about leading economic indicators, key business drivers, customer behavior, and supply chain performance has never been greater; however, we have only just begun to harness the potential for managing performance. Effective integration of these rich data sets into our performance management processes can revolutionize the quality and timeliness of the insights available to managers. The benefits are obvious: earlier identification of potential opportunities and threats, insightful tracking of customer and supplier behavior, and continuous monitoring of key business indicators. Instead of relying on static budgets and out-of-date forecasts, managers can track the real-time flow of business activity, which can only improve decision-making speed and confidence. It's a nice dream, isn't it?

IT ROI—An Oxymoron

To many business managers, the only certainty about IT projects is that they will be both late and over budget. In response, IT executives have expended tremendous effort in developing sophisticated project management processes, spent vast sums on training IT staff in the art of project management, and deployed complex methodologies to ensure that the latest ERP implementation does not morph from a project into a career. And then what happens? The technology becomes so embedded in the way we work that we cannot isolate the IT

> "They have computers, and they may have other weapons of mass destruction."
>
> Janet Reno, former Attorney General of the United States

components from the process and people elements. IT is no longer in control of the results, and we can forget about measuring the return on investment that is directly attributable to the technology. It's like trying to isolate the marginal value of the cheese on a pizza or the contribution of Ringo to The Beatles.

Measuring the return on technology investment has been the Holy Grail for CEOs and CIOs for years. Managers and consultants expend tremendous effort trying to quantify the returns in terms of shareholder value, sales growth, and cost reduction from investments in each new wave of technology. Each generation from mainframes through personal computers, client server, and enterprise resource planning (ERP) to the Web has promised unmatched ROI—but hard facts are scarce. The results have been inconclusive and seem restricted to broad statements about productivity increases being somehow tied to technology investments. This loose causal relationship is discomforting for many business leaders. The primary reason for dissatisfaction is straightforward. Asking the question, "What is the return on our technology investments?" is pointless. There is no meaningful answer.

Today, it is impossible to isolate the technology benefits of any project. How valuable would iTunes be without the music? What about Facebook without friends? The pervasive impact of technology now means that it is so inextricably intertwined with other aspects of the business that IT ROI is an oxymoron. This was not always the case. In the early days of IT there was a clear distinction between the technology and the other elements of the business. Inputs and outputs were highly regulated as manual work was handed off to IT, or in those days, the data processing department, and the data was keyed into terminals hooked up to computers that resided in remote, climate-controlled data centers. However, the advent of the personal computer, the Web, and all things wireless has obliterated the once-distinct boundary between technology and people.

Of course, there is another explanation that has more than a grain of truth. Many technology investments have failed to deliver the expected returns, not because of technology failures, but because of poor design, weak project management, and inadequate user training. As we discussed earlier, too many investments simply automated inefficient processes or delivered incredible functionality that no one fully understood how to use. How much of the available functionality in Microsoft Excel does the average user actually use or, perhaps more interestingly, even know that it exists? The return on technology investments is only as good as the impact of its usage. For example, the value of having a GPS system in you car is only realized if you, as the driver, take notice of the directions you are being given. The technology may work perfectly, but there is no guarantee that value from its use will be realized.

So how should IT investments be evaluated? First, abandon the idea that there are IT projects—there are no such things anymore. There are only projects that create something new or improve something that already exists of which technology is a component, be they cool products, more efficient customer service, or more productive employees. Therefore, the evaluation of return on investment needs to match the total investments with the total returns, regardless of the nature of each.

For example, consider the investment in a new customer relationship management (CRM) system. Typically, the expected benefits from such a system would be expressed in terms of improved customer satisfaction leading to increased retention and/or use of products and services, together with an enhanced ability to target customer needs. However, the implementation of the new system is only one element in ensuring that full value is realized. Having perfect customer information without adequately trained customer service representatives to interpret and act upon that information or without providing the insights derived from your CRM system to your sales force or product development organization will ensure that the return on investment is not maximized.

A better way of estimating the benefits is to address the value of all the elements that must come together for the investment to pay off. So in the example above, the evaluation would address three elements: the benefits from the technology itself such as consolidation of data, shorter processing times, and reduced data input errors; the value of new or changed processes to communicate the insights gained from better customer information such as providing better information to the sales force so they can close more deals or to the product development team to refine and design better products; and the increase in employee productivity and performance from training customer service representatives to both interpret and respond to the new customer information to deliver better service or identify new sales opportunities with existing customers.

Above all, when attempting to calculate the return on investment, keep the math simple. Many ROI calculations require a PhD to decode; this simply heightens suspicion that some creativity has been applied to the process.

For example, assume you have $100 million in sales and your cost of goods sold (COGS) are $55 million and selling, general, and administrative expenses (SG&A) add another $20 million. If the unrealized portion of your return on technology-related projects equals a modest 5 percent of COGS and 10 percent of SG&A, the incremental earnings opportunity is $4.75 million. Assuming a conservative price to earnings ratio of 12, the result is the creation of over $57 million of shareholder value. Not a bad justification for paying more attention to your IT investments.

Hype Versus Reality

Picture the scene—the CEO paces in a conference room, brandishing a thick report. He gazes impatiently at his senior managers. "You've all read this," he says. "Top-shelf consultants; two million bucks; pure strategic thinking. This could put us years ahead. The board is psyched. I'm psyched. It's a brilliant plan. One question: Given our current technology, is this implementable?" The response, from five different chairs in the room: "No." The CEO looks frustrated but not surprised.

For years, the hype about technology has greatly exceeded the reality. In the 1980s executive information systems and decision support systems were going to revolutionize management; by the 1990s it was data warehouses, client-server, and ERP, then of course, the biggest hype of all, the Web. Ironically, the scene described above is not drawn from an executive suite but from a television advertisement for IBM that ran during 2002. It accurately captures much of the frustration managers feel about the gap that exists between the promise of technology and the reality. As you may have surmised if you have made it this far, I am somewhat cynical about management fads, best practices, and all the other blather that surrounds modern management, so brace yourself for a shock. Today, I believe that for the first time since I started studying computer science at Leeds University in 1980, the hype about the potential of technology actually matches the reality. The last few years have seen the convergence of hardware, software, and networking technologies to such a degree that you can pretty much do whatever you want to do. Technology is no longer the problem—we are.

Cool but Pointless

The last thirty years have clearly been the computer age. More specifically, the combination of computer hardware, software, and communications has transformed our lives. Where would we be without cell phones and the Internet? Where would our children be without Facebook, Twitter, and text messaging?

With such an explosion of innovation, there is always the risk of creating cool but pointless products or applications. In the late 1990s, Pets.com became one of the hottest dot.com companies in a very overheated field. Its glove puppet mascot launched in August 1998 became an advertising sensation with its own balloon in the Macy's Thanksgiving Day Parade; unfortunately, the company was less successful. Online pet food was not a killer application, and Pets.com completed a roundtrip from creation to liquidation in just over two years—going from an IPO on Nasdaq to bankruptcy in just nine months. Bad ideas still persist; in 2008, Facebook offered an application to its subscribers that gave them the really cool feature of being able to order their pizza up to three weeks in advance! Personally, I would add electric candles, fondue sets, and the ability to watch movies on a two-inch screen to the list, but I suppose someone must value them.

I learned my own lesson about cool-sounding but pointless technology back in 1986. I was consulting with a fast-growing London-based securities trading house that was building a very strong business in trading shares, options, and warrants issued by Japanese companies. The Japanese economy was the strongest in the world at the time, and Japanese companies were increasingly using global markets to raise capital. Even then securities trading was one of the most technology-intensive businesses in the world—speed and information were everything.

At the time, few of the major financial information services provided fast, in-depth information on Japanese companies. Traders had to rely on Japanese information services, which were targeted at local Japanese players and therefore broadcast their information in Japanese. Some services offered an English translation 15 to 20 minutes later, but in the fast-moving and volatile world of securities trading, this was akin to trying to compete with Tiger Woods while using hickory-shafted golf clubs.

The traders at our client saw an opportunity if they could exploit the delay between the Japanese news service and the English translation becoming available. They could gain a significant competitive advantage if they had access to an English translation before their competitors. Inquiries to the information service provider indicated that a simultaneous Japanese/English service was three to five years away. Armed with this information, the company embarked upon a project to develop an in-house computer system that would translate the incoming Japanese feed into English with a delay of 30 to 45 seconds. The cost would be £3 million (about $4.8 million at the time). Based upon the potential upside to be gained by having a 15-minute advantage on the rest of the market, the payback could be huge. I sat there impressed with the elegance of the solution but something bothered me. Was this really the best answer?

We asked a few questions, and the traders told us that when news broke on the Japanese-language version of the service, one of their Japanese-speaking colleagues would notice it and shout out the news to whoever needed to know. This worked well for the big news, but these Japanese-speaking traders did not have the time or knowledge to do this for all the companies that each trader was tracking. We summarized the problem thus: "What you really need is not just a faster English-language version but also a mechanism to highlight news that is directly relevant to the companies you are tracking." The traders agreed, so we offered an alternative solution. Instead of building an expensive computer system, why didn't they hire two or three of the brightest bilingual English-Japanese students they could find. Set them up in the trading room with a dedicated terminal from the Japanese information service. Make sure they are briefed on the companies that each trader follows, and then when they see news that is relevant to a particular trader, they can call the trader up or shout the news out to him. That way, the traders will get rapid translation, selectivity in what is translated, and personalization of the information to each trader's needs without spending a penny on a new computer system. Oh, and another advantage was that this solution could be implemented really fast.

Three weeks later, two bilingual business graduates had been hired, and the company had achieved a major lead on the market. Management estimated the innovation contributed almost £4 million to profits in the first year at a total annual cost of approximately £150,000. The moral of the story is not that technology is bad—just that it is not always the best answer.

Whatever Happened to Real-Time Processing?

On September 5, 1951, operators flicked the switch on LEO, the Lyons Electronic Office, and the first business computer application stuttered into life as the bakeries valuation program was executed. The age of business computing had begun, not in California but in a humble British baking company. Just over two years later Lyons automated its payroll process, reducing the time to calculate an individual's pay from more than eight minutes to 1.5 seconds. The world has not been the same since.

The relentless advance of technology is undeniable. Numerous real-time applications allow for instantaneous transacting of business 24 hours a day all over the globe, but in one crucial area remarkably little has changed. The way we plan, forecast, report, and control business has barely changed in over half a century. The general ledger is closed on a monthly basis; accounts are reconciled on a set schedule; plans and budgets are developed annually; forecasts are updated quarterly; and performance is reported monthly.

While there has been significant automation of basic accounting tasks, and almost every business now runs an integrated suite of financial applications (some more than one!), the underlying processing philosophy is tied to an accounting calendar that bears little or no relation to the real-time nature with which virtually all business is conducted. In less volatile times the approach of recording transactions and verifying their accuracy sometime after they actually occurred worked well. Early computers worked much better when transactions were batched up into groups that could then exploit a computer's ability to rapidly repeat a single task many times over. This also fit in with the accountant's view of the world that is directly tied to a fixed, calendar-based schedule of monthly, quarterly, and annual tasks. For decades the process worked reasonably well, and then in the 1980s change started to accelerate. Globalization picked up pace as the Japanese, Korean, and other Asian economies began to become world players. Multinational companies such as Coca-Cola, Siemens, Procter and Gamble, and Toyota started to develop a true global presence. Global telecommunications became a seamless reality, and computing moved from the mainframe to the mini-computer and the desktop. The 1990s simply accelerated the change as networks took hold and the Internet became a ubiquitous asset for commerce globally. Real time equates to buying time. Instead of waiting for monthly reports or quarterly forecasts, organizations need near instantaneous communication of material information to decision-makers. Information, intelligence and insight delivered to the point of impact allows for fast, confident decision-making. The technology can do it—can your processes?

Breaking Down the Barriers

"We are deploying state-of-the-art technology. Our infrastructure is predicated on the ISO seven-layer model using multiple industry standard protocols such as TCP/IP, 802.1(b), and X.25. Our WAN/LAN configuration optimizes performance and redundancy while facilitating dynamic access to our best practice toolset encompassing ETL, RDMS, MOLAP and ROLAP, SQL, and XML. All this is wrapped in a fault-tolerant, 24/7 environment with multiple back-up and contingency schemas."

Clear as mud don't you think? Ever since the first programmer scratched out a few lines of code, the language of IT, much like that of finance, has sought to confuse rather than clarify. This mattered little until the 1980s since computers were largely segregated from the real world in large, faceless data centers, and interaction with the general populace was limited to the occasional printout on the then-ubiquitous green-and-white lined paper. However, in 1981, a major disruptive force emerged in the shape of the personal computer. As PCs started to become widely deployed, the effect was to move much of the control of computer processing from the remote, isolated data center and the bearded, sweater-wearing programmer to the desktop of the office worker. The visible focus of IT became the desktop, then the laptop, and today manifests itself through a myriad of wireless devices.

As the use of computers widened, so did the linguistic gulf between the "techies" and the "users." Sophisticated methodologies for system design and development emerged and defining user requirements became an essential part of every project. Unfortunately, all too often these attempts to bridge the divide simply pushed IT projects to be delivered late and over budget while also leaving the user underwhelmed.

Over time the complexity increased as client-server computing, enterprise resource planning (ERP) applications, and all things Internet came to pass. Late, over-budget, and failing to meet requirements no longer was simply an interdepartmental squabble but a major business problem visible to customers, suppliers, competitors, and the media. IT organizations have tried to adapt, but many still fall far short of realizing much-vaunted business partner status. So how do you get your IT organization to shape up? It is all about getting the right leadership. Traditionally, many companies viewed IT as either a technical function and appointed technicians to leadership positions rather than managers with the required business savvy or, IT was viewed as a back-office function and therefore a good candidate to be run by a burned-out executive on the glide slope to retirement. In today's instrumented world, the skills required of a CIO are largely the same as those for any other capable executive: leadership, talent management, financial acumen, negotiation, decisiveness, critical thinking, and client focus. Knowledge of the optimal way to structure databases to support queries on sparse data sets is not high on the list.

Today, managing IT is a managerial role not a technical role. Most software is packaged with custom development—a very small part of most organization's IT portfolio. As technologies become increasingly complex and critical, companies are recognizing that is impractical to try to operate all the key computer and communications systems internally. Simply recruiting appropriately skilled staff and keeping their skills up to date is too costly for most companies. As a result, many of these activities are being outsourced, with the internal IT organization playing a supplier and customer management role focused on setting standards, defining business needs, evaluating sourcing options, and managing service delivery. The sooner IT takes its rightful place as a service delivery organization rather than a technical organization, the sooner the real value can be unlocked.

Why Do We Fix Costs in a Variable Revenue World?

Paying workers not to work, paying for services that you don't use, or entering into long-term fixed price contracts when your income is uncertain does not make much sense. Yet nearly every company does it. Many have consciously made these choices, and the results are becoming increasingly painful. Globalization, competition, uncertainty, and volatility are combining to make revenue an increasingly variable (and valuable) item. At the same time as volatility has increased, many organizations have successfully managed to convert what were once largely variable costs into fixed costs. This works well when revenues are growing—after all, if the next dollar of revenue costs nothing to earn, profit margins are rather good. However, as soon as there is any downward movement in revenues, the pain can be severe. There have been two primary drivers of cost conversion: substituting variable labor costs with fixed technology costs and converting variable labor costs into fixed labor costs through successive rounds of contract renegotiation.

No one doubts the enormous impact that computer and communications technologies have had on business over the last forty years. Technology has transformed long-established industries and created many new ones. From a cost standpoint, technology has delivered substantial economies of scale through its ability to process many more transactions per unit than the technology it replaced—people. This simple effect has driven productivity growth rates that have contributed much to economic growth. However, there is a downside in times of volatility. In the days before automation, if business activity dropped by 10 percent, a business could simply reduce its workforce by 10 percent and largely keep its costs in line; however, it is difficult to fire a mainframe or downsize a server. In other words, while technology may be able to process a million transactions for the same cost as a thousand transactions, the reverse is also true; it will cost much the same to process a thousand transactions as a million transactions.

The second effect has been the trend in many industries where organized labor has been able to wield bargaining power for management to progressively guarantee elements of compensation and benefits regardless of the level of business activity. This is most notable in the automotive and airline industries, both of which have experienced

Mythbuster Wisdom: An English History Lesson

The disastrous economic consequences of dealing with fixed labor costs were on clear view in the UK during the 1970s. Since the end of World War II, successive governments had progressively expanded government ownership of key industries. By the early 1970s, British Airways, British Telecom, British Gas, the electric utilities, the coal mining industry, British Rail, British Leyland (essentially the whole UK car industry comprising Rover, Austin, Morris, Jaguar, Triumph, Mini, and Land Rover), and Rolls Royce (the aero engine, not the car company) were all under government ownership and operating with restrictive labor contracts that largely fixed employment and wage levels. The result was the effective bankruptcy of the UK economy. I well remember most of Britain operating on a three-day work week, doing my homework by candlelight as the power workers were on strike, baking bread as the bakers were on strike, and taking our rubbish to the dump as the refuse workers were on strike. In 1976 the UK Chancellor of the Exchequer (equivalent to the U.S. Treasury Secretary) had to go "cap in hand" to the International Monetary Fund and beg for a bailout in scenes that foreshadowed the bailouts of the banking and automotive industries in late 2008. The crisis paved the way for Margaret Thatcher to gain power in 1979 and begin a radical reshaping of the UK economy that left the country with no car industry, no mining industry, and the privatization of almost all other state-owned industries. The UK effectively became a variable cost economy again.

tremendous revenue volatility in recent years. Both industries are spending billions on restructuring that is largely aimed at making labor a variable cost again.

For decades the renegotiation of labor contracts in the automotive industry took on the tenor of a Cold War standoff. Management and labor engaged in a semi-public battle to make their cases. Management preached reasonableness and restraint while labor pointed to growing sales, profits, and, most pointedly, management compensation in their quest for a fair wage. For thirty years or more, labor usually won. Contracts became rich with guarantees and special provisions that covered not just the working day but also retirement. By the late 1960s automotive workers were at the pinnacle of the blue-collar economy. Highly paid and well provided for both at work and in retirement, they were the envy of many. But times were changing. The fifty-year growth of the American automotive industry was coming to an end. Every American family now owned a car, if not two cars; Japanese competitors were beating the Americans on price, fuel economy, and above all, quality; and gasoline was no longer a cheap commodity as OPEC flexed its muscles.

Despite these challenges, the automotive worker was all right. Wages were largely guaranteed whether cars were being built or not. For the next thirty years, General Motors, Ford, and Chrysler paid a steep price for making what should have been their biggest variable cost into a fixed cost. By 2007, at General Motors, more than $1,600 of every vehicle's cost was simply to cover the health and retirement benefits of current and former workers—a burden not shared by their foreign competitors. In addition, contract terms covering items like work rules, line relief, and holiday pay added a further $630, while the burden for paying union members for not working added another $350. The price of such largesse has been huge. U.S. market share has fallen from over 60 percent to under 25 percent, and the trend remains downward. Then the global economic crisis effectively buried the company save for bankruptcy, and a government rescue that left the U.S. taxpayer owning 60 percent of GM, once the world's greatest company.

Mythbuster Wisdom: General Motors—A 30-Year Slide
1979: GM's worldwide employment peaks at 853,000; in 1980 GM lost $763 million, its first loss since 1921.
2008: GM's worldwide employment is 235,000; losses in 2007 and 2008 totaled $68.6 billion.

After years of reasonable growth, automotive sales in the United States peaked at 17.3 million vehicles in 2000. The next three years saw a steady decline to around 16.6 million units in 2003, a modest decline of 4 percent; yet profits at GM and Ford declined by 26 percent. Sales made a steady recovery, climbing back to 17.1 million by 2007 and then all hell broke loose as gasoline soared to $4 a gallon and the U.S. economy hurtled into recession. Vehicle sales collapsed to less than 14 million units, an 18 percent decline in one year. The impact on profits was predictable. GM recorded losses of almost $31 billion in 2008, while Ford, which avoided the need for government help, lost $14.6 billion.

The cost of paid idleness through jobs banks was significant for the automotive companies. Funding the jobs banks for the big three in the 4-year UAW contract negotiated in 2003 was $2.1 billion for GM, nearly a billion dollars for Ford, and about $450 million for Daimler Chrysler. Nice "work" if you can get it. In January 2009, the United Automotive Workers finally agreed to end the jobs bank at General Motors where idled workers were assigned on close to full pay and benefits. There were 1,600 people enjoying well-paid idleness at the time.[5]

While less obvious than in the automotive industry, the airlines have suffered in much the same way. During the 1950s and 1960s the indus-try enjoyed explosive growth and well-organized labor groups, espe-cially those representing pilots, secured rich contracts. The 1970s saw rapid increases in fuel costs and deregulation in the U.S. market. Prices fell and competition became intense, yet labor costs were largely fixed. Perhaps more damaging in the short term were the rigidly defined roles and staffing levels that were built into contracts. New competi-tors, like Southwest, successfully exploited these rigidities to develop a new competitive model, which, among other things, employed a much more flexible use of labor. The sight of air crew cleaning planes or assisting with baggage became common—but not at the legacy airlines. Such rigidity was one contributor to the parade of airline deaths—Braniff, TWA, Pan Am, and Eastern—and bankruptcies—United, Delta, Northwest, Continental (twice), and USAirways—that have marred the industry over the last twenty years.

As the *Wall Street Journal* commented in July 2009, "Running an airline is one of the more reliable ways to lose money."[6] Since 1980, the revenues for the world's airlines have grown from just over $87 billion

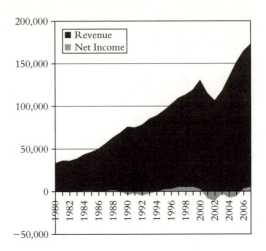

Figure 11.3   Annual Profits for Airlines
SOURCE: Air Transport Association

to more than $450 billion in 2006. This translates into a pretty impressive compound annual growth rate of 10.1 percent outstripping many other industries. Yet despite such robust revenue growth, the industry has failed to make any money at all over that period, with cumulative losses outweighing cumulative profits by almost $8 billion. A look at the pattern of profitability over the period illustrates the impact of high fixed costs (see Figure 11.3). Profits were good between 1986 and 1990 and even better during the boom years from 1997 until 9/11.

It is both ironic and sad that two great industries that largely symbolized America's economic growth should have both become symbols of the dangers of failing to adapt to the modern world.

Fixing variable costs can be very attractive when businesses are growing. Predictability allows for more effective planning and rising profitability; but the benefits are greatly outweighed by the risks when growth slows or other costs change dramatically. It only takes a very slight slowdown in the growth rate for fixed costs to become an albatross.

Both the automotive and airline industries sowed the seeds of fixed cost hell before IT became material. Since 1980 IT costs have been the fastest growing expense for most organizations. According to the Gartner Group, global IT spending in 2008 was around $3.4 trillion.[7]

This is only slightly less than the GDP of Germany, the world's fourth largest economy.

It is not unusual for technology-intensive businesses to spend more than 10 percent of their revenue on IT, and the proportion is growing. In the early years nearly every technology investment was a buy or build decision. Companies wrote large checks to IBM and others for hardware and employed legions of programmers to develop and maintain software. By the 1980s, the first commercial software applications started to appear, and the need to build custom software diminished. However, technology was now being deployed throughout the organization as the personal computer and the network took hold. Automation of transaction processing delivered massive economies of scale and allowed organizations to eliminate millions of clerical jobs while accommodating sizable growth in volumes without hiring large numbers of new workers.

However, the transition meant that while in the past a decline in demand could be offset by a reduction in labor, unless you were a car company or an airline, it was tough to fire a mainframe as the substitution of variable labor costs with fixed technology costs added yet another rigidity to an organization's operations at a time when volatility and uncertainty were increasing.

Centralized or Decentralized? What a Dumb Question!

For decades companies have argued as to whether a centralized or decentralized organizational model is best. In IT, the debate has been particularly intense with corporate CIOs arguing for centralization by emphasizing the benefits of standardization and scale economies while local operating units respond that flexibility and responsiveness is key and that the cost benefits of centralization are largely illusory. It is a fun debate—unfortunately, it is a pointless one. IT can only operate as a networked, or balanced, organizational model that is neither centralized nor decentralized. Leaders are recognizing that the age-old debate about the relative merits of centralization or decentralization is pointless since the answer is neither and both. Ironically, it is technology that is making the question redundant. The truth is that activities that are more homogeneous and location independent tend to benefit from more central coordination, while those that are more unique and localized tend to be best managed close to the customer. In fact, for many organizations, the centralization of IT actually meant that IT became so disconnected from the business that the IT versus user gulf became a chasm of conflicting goals, miscommunication, and distrust. Thankfully, most IT professionals are emerging from their bunker down in the data center and becoming full participants in key business processes such as product development, marketing, logistics, and customer support. The traditional approach of users defining requirements that are then thrown over the wall to IT to build is being replaced by a collaborative, cross-functional approach akin to the vaunted platform teams that transformed automotive design processes in the 1980s. These multi-skilled teams seek to leverage the collective knowledge of all participants to ensure sharper definition of requirements, better design, and faster deployment of technology-enabled solutions. Key to the transformation is a willingness of both IT and non-IT professionals to change entrenched behavior patterns. One notable example has been the need to reach common ground in terms of language. Historically, some IT professionals enjoyed using complex technical jargon to befuddle the humble user, while non-IT professionals steadfastly refused to make any attempt to understand even the basics of the technology that underpins their business. Sadly, such game playing is all too prevalent, and the opportunities to use technology effectively at lower risk and cost are lost.

Successful use of technology demands that it be woven into the very fabric of the business in much the same way as finance or human resources. Only then can all the elements work together to harness technology's undoubted potential to create value. Far from having its role diminished, the IT organization is a critical enabler of business strategy.

Outsourcing—the Myth and the Reality

Outsourcing is a trillion-dollar business and, along with its close relative offshoring, has experienced explosive growth in recent years. The basic idea is that a third party can provide services that demonstrably lower operating costs, increase service quality, reduce business risk, secure scarce skill sets, and allow the organization to refocus on what it does really well. It is a very seductive argument.

Outsourcing now covers almost every conceivable activity from providing legal services to cleaning bathrooms, but one of the biggest outsourcing markets is in Information Technology which the Gartner Group estimated to be $173 billion in 2007.[8] For many, the motivation was simply to reduce costs by taking advantage of lower cost labor in other regions of the world; others saw outsourcing as a way to access specialized skill sets that they could not justify hiring solely for themselves; while a third group simply wanted to leverage the capital investments made by others in processing, networking, and communications thereby eliminating a significant drain on their own capital spending. All are valid reasons, but for many an even more significant benefit can be the cost elasticity that outsourcing provides. Instead of paying the full costs for a whole factory regardless of how much the factory is producing, the company simply pays for the output it consumes. The outsourcing of IT operations can convert the high upfront capital cost of hardware and software plus the hefty ongoing cost of maintenance and support to a variable cost dictated the level of business activity. Similarly, software as a service or SaaS (to give it its essential technology acronym), offers the same option for software. Historically, organizations had to buy the software they use and also invest in the infrastructure to run it (computers, networks, and support staff) regardless of the level of usage. Software as a service allows organizations to rent the use of high-quality software over the Internet and pay on a per-user or per-transaction basis, eliminating the need to tie up scarce capital and other resources. SaaS was a $9 billion market in 2008 and was projected to double by 2012.[9] Selective use of outsourcing can be an effective element in managing costs when operating in volatile or uncertain markets.

For the last 20 years, CEOs and CIOs have heard the same arguments for outsourcing: Costs will go down; valuable internal resources can be better employed on strategic tasks; and risk will be transferred to a third party, much like buying insurance. However, for many, the analogy with insurance has unfortunately proven all too real. High deductibles, exclusions from coverage, questionable service, and opaque pricing have all raised questions as to outsourcing's value. Knowing all

Mythbuster Wisdom: Top Offshoring Locations[10]

Argentina, Australia, Brazil, Canada, Chile, China, Costa Rica, Czech Republic, Egypt, Hungary, India, Ireland, Israel, Malaysia, Mexico, Morocco, New Zealand, Pakistan and Panama, the Philippines, Poland, Romania, Russia, Singapore, Slovakia, South Africa, Spain, Thailand, Ukraine, and Vietnam.

This list highlights some of the risks associated with offshoring. In a twelve-month period from mid-2008, organizations had to deal with terrorist attacks in Mumbai, Taliban insurgency in Pakistan, a major earthquake in China, the H1N1 virus in Mexico, airport blockades in Bangkok, and deep economic crises in Argentina, Ireland, Romania, Russia, and the Ukraine.

this, how do you ensure the realization of outsourcing's often touted but infrequently realized benefits?

The first step is to remain objective. Too often outsourcing decisions are made for emotional reasons with the argument going something like this: We are not very good at doing X (insert the function or activity of your choice), we don't know how to fix it (or can't be bothered), and it costs a lot; so let's outsource it. After all, everyone else is doing it, so it must be okay, and then we can make it someone else's problem. Unfortunately, this approach typically leads to worse service at higher cost and actually makes the problem more visible and painful than when it was buried inside your own organization.

The key to outsourcing success is that for each expected benefit, there must be quantifiable metrics for which someone is held accountable, and those metrics must be built into contracts with service providers and internal process owners. Understanding the economics provides a clue as to how to ensure success. Outsourcing basically has three immutable truths.

First, if you outsource an inefficient process, the contractor will charge you for your inefficiency and use it to make a profit on the deal. One of the easiest ways for an outsourcer to make money is to take your inefficient process, clean it up, and reduce costs by 60 percent, giving you half of those savings staggered over the life of the contract while pocketing the rest. This realization leads to a very simple maxim for addressing the economic viability of outsourcing: *First, seek to eliminate the activity. If you cannot eliminate it, then simplify the heck out of it, then automate it, and only then, if some of it is still left, consider outsourcing it.*

Second, instead of comparing the current cost of an inefficient process to an outsourcer's best bid, use the lowest price you can achieve internally as the starting point of negotiation. *It is not your current cost, but your lowest achievable cost that is the baseline for evaluating the economics of outsourcing.*

Third, service providers negotiate outsourcing contracts everyday—you don't (hopefully). However, that also means that the provider will have much more experience in negotiating such contracts, and that leaves you susceptible to one or more of the basic outsourcing traps. A popular gambit is to base everything in the contract on the current level of service. Initially, this term can appear attractive as it guarantees the current service level; however, if the current level of service is so good, why are you outsourcing in the first place? The fix is simply to insist that service levels are tied to today's best benchmarks. After all, today's service level will probably be obsolete tomorrow. *Build benchmarks into the agreement that ensure service levels keep pace with the latest best practices—not just those that prevail at the time the contract is signed.*

A second trap that should make you very nervous is when you spy statements in the contract like, "everything outside the terms of this contract is extra and will be charged at standard rates." It sounds innocuous, but this is the kiss of death to the economics of any contract. Over the life of the agreement your needs will change, and you will never be able to anticipate them up front, so plan for ambiguity and ensure the contract offers flexibility. The supplier won't like it, since there is a real risk it will have to work hard to meet your needs—so go for it.

Getting the contract right is just the first step; then the hard work starts. Make sure that ownership, management, and accountability are retained internally. Service levels must be agreed upon up front and monitored routinely for compliance and continued applicability. Supplier schedules and status reports need to be integrated into internal planning and management processes. Gain-sharing arrangements should be set against credible benchmark targets and partner incentives linked to improvements in overall business performance.

Qualcomm, the wireless technology company that had sales of $11 billion in 2008, has avoided many of the perils associated with huge IT investments and outsourcing. First, the company did not follow many others in investing large sums in implementing a single, companywide ERP system. The business did not need it. Instead, the company invested in building a sound foundation of high-quality data and then allowed individual businesses to deploy the best solutions for their specific needs. For IT, this translated into deploying small development teams operating with a reasonable degree of freedom and employing rapid development approaches to meet individual business needs. Such an approach allows businesses to quickly reprioritize projects based upon changing business needs or changes in the external environment.

Maintaining flexibility also extends to Qualcomm's approach to outsourcing. The company has not outsourced any core function completely. Outsourcing is used as the "flex" in resourcing, thereby enabling the company to rapidly adjust capacity, either up or down, in response to market trends and business needs. By retaining core capabilities in house, the company can manage service levels while also being able to size capacity to current needs.

Today you can outsource just about anything. One of the most intriguing trends is the increasing use of hosting services, whereby a third-party service provider acts as a host for one or more of a company's service needs. These can range from management of a website through the provision of application processing capabilities over the Web. Ironically, hosting or SaaS marks a return to vogue of timesharing services that were popular in the 1960s. The difference now is that instead of the driver being the prohibitively high costs of computer technology, it is the very low cost and high speed of communications that make it more attractive to rent rather than buy. All these trends point to the need for CEOs and executive management to be skilled in the negotiation and management of third-party service agreements, so that companies can retain their competitive edge in the ever-changing world of business.

Information technology has become the second most important ingredient for almost all organizations after people. While technology has advanced in accordance with Moore's Law, our ability to effectively manage such technologies more often resembles Murphy's Law. Common sense is often the missing ingredient.

So What?

- There is no such a thing as an IT project anymore.
- Evaluate ROI by comparing total investments with the total returns.
- Set clear criteria for project abandonment.
- Link rewards to results, not plans.
- Focus on results realization rather than task completion.
- Embrace uncertainty and plan accordingly.
- If you automate an inefficient process, you just get bad data faster.
- Automation can replace variable labor costs with fixed technology costs.
- If you operate in volatile markets, consider renting technology rather than buying it.
- True innovation may require that you build it.
- If you outsource an inefficient process, the outsourcer will charge you for your own inefficiency and still make a profit on the deal.
- The real long-term value of outsourcing may not be cost reduction but cost flexibility.

Notes

1. SAP Earnings Release, October 28, 2008.
2. Ibid.
3. Ibid.
4. Ibid.
5. Mike Ramsey and Jeff Green "UAW to End GM Jobs Bank," *Bloomberg News,* January 28, 2009.
6. "Airline Sectors Woes Slam a Highflier," *Wall Street Journal,* July 2, 2009.
7. Gartner Inc., "Gartner Says IT Spending to Slow in 2009," Press release, Stamford CT October 13, 2008.
8. Gartner Group, IT Outsourcing Worldwide 2007.
9. Robert Mahowald, "SaaS Market Size," IDC, January 30, 2009
10. Ian Marriott, "Top 30 Countries for Offshore Services in 2008," Gartner Inc., London, December 11, 2008.

Chapter 12

Why Accountants Rule
the World

To an optimist, the glass is half full; to the pessimist, it is half empty; and to the accountant the glass is twice as big as it needs to be. I know it is not the best joke in the world, but it does accurately sum up many people's feelings toward accountants—always looking to cut. The role and influence of accountants has grown significantly from the humble origins of the bookkeeper in the green eyeshade painstakingly entering numbers in a ledger. Today, accounting underpins almost everything in business, and the results are not always pretty. Hattie Jacques, Cruciant's financial controller, prides herself on the pristine nature of the company's books and her team's ability to manage expenses down to the last cent.

Fiction: Closing the Books, October 11, 2007

Henry walks into Hattie's office and asks how the process of closing the books for the third quarter is going. Hattie replies, "We are in pretty good shape, all the sub-ledgers are posted to the general ledger, and we are going through the accruals and also reconciling the intercompany accounts. We are on schedule to have the books closed in another three days."

"Any issues I should know about?" Henry inquires.

"Only one material matter," replies Hattie. "We have found a few discrepancies in the revenue recognition for the European operations. It looks like they have booked a few contracts before shipment actually occurred. I am looking into it, but it may require us to restate about $17 million in revenue."

"So what happened?" asks Henry.

"Well, I am not exactly sure yet," responds Hattie. "I don't think it is anything fraudulent. I suspect it may be due to the different accounting rules in some European countries. We have to keep two sets of books: one for local reporting and then one for U.S. GAAP reporting, and I think the entries may have been switched by mistake. I should know by tomorrow morning."

"OK, keep me posted. If it is material, I will have to brief Steve, although he won't understand what I'm talking about," says Henry as he leaves the room.

Ten Minutes Later . . .

"Henry, why does it take so long to close the books at the end of the month?" asks Steve. Henry is about to respond when Steve continues, "No, don't bother telling me. I won't understand it. All that accounting crap makes no sense to me. It just drives me crazy that we have to wait two weeks at the end of every month to get numbers about stuff that has already happened, and when we do, it takes another five days to rework the accounting reports into a management view that people can actually use to make some decisions—it is crazy." Henry nods but says nothing.

One Month Later . . .

Hattie is updating the executive team on a range of accounting issues—her update is just entering its third hour. A number of members of the management team are struggling to stay awake. Steve is furtively tapping on his Blackberry under the table.

"FAS 157 on fair value measurements will force us to use market-based measures to value assets starting with our next financial year. You will probably gather that this could negatively impact asset valuations on our balance sheet, and we will probably have to take a charge in the first quarter to reflect the revaluation. The impact on earnings could be as high as $15 million."

Steve looks up and almost shouts, "You mean we are going to have to take a $15 million hit to earnings and see our stock price tank because a group of accountants have decided that the way we added up the numbers is now wrong even though it was right last year?"

Henry intercedes, "Steve, these things happen pretty regularly, and it is not as if we are the only company that is going to be affected. I don't expect the market will take much notice." Steve shakes his head but says nothing. Hattie continues:

"That is all for the financial accounting side of the house. With regards to management accounting, we expect to have the FTE acquisition fully reflected in our management reports by the end of the second quarter."

"Why so long?" Steve asks.

Hattie responds: "As you will remember, FTE's systems were all over the place so it has taken a long time to map all the data in their systems to ours. We have also found that they used a different costing methodology, so none of the product costing or profitability models worked properly. At the same time we have been implementing activity-based costing, which has driven a lot of new data requirements in order for us to be able to accurately reflect the whole cost structure of the business."

Steve sighs and thinks that it really shouldn't be this complicated to simply report about how the business is doing in the way that he manages it but he decides to save that debate for another day.

Facts: Death by Accounting and Other Fatal Diseases

Before alienating all my clients, I should make clear that some of my best friends are accountants. I myself have studied and worked in accounting- and finance-related roles for nearly thirty years. My diploma verifying my Bachelor of Science in Accounting from the University of Leeds hangs on my office wall as I write these words, and I am a proud alumnus of the accounting firm Deloitte, Haskins and Sells. Despite being steeped in accounting law (or is it lore?), I struggle with the basic lack of relevance that accounting has to much of life. The average person has no desire to be able to read a profit and loss account or balance sheet, yet the American Institute of Certified Public Accountants (AICPA) defines an accountant's purpose as "making sense of a changing and complex world."[1] Next time you read through a set of financial statements, ask yourself whether they are fulfilling their stated purpose.

> **Mythbuster Wisdom: The Truth About Accounting**
> Accounting is a bit like law—a necessary evil, and as your career progresses, it becomes more necessary and more evil.

When was the last time you heard someone describe an accounting report as crystal clear, insightful, and directly relevant to the decisions that need to be made? To be fair, the accountant is fighting a losing battle. Offering clarity about ever more complex business structures is fraught with difficulty, but there is no excuse for not getting some of the basics right. After all, there were just over 338,000 CPAs in the United States as of August 2008, and that was 13 percent more than in 2007.[2] Elsewhere in the world, growth has been even more impressive with the number of accounting professionals in China growing by 35 percent and in Russia by 20 percent. Accountancy is one of the fastest growing industries in the world. No doubt future growth will be equally impressive as new rules and regulations emerge in the wake of the economic debacle of 2008–2009.

The AICPA defines the value-adding role of the CPA as communicating the total picture with clarity and objectivity; translating complex information into critical knowledge; anticipating and creating opportunities; and designing pathways that transform vision into reality. Laudable goals indeed but difficult to achieve when accountants spend countless hours wading through the minutiae of financial transactions to ensure the right number is put in the right bucket. Their task is not made any easier by the need to apply ever more complex rules. Consider the following rule, which relates to accounting for credit derivatives, the cause of much of the financial angst of 2008:

> "If the notional amounts of the fixed-rate bonds and the variable interest rate swap do not match (thereby creating the possibility that the financial instruments held by the special purpose entity might not provide the necessary cash flows to the swap counterparty), the variable-rate interest provisions would have to be evaluated for an embedded derivative under paragraph 13 because the underlying is an interest rate or interest rate index."[3]

Got that?

Accounting—An Alternative Reality

To be fair, the task of creating a common approach to reporting on the performance of myriad different types of organization is no easy task. Unfortunately, in the quest for comparability, any semblance of clarity has been lost. Financial statements do not provide a real worldview of how an organization actually operates. The mismatch between the accounting and management view is the result of the longstanding practice of allowing external reporting standards and rules to dictate the internal view that is used for management decision-making purposes.

External reporting seeks to normalize all the inconsistencies and differences between the ways different businesses account and report their results, thereby allowing many different businesses to be viewed in a standardized manner. It is a sort of accounting communism— everyone should look the same. Given that the audience for external financial reports is shareholders, investors, and regulators, the goal of consistency is reasonable. However, that does not help managers when they are trying to make decisions.

The origin of the reliance on an external or regulated view of a business stems from the creation of the basic processes to account and report on an organization's activity. Because the production of financial statements was a statutory requirement, the finance department's first job was to meet those requirements. As technology began to impact business, some of the first software applications were accounting oriented. As a result, the general ledger, the heart of any accounting system, became the central and often only source of financial data. Because the ledger's primary function was to support the accurate accounting of an organization's activity according to external accounting rules and regulations, it was structured to meet that purpose. The same reports became the de facto standard for internal management use and the basis for the majority of management reporting was established. Over time, managers began to recognize the limitations of the external accounting view, and many organizations set up an alternate or management accounting view that sought to better represent the business as it was actually managed.

As technology made its presence felt, new reporting mechanisms such as data warehouses and performance management systems were developed to support management accounting and reporting. Unfortunately, at their core, these new systems retained much of the structure of the external financial reporting systems, and much of the potential was wasted. Finance teams got around these constraints by creating numerous spreadsheet-based reports and analyses that allowed them to circumvent the rigid view embedded in the general ledger. Today most companies report vital business data from hand-built spreadsheets that reside on a single individual's computer with little assurance of security or integrity. Critical business decisions are made based upon manually input data that has been run through handcrafted formulas developed and maintained by a single person. Pretty scary, don't you think?

Despite the laudable goals of the AICPA, many managers do not yet see their accounting colleagues as the primary source of clear, relevant, and timely information, which may go some way to explain why only 39 percent of the Chief Financial Officers of Fortune 1000 companies were CPAs in 2008 while more than 60 percent possessed an MBA.[4] The numbers of CPA's taking on the CFO job are improving, with a 10 percent increase since 2003, probably due to the focus on accounting integrity ushered in by the Sarbanes-Oxley, but accountants are not yet on the front line.

The need to offer credible management views of the business while continuing to meet ever-changing external reporting standards is perhaps the biggest challenge finance professionals face.

Accounting Irrelevance

In 1987, Thomas Johnson and Robert Kaplan published *Relevance Lost: The Rise and Fall of Management Accounting.* The underlying premise of the book was that financial accounting—that is, the preparation of financial statements in compliance with applicable accounting standards—had become so dominant in organizations that management accounting, the presentation of financial information to help managers within the organization make better decisions, had been overwhelmed to the detriment of business. The book caused quite a stir and triggered much debate about new management tools. Johnson and Kaplan proposed that management accounting systems needed to measure nonfinancial indicators based on the firm's strategy.[5] This should include measures of internal process failure, such as rework; external failure, such as customer complaints; productivity measures; and measures of innovation, all of which have received significant focus in recent years but are rarely reflected in the financial reports that investors use to assess the health of an organization. In subsequent years, activity-based costing and the balanced scorecard became popular—both tools were more focused on management decision making as opposed to external reporting.

Despite the many additions to the toolkit for accounting and reporting, the financial crisis of 2008–2009 seemed to confirm that much work remained to be done. In November 2008 at the height of the financial crisis, Steve Schwarzman, chairman and CEO of the Blackstone Group, one of the world's largest private equity firms and a former Managing Director at defunct Lehman Brothers, described his recommendations for preventing a further crisis.[6] His seven points with my commentary in italics were:

1. Establish a common set of accounting principles across borders. *Yes but whose principles should we use? And there's the rub, politics trumps common sense every time.*

2. Structure regulatory oversight in a consistent manner with a single financial services regulator in each market. *Common sense, you think, but think of all those cushy bureaucrats who would lose their jobs.*

3. Financial statements should be fully transparent with nothing eliminated. *Sounds simple, and you would have thought Enron would have taught us a lesson.*

4. All financial instruments need to be fully disclosed to the regulator and monitored by the regulator. *Credit default swaps, all $60 trillion of them and one of the major causes of the 2008 liquidity crisis, were largely unregulated.*

5. Regulators should have oversight of all participants in a market regardless of their legal status, domicile, or charter. *So we can fully expect the French and Germans to acquiesce to U.S. regulation based upon its track record over the last few years?*

6. Abolish mark to market accounting for hard-to-value assets. It's difficult to mark to market when there is no market. *See the Mythbuster Wisdom sidebar "The Hypocrisy of Marking to Market" on page 254.*

7. Move from a rules-based regulatory system to a principle-based system. *As Schwarzman rightly points out, there is no way a rules-based system can keep pace with the speed of evolution and innovation in the global financial marketplace.*

For a sophisticated and very rich financial market player, these principles reek of common sense. Shocking, isn't it?

The Myth of Cost Allocations

Has Warren Buffett ever invested in a company because it has a really cool way of allocating IT costs out to the different business units? Do CEOs rhapsodize about the precision of their company's method for allocating overhead costs to each individual product? I thought not.

Organizations spend enormous amounts of time and energy defining, debating, and negotiating arbitrary and meaningless allocation rules and transfer prices. The original premise made perfect sense. Each product, department, or business unit should bear its fair share of overhead if it is to truly understand its contribution to the enterprise. After all, someone has to pay for the corporate jet, right?

Unfortunately, this simple goal has given birth to a whole industry called cost accounting that in turn has spawned numerous subdisciplines such as product costing, process costing, standard costing, and more recently, activity-based costing. Many companies use two or more costing systems, offering myriad opportunities for complexity and confusion.

Cost allocations are an insidious plague. They start out innocuously enough as managers attempt to better understand the true costs of a particular operation, product, or department by allocating costs that are not directly incurred. Pretty soon, a cost accounting department is created, the allocation process expands to more and more cost elements, and the allocations are pushed down to lower and lower levels in the organization. After a couple of years, the consultants arrive to fix the process, and the organization embarks on a rigorous activity-based costing project. New allocation rules are defined, algorithms are created, and systems are implemented. Costs are broken down into such detail that the organization starts to develop price lists for different activities so that "customer" departments can negotiate with "supplier" departments and everyone can pretend they are real business people. Eventually, everyone is spending so much time analyzing and managing costs down to the last cent that no one notices that the business is tanking. Extreme? Maybe, but American manufacturing companies led the way in developing detailed cost accounting mechanisms, and there are not many left now, are there?

Of course, once an organization has designed a sophisticated costing methodology, there is then a need to report and budget around it. This leads to some entertaining but not very productive discussions such as:

"I can't control it, so why allocate it to me?" For many managers, a very large portion of their total budget is made up of costs allocated to them by other departments over which they have no control. The appearance of such costs implies accountability without responsibility (the business version of taxation without representation and look where that ended up) and undermines management ownership of budgets. It also serves

as a distraction from the real job of managing those resources that you do control.

"My budget has been cut, so you must cut the costs you allocate to me." Put yourself in the position of a manager who has been told to cut his budget by 10 percent. Which of the following approaches would you take? Option A is to go through the painful exercise of reviewing the staffing and spending levels in your own organization in order to cut costs. Option B simply requires you to go to the managers of the departments who are allocating costs to your budget and demand that they cut the amount of the allocation. An easy choice, but one that adds no value at all since if the costs are not allocated to you, then they still must be allocated somewhere else. Never mind that the conversation has zero productive value in the first place.

"I can get it cheaper down the street than the price corporate charges." This is a classic debate that occurs whenever a central function charges a local function for goods and services. For example, corporate has negotiated a companywide deal for the purchase of office supplies that requires all managers to buy at a standard price from the vendor's catalogue. However, some managers in the field complain at being forced to pay higher prices than they can get from a local supplier. One company set its internal cost allocation for a computer at $5,500. It explained the high cost by pointing out that in addition to the computer, the company also provided security, network, backup, help desk, and numerous other services for each user. Fair enough, but do these services really demand a 400 to 500 percent markup? Such behavior further destroys the already dubious credibility of many central functions that incur cost but appear to add little tangible value.

"I don't use the corporate jet. So why should I pay for it?" This is a favorite when allocations are not tied any service or value derived. Seeking to charge out for items that an entity does not use (or is not even allowed to use even if it wanted to) is a recipe for frustration and yet another excuse to avoid talking about the things that matter.

The mantra of cost allocation should be stamped on every accountant's forehead—keep it real and keep it simple. Where possible, avoid allocations all together and focus on usage charges that relate to some variable that makes sense. If you must allocate overheads, do it as flat tax on each business. For example, charge every business a fixed percentage of revenue or expenses to cover overhead expenses and avoid getting into meaningless debates over items that have no impact upon overall performance.

Time saved by simplifying or even eliminating cost allocations can be much more profitably spent on seeking ways to increase cost flexibility or leverage, the objective being to drive positive cost leverage in a rising revenue environment and at least maintain constant leverage in a falling revenue environment. What does this mean in English? Simply put, you want each incremental dollar of revenue to cost less than the previous dollar to earn; when revenues decline you want to be able to reduce your cost structure accordingly. One related benefit of blowing up much of the cost accounting, cost allocation, and transfer-pricing spaghetti that clogs up business would be to reduce the number of accountants needed to manage the whole mess.

Making the Numbers or Making The Numbers Up?

Missing your quarterly earnings estimates or perhaps, more important, missing the estimates of Wall Street analysts can be very harmful to your stock price. Like a jilted lover, the stock market can exact painful revenge by wiping out millions in shareholder value in seconds. Miss a second time and make sure your resume is up to date.

Public company executives have long lamented that the need to meet Wall Street's quarterly expectations hinders their ability to invest for the long term. These concerns are always amplified in times of economic turbulence. The arguments tend to center on the short-term focus that meeting quarterly expectations induces in management. For many companies the last week of the quarter results in a mad rush to book new sales before the end of the quarter and defer expenses to the next quarter in order to make the numbers. Public company executives periodically look at their peers in privately held companies with envy at not having to submit to the quarterly examination by Wall Street. Of course, if the reason you are privately held is as a result of a private equity deal, you probably have the burden of making sure you generate enough cash to service what is often a crippling debt load, as companies such as Chrysler and Harrah's found during 2008.

Many see the quarterly earnings game as a distraction. A number of high profile companies, including Google, Coca-Cola, and AT&T, simply refuse to provide earnings guidance, leaving analysts to make up their own numbers. In December 2008, General Electric joined this elite group. GE had a good track record of consistently meeting its earnings estimates, although some commentators suggested that the ability to manage earnings in its financial services businesses contributed to its success. However, such flexibility disappeared during the meltdown in the financial services industry during 2008. The result was two missed quarterly earnings estimates leading management to drop out of the earnings estimation game.

Wall Street argues that consistent quarterly performance and sustainable long-term growth are synonymous and that the former is a prerequisite for the latter. Both arguments have merit. The pressure to make the numbers is intense. During the telecom meltdown, once-high-flying companies such as telecom equipment maker Lucent (–89 percent in 12 months) and Nortel (–85 percent), were punished severely for missing their numbers. In both cases, short-term misses presaged terminal declines. Given the implications, it is not surprising that managers will delay future investments, cut costs, or take other, often drastic—or in the case of Worldcom and Computer Associates, illegal—action to make the current quarter in the hope that the shortfall can be made up in the next period. Sometimes this works; however, more often it simply delays the inevitable.

Two recent phenomena have amplified the impact of quarterly results. First, the level of individual stock ownership has increased significantly over the last twenty years. If a company misses its numbers and the stock halves in value, it makes news on CNBC and at the water cooler the next morning. Second, employee ownership of shares is now widespread. In good times, a rapidly rising stock price is a powerful motivator and can serve as a catalyst for further performance improvements. However, if your options are so far underwater that you need Jacques Cousteau to find them, the motivational impact is going to be limited.

Investors and analysts argue that the discipline of consistently improving performance on a quarterly basis provides both the funding and the confidence to make longer-term investments. They also argue that it is a powerful measure of management's effectiveness and acts as a scorecard for investors to monitor the effective utilization of their capital.

In recent years, the most often heard phrase from business leaders on earnings calls has been that they are suffering from a lack of visibility. In 2008, as credit markets seized up and consumers put their wallets away, making all prior forecasts obsolete, the shock to the system was profound. Only months earlier, many of the same CEOs were predicting that the rapid growth rates of the past few years were here to stay as technology created a new economy where demand apparently knew no limits and productivity improvements were a permanent fixture. The vision turned into a mirage and sent companies scrambling to the old standbys of layoffs, hiring freezes, and expense controls.

The crash of 2008 also showed that many of the massive investments in new technologies that promised instant visibility into operations and performance were flawed. Investments in customer relationship management and supply chain technologies were supposed to provide clear visibility into customer buying patterns, production scheduling, inventory, pricing, and the like. Similarly, the linkage of these new internal systems to those of partners and customers was expected to provide greater insight into overall supply and demand patterns. Hence, performance was supposed to be more predictable. Clearly, the results were not what was expected. The warning signs were there almost a decade earlier when Cisco, a poster child for leveraging technology, took a $2.2 billion excess inventory charge for its fiscal third quarter ending April 2001.

So why has there been an apparent failure to fully realize the expected benefits? Is it simply that business cycles are unpredictable or are there other explanations? As discussed in Chapters 5 and 6, predicting the future is an exercise in being wrong most of the time. Part of the problem is that for most organizations, revenues will always be more volatile than costs. When a customer stops buying, it does not automatically reduce the costs of his or her suppliers. When donors stop giving, a not-for-profit's costs don't automatically reduce. However, in many situations organizations do little to help themselves. Couple these findings with the failure to successfully integrate basic financial systems following acquisitions and the problems become easier to understand.

One $5 billion company is still wrestling with over 400 different financial systems, including more than 30 general ledgers.

Simply put, today's management processes and systems do not get the job done. They cannot cope with the speed, volatility, and complexity of today's business environment. My own research shows that the best organizations don't make excuses. They have a very different profile and have successfully revamped their management processes to address both the short-term and the long-term goals. They share four characteristics: focus, integration, technology leverage, and speed. First, they focus on those key variables that are most critical to their business. Instead of drowning in data spewing out of their ERP systems, they have developed a small set of continuously monitored, well-understood measures that provide rapid insights into both the "what" and "why" of performance. These measures include key predictive or leading measures as well as external or market based measures. In addition to having the right measures, they are complemented by exception-based reporting of any material event that merits attention. Instead of a system that delivers exhaustive reporting of irrelevant data, they have selective reporting of useful information.

Second, leading companies have been successful in integrating all their key management processes to ensure alignment. This includes strategic planning, business planning, budgeting, reporting, forecasting, risk management, project management, and perhaps most important of all, compensation. Many organizations have a disconnect between what is described in the strategy and what is budgeted, reported, and rewarded. For example, strategies often talk about innovation, customer attraction, and the like, yet rarely can you find a line item in a budget that defines how much is going to be invested in these items. Leaders can look at their budget or a monthly management report and quickly discern what are their key strategies or initiatives and how progress is tracking. This linkage is crucial if the impact of short-term actions to meet quarterly performance targets and also to achieve long-term strategic goals is to be understood and effectively managed.

Third, leading companies are successful in effectively leveraging technology to support better decision making and execution. It is logical that this is an easier task for companies that have successfully focused and integrated their management processes, since they have already eliminated a lot of the unnecessary data and process inefficiencies. It is a lot easier to automate a simple process than a complex one. The simplification of the data collection, manipulation, and reporting processes has the added benefit of freeing up analyst time to focus on deriving insight in support of better decision making. For the best, this results in a doubling of the time devoted to analysis while needing only two-thirds of the headcount. This in turn allows them to both attract and retain the best talent further enhancing the quality of analysis and decision making.

Fourth and largely enabled by the first three principles, the best organizations execute at speed. From closing the books to making a decision, they do not waste time. They are able to rapidly assess both the short- and long-term implications and scenarios associated with their decisions so that the appropriate trade-offs are understood in advance. This gives them the added benefit of being in a position to better manage expectations. Analysts and investors hate surprises.

Smart organizations understand that they will make bad decisions—the key is that they can identify their bad decisions faster than their competitors and then take corrective action before too much damage is done. Their GPS system tells them the instant they deviate from the planned course and provides insight into the actions that can be taken. Organizations that successfully balance short- and long-term growth are constantly evaluating the choices and tradeoffs inherent in any decision. They define clear criteria for making investments, but more important, they define criteria for abandonment. Those are the conditions under which they will cease investing or stop a project. This ensures that changes in the real world that inevitably occur during any long-term project are not ignored.

There will always be inevitable tension between meeting quarterly expectations and sustaining long-term growth. Painful tradeoffs will have to be made regardless of how effective your management processes are. However, by focusing on the right information, processes, and technology support, you can buy yourself time. Companies with long track records of success such as Apple, BMW, Exxon Mobil, General Electric, Toyota, IKEA, Johnson & Johnson, Nestlé, Nike, and Samsung tend to exhibit many of these characteristics.

As one CEO described it to me, "By having the right information, the right processes, and the right technology, you are removing
all my excuses. Effectively what you are doing is isolating management
stupidity as the only reason for making poor decisions." This is true;
however, in the long run no company can survive if it cannot provide
products or services that people want at a price they will pay, and which
provides a reasonable return to investors.

**Mythbuster Wisdom: The Hypocrisy of Mark-to-Market
Accounting**

During the economic meltdown of 2008, a rather obscure
accounting rule emerged as a real devil in the details. Bankers,
politicians, and commentators all lined up to lambaste the so-
called "mark-to-market" rule as one of the primary causes for
bank's bleeding so much red ink that the taxpayer had to step
in with multiple bailouts. Many on Main Street were bewildered as to how a humble accounting rule could cripple the
financial system. So what is the real story?

The accounting rule in question has the sexy title of FAS
157. This means that it is one of many Financial Accounting
Standards issued by the Financial Accounting Standards Board
(FASB). I suspect that the fact that it is Standard number 157
adds weight to the "confuse rather than clarify" argument
against accounting. FAS 157 describes the accounting rules for
valuing marketable assets and liabilities. The standard requires
that companies record the value of marketable securities at their
market value as opposed to either their purchase price or the
expected value when they are sold. So if you buy a security
for $100 and its value declines to $75, you should record its
value as $75 and report a loss of $25, regardless of whether
you actually sell it. The intent of the standard is to help investors understand the value of these securities at a point in time.
Sounds very reasonable, doesn't it? After all, if your home value
goes down by 25 percent, it makes little sense to value it at

what you paid for it. Similarly, if it goes up in value, you would like to recognize the increase in value, particularly when you apply for a home equity loan.

The problem occurs when the market for the security disappears or the value of the assets decline so dramatically that they become virtually worthless and can only be sold for a fraction of their original cost. This is what happened to many mortgage-backed securities during 2008—they became distressed. Such a quaint term, which for me conjures up a mental image of a poor little mortgage-backed security sitting on a park bench with tears streaming down its face, or perhaps more appropriately, sitting alone in a bar knocking back a fifteenth glass of Kristal and bemoaning the repossession of the Ferrari. Anyway the value of these securities dropped so much that when marked to market, the value was no longer sufficient to support the loans that had been taken out to buy them in the first place, hence lenders demanded repayment, triggering defaults all over the place. William Isaac, a former head of the FDIC, led many of the critics by commenting that, "The accounting system is destroying too much capital."[7] That may have been so, but the root cause of the crisis was lending too much money to too many people with insufficient means to repay the loans when the value of their homes fell below the outstanding mortgage balance. Fair value accounting simply recognized this fact. It is a bit like blaming the medical laboratory for reporting that your cholesterol is too high. However, critics argued that forcing the value of mortgage-backed securities to be marked down so severely was not realistic because the holders were not planning to sell them. The market for these assets became so distressed that holders of mortgage-backed securities could not sell them other than at fire-sale prices, which may be below the true value of the cash flows related to the security. The argument has some merit, but it is tough to escape the conclusion that many buyers took on risks they did not fully understand.

Some finance executives saw through the "blame the accounting rule argument" and responded to Isaac's criticisms with some wit (a talent for which accountants are not normally renowned). Comments included:

- "Isaac's argument is like blaming the mountain for the plane crash. Let's just give the drunk pilot another Scotch and assume the mountain away."
- "Now I know why the Cubs lost in playoffs. It was the scoreboard operator, not the pitching, hitting, and fielding."
- "From 2004 to 2007 not even one of these Masters of the Universe raised their hand and proclaimed, "Geez, my bonus check looks too large—better double-check it.""[8]

Underneath this debate there is an underlying hypocrisy. When the value of these securities was soaring as home prices moved ever upwards, no one complained about mark to market, since the increasing values could be used as security for even bigger loans. Not too many people complained when the value of their home increased, allowing them to tap a nice home equity line to buy a new boat!

An Accounting Conspiracy Theory

In the late 1990s there were growing concerns about the potential conflicts of interest that could (did) exist between the auditing and consulting arms of the big four accounting firms. In many cases the fears were well founded; captive audit clients with long-term relationships to the accounting firm represented juicy targets for the new, slick management consulting arms that emerged in the 1980s. I can personally vouch for the paper-thin Chinese walls that existed during my own tenure with a large accounting firm in London from 1985–1989.

In order to stave off possible regulation, three of the big four firms voluntarily divested themselves of their consulting arms. Price Waterhouse Coopers sold its consulting arm to IBM, but only after a truly comic moment in the history of corporate branding when the firm initially proposed renaming itself "Monday." Arthur Andersen formalized the split of Andersen Consulting, which then morphed into Accenture, and KPMG gave birth to Bearing Point. Only Deloitte resisted the change. For the three brave firms, the splits removed some hugely profitable businesses from under their corporate umbrella, leaving behind relatively slow-growth audit, tax, and accounting businesses. Not long after the splits, Enron happened and the world changed. This had two consequences. Everyone at Accenture breathed a huge sigh of relief as its former parent, Arthur Andersen, evaporated in the fallout from its involvement with Enron. Second, accounting became cool again and with the passage of Sarbanes-Oxley, the firms were thrown a hugely lucrative new line of business in the form of Sarbox compliance.

A more cynical person than I could postulate a conspiracy between the well-connected and lobbied-up accountants and Congress. This was a government bailout at its purest. The trend continues to this day as with the wave of Sarbox-generated work drying up, the SEC has thoughtfully announced a multi-year process to eliminate America's indigenous accounting rules named GAAP (which stands for Generally Accepted Accounting Principles), which were of course designed by the accountants, and replace them with a new international standard called IFRS (which stands for International Financial Reporting Standards), thereby ensuring the accounting firms yet another lucrative, multi-year stream of new work as they assist their clients in the switch.

A final note is that while nearly everyone agrees that simplicity and consistency are laudable goals for accounting and taxation, what would such simplicity and consistency do for the revenue of accounting firms?

So What?

- While correct accounting of any organization's operations is essential (you can go to jail if you fail to do it), it rarely provides a useful management view.
- Managing real-time businesses requires real-time information and real-time decision making.

- Accounting is here to stay, so if you aspire to a business leadership role, you will have to understand at the least the basics and, as you rise higher in the organization, much more.
- There is a trend toward global standardization of accounting rules—this is not the same as having clear and simple rules.
- The more creative organizations, especially banks, get into the development of ever more sophisticated financing instruments— the more complicated the accounting becomes. So you get what you deserve.
- Beware the behavioral side effects of excessively complex cost allocation mechanisms—they can be counterproductive and distracting from the real objectives of delivering superior performance.

Notes

1. CPA Vision Project, aicpa.org, July 2009.
2. American Institute of Certified Public Accountants. www.aicpa.org, May 2009.
3. Financial Accounting Standards Board, "FASB 133 Implementation Issue: Exception Related to Embedded Credit Derivatives," FASB.org January 2009.
4. Alix Stewart, Making the Leap, *CFO* Magazine, November 1, 2008.
5. Thomas Johnson and Robert Kaplan, *Relevance Lost: The Rise and Fall of Management Accounting* (Cambridge MA: Harvard Business School Press, 1991).
6. Steve Schwarzman, "Some Lessons of the Financial Crisis," *Wall Street Journal,* November 4, 2008.
7. David M. Katz "Former FDIC Chief: Fair Value Caused The Crisis," *CFO* Magazine, December 2008.
8. Ibid.

Chapter 13

The Synergies Will Be Massive!

I t was not that long ago that mergers and acquisitions were relatively rare. Now it is an everyday activity—no self-respecting CEO can survive on organic growth alone. It is all about the deal. After all, it is a lot quicker and easier, although not always more effective, to buy a business than build one, and there is also the allure of the Holy Grail of mergers and acquisitions (M&A)—synergy. In 2007, global M&A transactions reached a total value of around $3.6 trillion. In 2008 the value dropped to $2.9 trillion—still not too shabby. The global credit crunch is likely to be a mere hiccup in the accelerating wave of acquisitions and divestitures that seek, often illusively, to increase value. Much of the growth has been spurred by the rapid rise of private equity as a force for corporate restructuring—20 percent ($720 billion) of 2007's M&A deals were private equity buyouts. Steve Borden at Cruciant loves doing deals and has been eyeing a lucrative private equity play for some time.

Fiction: The Myth of Synergy—August 2006

Martin James, a top investment banker with Silverman Penney, calls Steve to pitch an idea. After the usual pleasantries surrounding the current state of the markets and a chuckle at the recent demise of a competitor's CEO who was found to have installed a rather classy, but very expensive, lady friend in the company's Park Avenue apartment, Martin asks Steve if it is time for Cruciant to put some of its cash to work. Steve knows a pitch is coming, but he is not averse to listening. James has a good track record, bringing a couple of interesting opportunities to Cruciant's attention in the past. "You know us, Martin, if the price is right and the strategic fit is clear, we are always interested. So tell me more."

Martin goes on to describe the potential acquisition target: "You know that FTE Inc. has had a few problems with recent product launches, don't you? Well, one of my colleagues in Hong Kong tells me that the Board is open to offers, and with the stock down 30 percent in the past six months, there is clearly a deal to be done. Our analysis shows that while the launch problems have been significant, the underlying franchise is strong. Customers love FTE's service, and contract renewals are running at 90 percent. This is a company with a solid base; it just cannot seem to grow. They spin off lots of cash, which is always worth having; and with Cruciant's outstanding product development and marketing capabilities, you should be able to fix their problems pretty quickly. The synergies could be huge; not just in the traditional back-office areas, but their market footprint and product mix seem wholly complementary to Cruciant's. Based upon the preliminary numbers my guys have run, if you could do a deal at $60 per share, you could fund the complete acquisition with debt serviced by FTE's strong cash flow. Even if you only realize 10 percent synergy savings, the deal is accretive by a couple of cents in year one and up to 12 cents in year two." Steve responds that the deal looks attractive and asks Martin to have his team develop a full analysis.

Three weeks later, Steve places a call to FTE's Chairman, and a week later the deal is announced at $62 a share, valuing FTE, Inc. at $1.1 billion. At the press conference, Steve describes the deal thus: "The combination of Cruciant and FTE redefines our industry. By combining the undoubted strengths of our two great companies we will be able to offer our customers an unparalleled value proposition serving all business needs. With this deal Cruciant confirms its position as the preeminent player in a rapidly growing market. The synergies extend from our core research and development operations all the way through to the rationalization of back-office operations. The combined revenue and expense opportunities are unprecedented and should allow our shareholders to rapidly realize the benefits. I have tremendous respect for FTE's history and reputation and feel honored to be chosen to lead the combined business. Look for the combined company to assert its presence in the marketplace in short order."

March 2008

Henry walks briskly into Steve office. "Steve, we have a problem."

"What's up?" Steve replies.

"Our fabrication business in Malaysia has been having a problem with one of its customers not paying its bills and has put a hold on all future shipments," Henry explains.

"Why should we be worrying about that? It's a small local matter, and Chen Li and his team do a good job out there," comments Steve.

Henry frowns and responds, "It is not quite that simple. Let me explain. The customer in question accounts for only about $100,000 in business. They are 90 days past due on about $35,000 of receivables, and according to local policy, Chen Li did the right thing. However, the customer is a small subsidiary of Giant, Inc., our biggest customer. Apparently, the local Giant manager sent a message to Giant HQ saying that Cruciant was stopping shipments and that the reason the bills had not been paid was a dispute over pricing. I have not gotten to the bottom of whether the pricing dispute is real, but that's not the main point. Apparently, Craig Lucas, Giant's CEO, has gotten wind of this and is hopping mad. If he hasn't contacted you already, he will soon. We do about $75 million of business with Giant every year, and if you don't calm him down this could be a big problem for us."

Steve exclaims, "How can this happen?"

Henry replies: "Well, it's a function of the fact that we have not yet finished migrating the Malaysian operations onto our enterprise systems. If you remember, the business was part of the FTE acquisition and we have been having some problems with the integration. As a result, we have no ability to consolidate total risk exposure by customer, so we have been using a system of local limits to control past due accounts. Most of the time it works well, but in this instance it has come back to bite us."

Steve nods his head slowly, "Well, call Chen Li immediately and tell him to resume shipping. I am not going to risk $75 million for the sake of $35 grand. I will call Lucas now and apologize. But Henry, make sure this never happens again. It's ridiculous."

April 2008

Henry and Steve are reviewing the results for the first quarter.

"How come the expense reductions are about $50 million lower than we expected when we closed the FTE deal?" Steve asks.

"It's a bit of mess actually," replies Henry. "There are three things that make up the shortfall. First, when we closed the deal, we thought there would be about $20 million in savings from moving FTE workers over to our pay and benefits programs. We have realized some of that but it turns out that most FTE managers have two-year rolling contracts that have a one-year notice period, so we cannot do anything to those contracts for another six months. Second, we expected about $15 million in savings from rationalizing all of their computer systems. That number still looks good, but it is taking longer and costing more to get those savings. IT tells me that FTE has more systems than we anticipated and many of them are poorly documented. You will remember the Malaysian problem with Giant last month. That is a good example. Finally, we saw some opportunities to rationalize marketing and product development—however, it does not look like those are real. FTE had basically stopped all product development to conserve cash and get ready for a sale so there was nothing to cut—somehow we missed that in our due diligence, and they were not totally open with us about it during negotiations."

Steve sighs, "So the bottom line is the savings are not real, and when we combine that with the falling market share for most FTE products, the future looks bleak, doesn't it?"

"I'm afraid so," Henry responds. "My team are looking at some numbers, and we think there is about $40 million to be gained by shutting down FTEs SE Asia operation, which accounts for about 35 percent of their costs, but only about 20 percent of revenue. Given the state of the economy out there, that might be the best thing to do."

Facts: Synergy—Much Touted, Rarely Realized

Has there ever been an acquisitive CEO who did not boast about the synergy of a deal? Yet despite the euphoria that typically accompanies any deal, the track record of realizing results is patchy at best. Robert F. Bruner in his 2005 book, *Deals from Hell,* commented on the overall profitability of mergers and acquisitions: ". . . the average, benchmark-adjusted return to corporate investment in M&A is close to zero."[1] That's not a lot of value for an awful lot of effort and investment banking fees. Bruner goes on to catalogue a number of very high-profile clunkers from the world of M&A such as AOL/Time-Warner, AT&T/NCR, and Mattel's acquisition of The Learning Company. To this list can be added Wachovia's purchase of Golden Tree Financial, Boston Scientific acquiring Guidant, Sears' combination with K-Mart, and Daimler's acquisition of Chrysler. Vaunted private equity players have not been much more successful. Daimler succeeded in offloading Chrysler to Cerberus, only for the company to hurtle into bankruptcy.

Paul B. Carroll and Chunka Mui in their book *Billion-Dollar Lessons* identified seven highly suspect business strategies.[2] First on the list was synergy, quickly followed by financial engineering, rollups, staying the course, moving into an adjacent market, technology leverage, and consolidation. Four items on their list directly relate to M&A, while the complete list covers just about every reason I have heard a CEO use to explain a strategy with the possible exception of achieving economies of scale.

Of course, at the time of a deal, optimism knows no bounds and much is promised, at least according to the people involved. Richard Parsons, Time Warner's President at the time of the AOL deal in 2000, commented,

"This is a defining event for Time Warner and America Online as well as a pivotal moment in the unfolding of the Internet age. By joining the resources and talents of these two highly creative companies, we can accelerate the development and deployment of a whole new generation of interactive services and content. AOL–Time Warner will offer an incomparable portfolio of global brands that encompass the full spectrum of media and content."[3]

Both companies had facts at their fingertips when justifying the combination. Synergies from the combination of AOL's technology platform and Time Warner's rich content were projected to deliver $1 billion in earnings during the first year; AOL would gain access to Time Warner's 13 million cable customers, while Time Warner could deliver content to AOL's more than 20 million subscribers; and the combined company would have revenues of more than $20 billion and a market capitalization of over $350 billion. Tough to argue with any of that, yet within three years the deal was being lambasted as "the worst deal in history" by Kara Swisher in her book, *There Must Be a Pony in Here Somewhere: The AOL Time Warner Debacle and the Quest for a Digital Future*. Swisher went on to comment, "a company without assets was buying a company without a clue."[4]

Mythbuster Wisdom: Forget Value Creation

- January 2001: Time Warner market capitalization at time of AOL deal: $164 billion.
- May 2009: Market capitalization when spinoff of AOL was announced: $28 billion.

Despite the deal's massive destruction of shareholder value, Time Warner's Parsons went on to become Chairman, and after retiring from that role, took on the Chairmanship of Citigroup as the bank sought salvation from government ownership. To be fair, Parsons was not one of the key architects of the deal—they were Steve Case, the founder of AOL, and Gerry Levin, Chairman and CEO of Time-Warner. Not long after the deal, both were gone.

Insiders are not the only ones who get caught up in the synergy of the deal. Scott Ehrens, a media analyst with Bear Stearns (at the time, still a respected investment bank) commented that together AOL and Time-Warner "represent an unprecedented powerhouse. If their mantra

Mar 5, 2009   Open 16.22   High 16.62   Low 15.40   Close 15.65   Volume 10,695,380

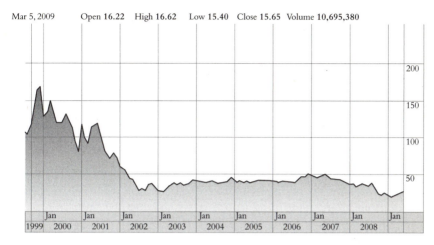

Figure 13.1   Time Warner Stock Price Chart
Time Warner Stock Price Chart from January 1, 1999 to March 5, 2009
SOURCE: BusinessWeek

is content, this alliance is unbeatable. Now they have this great platform they can cross-fertilize with content and redistribute."[5]

In May 2009, Time Warner finally threw in the towel and announced that it would be spinning off what was left of AOL into a separate company. In a rare act of executive contrition, Steve Case admitted to both his own and the deal's failings by commenting that Thomas Edison's quote that vision without execution is hallucination "pretty much sums up AOL/TW" and acknowledging "a failure of leadership (my own included)."[6] Interestingly for the one-time Internet pioneer, he used Twitter to provide his comments.

On a smaller scale, but no less spectacular, was Mattel's acquisition of the Learning Company in May 1999 for $3.6 billion. The logic for the acquisition was to add entertainment and educational software to Mattel's more traditional Barbie Doll and Hot Wheels brands. At the time it sounded very logical. Michael Perik, The Learning Company's chairman and chief executive, commented, "together we have the engine and the content to redefine leadership in the interactive world."[7]

The Learning Company was a fast-growing player in the educational software market and had established some strong franchises with games such as Myst and Carmen Sandiego. Mattel confidently predicted large and growing profits from the acquisition. Problems emerged almost immediately, and The Learning Company posted pretax losses of over $200 million for 1999. By February 2000, Mattel's stock was down from a high of $45 to $11 and CEO Jill Barad resigned, albeit with a $50 million payoff. In October 2000, Mattel sold The Learning Company for nothing except a share of any future profits. In just over a year, $3.6 billion had simply evaporated—so much for the purported synergy.

So why do so many deals promise so much and deliver so little? Much of the problem lies in the gulf between crunching numbers and the actual business of successfully integrating two organizations. Almost all deal logic is built upon financial models that incorporate numerous assumptions about everything from market share to the reduction in IT costs from combining two organizations. Very little consideration is given as to whether the practical act of integration and synergy can actually be achieved. As Steve Case, channeling Thomas Edison, pointed out, vision without execution delivers very little of real value. Effectively integrating two organizations poses a myriad of organizational, legal, technical, cultural, behavioral, procedural, and financial challenges, any one of which can be fatal to achieving the projected benefits. Companies with a strong track record in successfully making acquisitions such as Cisco, Johnson & Johnson, and Oracle have well-honed procedures that drive very disciplined integration—they also tend to purposely underestimate the expected benefits in an attempt to manage expectations.

Private Equity—It's Really Just a Corporate Enema!

In the last few years, private equity has assumed almost mythical status as a vehicle for making boatloads of money by taking poorly performing businesses and systematically driving up their value. Actually, a business does not necessarily have to be performing poorly. Any business that generates good cash flow is a ripe target.

Private equity emerged after World War II as a means for wealthy individuals to invest directly in businesses. It stayed largely under the radar for almost 50 years despite some significant successes. In 1957, American Research and Development Corporation, one of the first private equity firms, made an investment of $70,000 in Digital Equipment that was worth $355 million when Digital went public in 1968, an annual return of more than 100 percent. However, it was not until the 1980s that the general public first became fully aware of the private equity business during the leveraged buyout boom. The signature transaction was the Kohlberg, Kravis and Roberts (KKR) acquisition of RJR Nabisco in 1988. KKR and its partners won an intense and very public battle for the company by paying more than $30 billion, including assumed debt, a record that would stand for 17 years. The deal was populated with colorful characters and spawned a best-selling book by Bryan Burrough and John Helyar, *Barbarians at the Gate*,[8] and a television film starring James Garner. In a passage eerily prescient of the events that would transpire two decades later, the authors of *Barbarians*, closed their account with the following description of the investment bankers behind the deal: "The investment bankers were part croupiers, part alchemists. They conjured up wild schemes, pounded out new and more outlandish computer runs to justify them, then twirled their temptations before executives in a devil dance."[9]

The 1980s buyout boom triggered an unprecedented explosion in financial engineering as bankers, investors, and their hired brains sought to develop ever more sophisticated financing and trading strategies, often creating exotic new securities to support them. The pace accelerated as money poured into private-equity funds, managed by companies like Blackstone, Kohlberg, Kravis, and Roberts, and the Carlyle Group. Investors in private-equity funds included wealthy individuals, insurance companies, college endowments, and pension funds.

For the last twenty years, private-equity activity has largely followed the economic cycle; booming in the mid-1990s, slumping around the time of the dot.com bust and 9/11, and then booming more than ever, fueled by lots of cheap credit. In 2006, almost $700 billion was invested globally. That year, private equity firms bought 654 U.S. companies, eighteen times more than in 2003. It was a profitable business from 1987 to 2006: Private equity firms averaged annual returns of 13.2 percent while stocks in the Standard & Poor's 500 Index have averaged only 9.7 percent.

The boom lasted until 2008 when the credit markets choked off the lifeblood of the private-equity deal—debt. Sounds ironic, doesn't it? But private equity is actually fueled by debt—lots of it.

So what's the secret sauce? It is really simple. You find a company with lazy shareholders, high costs, a depressed stock price, not too much debt, and a reasonably solid business or some undervalued asset. You raise capital from investors, borrow like crazy, and then buy the company for 1 percent down and 99 percent borrowed (private-equity owners added $741 billion of debt to company balance sheets from 2004 to 2008). The new owners then fire all the current management team and bring in new managers at a low base salary but with lots of stock as an incentive. The new team hacks expenses in order to maximize cash flow to service the massive debt load. After a few months, the private-equity firm uses the increased cash flow to add on even more debt and pays itself and its investors a nice fat dividend. Alternatively, if the equity markets look reasonable, they take the company public again, pocketing a massive return on their minimal equity investment. Another set of lazy shareholders takes control and the cycle begins again. For many years this was a no-lose proposition. When Bain Capital took Dominos Pizza public in 2004, it realized a 400 percent payback on its original investment. CVC Capital Partners took British car and bicycle parts chain Halfords public in 2004 at a valuation of £593 million compared to a purchase price of £427 million two years earlier—a gain of 39 percent. Clayton, Dubilier and Rice tripled its investment when it sold Kinkos to Federal Express in 2004. Profits remained for some even amid the credit crunch. In May 2007, TPG Capital and Goldman Sachs netted a profit of $1.3 billion in seven months from their acquisition of wireless phone company Alltel and then its subsequent sale to Verizon. A study by the British Venture Capital Association (BVCA) showed that the average investment return on sales of private-equity-owned businesses during 2005–2007 was 3.3 times that of the benchmark FTSE All-Share Index.[10]

For the private equity model to work, two conditions are essential: access to lots of cheap debt and investors or companies who are willing to buy private-equity-owned businesses at a huge premium over the original purchase price. When both conditions are met, the two components of the revenue and profit model for private equity firms are in place. Typically, they take a 20 percent cut of any profits and a 2 percent fee based upon the value of the assets. However, that 20 percent looks even better if you use a small amount of your own money to buy the company. Watch how the machine works:

Cashflow Inc. is producing profits of $100 million a year. Leverage Capital buys Cashflow Inc. for ten times earnings or $1 billion. It puts in $200 million of its own money and borrows the other $800 million. For the next few years, Cashflow's profits are used to pay interest on the debt, and Leverage Capital gets to work on cutting costs and streamlining Cashflow's business. Helped by these changes and a strong economy, profits increase to $150 million a year. Five years after buying Cashflow, Leverage Capital sells the company for the same multiple—ten times earnings or $1.5 billion. After repaying the $800 million in debt, Leverage Capital is left with $700 million, a return of 350 percent on the original $200 million investment. Even better for Leverage, it gets to keep $140 million of the profit before distributing the balance ($560 million) to the investors who put up all the original money. Of course, Leverage didn't have to wait five years to get some money; it pocketed its 2 percent management fee of between $20 and $30 million a year to ensure that no one starved while waiting for the big payoff.

> **Mythbuster Wisdom: You Too Can Live the Private-Equity Life!**
>
> At the peak of the private-equity boom, private equity firms owned numerous household names. It was quite easy for your whole life to be serviced by the world of private equity.
>
> After waking up in your Hilton Hotel room, you roll out of the Sealy bed, pull on your trendy Tommy Hilfiger shirt and trousers purchased at Neiman Marcus and jump in your Dodge rented from Hertz. Tune the radio to one of Clear Channel's many radio stations and head to Dunkin' Donuts for coffee and doughnuts. Suitably refreshed, head over for a little shopping at Sears, pick up some gifts for the kids at Toys 'R Us, and then grab some lunch at the Outback Steakhouse. As you still have some time to kill, drive down to one of Harrah's casinos and make a few modest wagers. Then catch an MGM movie at the Regal cinema before heading off to the airport to catch your Midwest airlines flight. Upon landing, jump into your Jeep Grand Cherokee and head home after a brief drive through Burger King.

The BVCA study[11] mentioned above analyzed the source of the private equity profits and the results were interesting: 30 percent came from rising stock markets; 50 percent came from taking on more debt, i.e., leverage; and 20 percent from strategic and operational improvements. This explains the challenges faced by private equity during 2008–2009. Stock markets stopped going up, and debt ceased to plentiful, so 80 percent of the opportunity disappeared. But it was worse than that. The spectacular success of the previous few years led private-equity firms to pay ever-higher prices for companies; this of course required that they use even more debt. Many firms were stuck with investments in companies whose prospects were darkening fast. A string of private-equity-backed companies filed for bankruptcy, including Chrysler, perhaps the highest profile private-equity owned company of all. Cerberus, the private equity firm that led the purchase of most of Chrysler from Daimler, itself a failed acquisition, and its partners suffered a total loss of over $7 billion. Besides incurring major reductions in the value of their investments, many private equity firms found themselves in the uncomfortable position of actually having to run companies over the long term. For example, in 2003, hedge fund manager Eddie Lampert bought failed retailer Kmart out of bankruptcy. He succeeded in making money, or as one analyst commented, "He recognized Kmart was a cadaver and he monetized it."[12] A $1.1 billion profit in 2004 was not driven by higher sales but by selling off real estate. In 2005, Eddie decided to double-down by engineering an acquisition of storied retailer, Sears, for $12.3 billion and combining it with Kmart. No one expected that the combination of two fading retailers was going to keep the residents of Bentonville, Arkansas (Wal-Mart's hometown), awake at night. The game plan was to slash costs and sell supposedly undervalued real estate. Investors loved the deal and the stock price soared, but then reality set in. The cash flows from the retail business slumped, and owner Eddie Lampert found himself working as a shopkeeper. Then the real estate market tanked, making it difficult to sell off assets for a profit. Fast Eddie had his work cut out for him.

By 2008, many private-equity deals had failed to deliver the hoped-for quick flip for profit. As one commentator put it, the "next thing you know, bankers will be handing out copies of *Good to Great*."[13] No doubt some of the investors turned operators will be successful; after all, the private-equity compensation model can be very attractive to top-tier executives. In 2006, David Calhoun, one of GE's star executives, left to join VNU, a publishing and information management company that includes the Nielsen television ratings business, for a package estimated at over $100 million. An all-star team of private-equity firms including The Blackstone Group, Kohlberg, Kravis and Roberts, and Thomas H. Lee Partners had recently bought VNU for €8.6 billion and lured Calhoun to run it for them.

Despite the criticism of private-equity firms, they do serve a valuable role in keeping lazy boards of directors and management teams on their toes. As Geoff Cullinan of Bain and Company commented, "They get flak for being rape and pillage merchants, but if they do get rich, they only do it by making better companies."[14] However, for the humble employee it can be a painful experience. No matter, private equity is clearly here to stay, unless outsized profits are taxed out of existence.

Mythbuster Wisdom: Buffett on Private Equity

So what does Warren Buffett say about private equity?

"Some years back our competitors were known as leveraged-buyout operators. But LBO became a bad name. So in Orwellian fashion, the buyout firms decided to change their moniker. What they did not change, though, were the essential ingredients of their previous operations, including their cherished fee structures and love of leverage.

"Their new label became 'private equity,' a name that turns the facts upside-down: A purchase of a business by these firms almost invariably results in dramatic reductions in the equity portion of the acquiree's capital structure compared to that previously existing. A number of these acquirees, purchased only two to three years ago, are now in mortal danger because of the debt piled on them by their private-equity buyers. Much of the bank debt is selling below 70¢ on the dollar, and the public debt has taken a far greater beating. The private-equity firms, it should be noted, are not rushing in to inject the equity their wards now desperately need. Instead, they're keeping their remaining funds very private."[15]

Private equity is not always a winner. Of the 109 U.S. companies with assets of more than $1 million that filed for bankruptcy in the first 11 months of 2008, 67 (61 percent) were either owned by or had been spun off from private equity firms.[16]

One reason is that sometimes the assumption that strong cash flows will comfortably serve massive debt loads does not quite work out. In 2006 private-equity firms TPG and Apollo Management LP bought casino-operator Harrah's for $17.3 billion. Harrah's was lauded for its market-leading position and innovative use of computer-based analysis to gain a competitive advantage in a cutthroat industry. At the time, the deal was viewed as a license to print money. However, future growth was predicated on consumers continuing to gamble. As the real estate ATM sputtered and the economy nose-dived, the rosy projections of growth disappeared. By late 2008 Harrah's found itself laboring under $23.9 billion in debt. Huge debt payments siphoned off money that would have gone toward investments in the business, weakening the company's once strong competitive advantage.

While the wisdom of debt-fuelled private equity deals can be questioned, Harrah's at least anticipated that the future might not quite turn out as expected. Before the deal closed, the company ran scenarios to prepare for the eventuality that "the world got very bad." Unfortunately, by late 2008 as one executive commented, "the problem is that this is worse than the worst case scenario."[17]

So What?

- Realizing M&A synergies is not financial modeling; it is roll-your-sleeves-up work that requires focus, discipline, and leadership.
- Ultimately, successful mergers are reflected by the actions of customers in the marketplace—not by accountants in the back office.
- One plus one rarely equals two, never mind three.
- Executive ego is not a valid justification for making acquisitions.
- In a perfect world there would be no need for private equity. As it is clearly not perfect, the vultures are here to stay!

Notes

1. Robert F. Bruner, *Deals from Hell* (Hoboken NJ: John Wiley & Sons, 2005).

2. Paul B. Carroll and Chunka Mui, *Billion-Dollar Lessons* (London: Penguin Books 2008).

3. Time Warner Inc., "AOL & Time Warner Will Merge To Create World's First Internet-Age Media & Communications Company" Time Warner Press Release, January 10, 2000.

4. Kara Swisher, *There Must Be a Pony in Here Somewhere: The AOL Time Warner Debacle and the Quest for a Digital Future* (New York: Three Rivers Press, 2003).

5. Tom Johnson, "Internet Leader and Entertainment Firm to Join Forces; New Company Worth $350B," CNNMoney.com, January 10, 2000.

6. "Time Warner Brings Down Curtain on AOL Flop," *The Financial Times,* May 30, 2009.

7. Mattel Inc. "Cutbacks in Retailer Buying; Mattel and The Learning Company Agree To Merge" Mattel Press Release, December 14.

8. Bryan Burrough and John Helyar, *Barbarians at the Gate* (New York: Harper & Row, 1990).

9. Ibid. p. 514.

10. British Venture Capital Association and Ernst & Young, BVCA Annual Report on the Performance of Portfolio Companies, London: BVCA and Ernst & Young: 2008.

11. Ibid.

12. "Kmart Completes $12.3B Sears Acquisition," Associated Press Online, March 24, 2005.

13. Telis Demos, "Dealmakers Stop Leveraging and Start Managing," *Fortune,* May 25, 2009.

14. Toby Preston, "The Private Equity Rollercoaster," BBC News, January 9, 2006.

15. Warren Buffett, Letter to Shareholders, Berkshire Hathaway, February 27, 2009.

16. Peter Lattman, "Carlyle's Bet on Telecom in Hawaii Ends Badly," *Wall Street Journal,* December 2, 2008.

17. Tamara Audi, Peter Lattman and Jeff McCracken "Harrah's Changes Its Game," *Wall Street Journal,* October 27, 2008.

Chapter 14

Talent Matters

Is talent overvalued? Geoffrey Colvin's 2008 book, *Talent Is Overrated,* (Penguin Group, 2008) postulates that there is really no such thing as innate talent. Exceptional performance is only realized through hard work, practice, and repetition. If true, and I am only partially convinced, this is good news. No longer can we explain away our failures by referring to others as simply being more talented. They just work harder and smarter. Of course, hard work alone does not guarantee success but without it the odds are stacked against you. The best organizations and people work harder and smarter when times are tough, or in the immortal words of Billy Ocean's 1986 hit, "When the going gets tough, the tough get going." The ability to outperform in a downturn truly distinguishes the star performers. Like most if its peers, Cruciant's management constantly reaffirms that talent is its most valuable resource.

Fiction: A Corner Office on the 15th Floor of Cruciant's Headquarters—April 2008

Stephanie Ekblom is sitting in her new office. It is her first day at Cruciant. She has been hired as the Director of Financial Planning responsible for all of Cruciant's planning, budgeting, and forecasting on a global basis. This is a new position, created by CFO Henry Pritchett in recognition of the increasing complexity of Cruciant's business given its rapid global expansion. Stephanie was hired from a top consulting firm where she had done some great work for Henry over the past few years. She qualified as an accountant in Australia and had considerable experience working in Asia.

There is a knock at the door and Stephanie gets up, walks across the room, and opens it. Outside is a man with a trolley on which appears to be a selection of framed pictures. "Hello, I'm Fred from building operations. I've brought along some pictures for you to look at for your office," he explained.

"Oh, I get to choose pictures—how exciting," exclaims Stephanie, waving Fred into her office. For the next 20 minutes she sorts through the pictures and selects three for her wall, "I like these three—that one can go on the wall behind my desk," she says pointing to a framed photograph of Ayers Rock in Australia at sunset. " "It will remind me of home. The other two can go on this wall," she says pointing to her left."

Fred looks a little uncomfortable and says: "Well, ma'am, that might be a problem. As a Director, you can only have two pictures. You have to be a Vice President to have three."

Stephanie looks astonished: "You mean the company has rules as to how many pictures a person can have on their wall?"

"Oh, yes. There are also standards for the size of office and the type of furniture you can have. We simply took all the old United Integrated rules when we were spun off," Fred responds.

Stephanie laughs and then looks at Fred a little conspiratorially, before smiling and saying, "Well, Fred, if you don't tell anyone that I picked out three pictures, I won't either. So it will be all right, won't it?" Then she winks.

Fred half-smiles and reluctantly agrees, "OK. Because it is your first day I'll let you, but don't tell anyone about it or I could get in trouble."

"Don't worry, it will be our secret," Stephanie assures him.

(Author's note: This exact experience happened to me on my first day working at one of America's largest companies, except I did not wink at Fred.)

Two Days Later . . . 8 PM

Stephanie is sitting at her desk with Kevin Na. They are staring at a stack of printouts.

"So these spreadsheets are the forecast submissions from each of the country managers in Asia?" she asks.

"Yes," replies Kevin, "they send in their forecast on the ninth workday after the quarterly close; that was Monday. It takes my team a couple of days to check each one and work with the country managers to ensure the data is complete and accurate. After you and I have reviewed them tonight, I will go back and get any further questions answered. We will then start consolidating the forecasts and should have a draft for you to review with Henry early next week. It takes another three or four days to complete the forecast and it will be ready for the management meeting early next month."

"So the forecast will be based upon data that is already one month old before the management team gets to see it?" asks Stephanie.

"Yes, that is right," Kevin responds, "but it is better than it used to be. Asia used to have a one-month lag in reporting its actual results, so back then the forecast was based upon data that was two months old."

Stephanie is astonished but decides to keep quiet. She has 90 days to come up with a plan for improving all the processes, and at this rate a lot will need to change.

"OK, I understand," she says, "Now when I look at these spreadsheets they show the actual results for the year to date compared to the budget and then there is a forecast for each month for the rest of the year compared to the budget. Is that right?"

"Yes, that's right," Kevin answers.

"Is there anything that shows me the trend of actual results for the year to date or gives me a comparison to the last forecast? After all, the budget isn't really much use now with all the change going on, is it?" Stephanie asks.

"Oh no, the budget is very important. The budget is the basis by which all the managers get compensated, so it remains the benchmark," says Kevin.

Stephanie shakes her head: "So that's why when I look at the Philippines here and see that they are 12 percent behind budget through the end of the second quarter, their forecast shows that they will make it all up in the second half and still make the budget number? How can that be realistic given the delays in the new product launch program and the weakening economy?"

"I understand, but the local team will keep striving to make the budget no matter what," explains Kevin.

"OK, so this is not really a forecast at all, it is simply a mathematical picture of what would need to happen for them to get back on budget," concludes Stephanie.

Two hours later, Stephanie leaves the office with a stack of spreadsheets under her arm. Kevin told her that there was no way to access the forecast system from her home as the master was kept on a PC in his department, and the system was shut down at 5 PM each day. So she had a few more hours of severe eyestrain ahead as she sought to interpret the numbers being submitted for the forecast. Up until now, she had not seen one single explanation as to the changes in tactics that would be required to allow each of the countries to get back on plan. Well, at least she knew why they hired her, but it was not exactly the way she would have liked to get started.

The Next Morning

There is a knock at Stephanie's door, and Andrew Tompkins pokes his head around and says: "Hi, I'm Andrew Tompkins and I am here for our 10 o'clock meeting."

"Come in, Andrew, it is good to see you. I have been hearing great things about you. Now what do you want to see me for?" asks Stephanie.

Andrew is a senior financial analyst on Kevin's team. He has been with Cruciant for two years after getting his MBA from Wharton. Kevin rates him as one of the top performers on the team.

Andrew sits down and begins, "Well, I know you have only just arrived, and I think it is great that the company has brought you in. We certainly need to improve our processes and systems if we are to effectively run a global business, but truth be told I am not sure Cruciant is the right place for me."

Stephanie cannot hide her shock, "So are you saying you want to leave?"

"It's a bit more than that," replies Andrew. "I have been offered another job that I plan on taking, so I want to hand in my resignation. I am sorry to do this so soon after you arrived, but it is something I've been thinking about for a few months."

"Are you sure you want to do this?" Stephanie asks, "Kevin rates you very highly, and your performance reviews have all been excellent. You have a great future here. I saw you as a key member of my team as we try and change things around here."

"Thank you, and believe me I would have loved to work on the changes you talk about. I just feel that after two years of spending every day, most evenings, and the occasional weekend buried in the minutiae of budget and forecast spreadsheets that I am not getting the experience and exposure I need to develop. I did not go to Wharton to end up playing with Excel every day. It takes us so long to collect and check all the data that we have no time left to do any real analysis. Usually, Kevin is standing by the printer waiting for the final forecast to print so he can run upstairs to Henry's office to review it. We never have time to really understand the numbers or do any insightful analysis. I feel like I only use my brain for about two hours a week. It is time for me to move on. Maybe if you had come aboard a few months ago things might have been different."

Stephanie responds, "Well, I can't say I am not disappointed, but in the short time I have been here, I can certainly understand why you feel the way you do. If your mind is made up, I will not try to change it—even if I did, it would most likely only be temporary. I wish you tremendous success in your new job and from all I hear that should be guaranteed." She gets up and shakes Andrew's hand. As he turns to leave, she ponders her position. It is not really a big surprise that bright, ambitious professionals quit when they are forced to do so much "grunt" work. There will probably be more defections. From her consulting days she knows that often the only people who stay around when the processes are broken and the systems nonexistent are those who have no desire or aptitude for insightful analysis. She needs to change things fast. Despite all Cruciant's talk of valuing people, the processes and systems are not helping much in attracting and retaining talent.

When Is a Headcount Freeze Not Really a Headcount Freeze?—August 2008

Lance Headley runs Cruciant's purchasing organization. His team oversees the buying of over a billion dollars of goods and services that Cruciant needs to function: everything from desks and chairs to legal services. As part of the budget process, Lance is being forced to cut his costs by 20 percent and that means getting rid of people. He is not happy. His team's workload is not changing; in fact, the increasingly global nature of Cruciant's supply chain and the expanding array of sourcing options mean that everyone is working harder than ever. But the budget cuts and hiring freeze that CEO Steve Borden has ordered are essential if the company is to meet its aggressive earnings goals, so Lance will have to make some tough decisions. He lets go fifteen people from his team, including Sarah Lawrence, who has been managing Cruciant's purchases of advertising and marketing services for fifteen years. Sarah was a key member of his team, but Lance could see no other option, and one of Cruciant's ad agencies was offering to provide some of the same services as part of their existing contract, so Sarah's position was eliminated.

Two Months Later . . .

Lance is meeting with Phil the VP of Marketing. Phil is not happy. "Lance, this is a shambles. We have a major campaign coming up for the new product launch in Southeast Asia and none of the billboards, magazine slots, or radio slots for the ad campaign are lined up. What the hell is going on?

Lance: "I understand, but it has been really tough here since we had to make those budget cuts a couple of months ago. If you remember, our ad agency offered to take on some of the purchasing activities we used to do in house so I let Sarah, our in-house buyer, go as part of the cuts. We are now learning that the agency is not really set up to handle the contractual elements of the purchasing. They are all creative types and their attention to detail is not great. The problem is with the hiring freeze I cannot go out and get someone in house to take over the role."

Phil: "Well, we have to fix it. We never used to have problems in this area. When Sarah was here, she was on top of it all. She negotiated great deals and was incredibly well organized. Do you know if she has found a new job?"

Lance: "I don't think so. She was pretty upset when we let her go. The package we gave her was quite generous, so I think she is taking some time to decide what to do."

Phil: "How about calling her and seeing if she is interested in coming back?"

Lance: "But what about the hiring freeze?"

Phil: "Well, I have some money in my budget because we cancelled that campaign in Europe. I think I can take those funds and use them to pay Sarah if we hire her back as a contractor. Why don't you see if she is interested?"

Two weeks later Sarah is back at her old desk, doing her old job. She is not a Cruciant employee but working as a consultant. Cruciant is paying her $350 a day, and Sarah is delighted. Her twelve-month contract will pay her $80,000, which is $20,000 more than she was making as an employee. Even after paying for her own health insurance, she is still better off. She has barely touched the nine months' salary, about $45,000, that she received as severance. Lance is happy because he has a key resource back but has not had to increase his budget or headcount, and Phil is happy; he can now be confident his purchasing work will be professionally handled.

Facts: Talent Factories

Many companies have developed strong reputations as developers of talent. Need an aggressive numbers-oriented manager, then think GE; a well-trained radio and television producer, raid the BBC; a strategic-thinking CEO or General Manager, tap McKinsey; a top-notch brand manager, think Procter & Gamble or Coca-Cola; a manager for your new hedge fund or private equity group, look no further than Goldman Sachs.

> **Mythbuster Wisdom: It Can Be Tough At The Top**
> The near collapse of the banking sector during late 2008 exacted a high price. Almost 20 percent of the world's largest banks replaced their CEOs. According to a study by Booz & Co., more than half were pushed out.[1]

Be it the strength of their training programs (BBC, GE, Procter and Gamble) or their reputations as the home of the best and brightest (McKinsey and Goldman Sachs), these organizations have demonstrated a track record for producing a certain type of talent. Executives at other companies will often look for a "GE general manager" or a "Procter and Gamble brand manager." All of these talent factories recognize that they will not be able to, nor should they seek to, keep all their best talent. In fact, it is actually good for business to seed talent in many different companies. McKinsey's talented alumni represent a key source of new clients, while former Goldman dealmakers stay very connected with their former home. Such is the aura that surrounds many of these organizations that it is easy to assume that all their people are talented—yet another myth. In fact, many may have become alumni because they didn't make it. After all, GE routinely counseled out the bottom 10 percent of its employees—so beware the brand name on the resume—and make sure the credentials are real.

> **Mythbuster Wisdom: Are People An Expense Or An Investment?**
> Most organizations will happily acknowledge that people are their largest expense, but are people really an expense? Surely organizations invest in people? Yet few CEOs talk about labor costs as investments. One who does is Martin Sorrell, long time leader of British advertising firm WPP, the world's largest by revenue. Sorrell in a *Wall Street Journal* interview was very clear when asked about cost-cutting, "The only thing that we can affect in the short term is our investment in people. We invest about $9 billion in people and $350 million a year in capital investment."[2]

All GE Managers Are Gods

General Electric has topped numerous lists of companies that are the best at developing talent. The company's leadership programs, management practices, and career development are rightly lauded for developing one of the most able management teams in the world. So it is not surprising that GE has long been a source for companies looking for new leaders. More than 25 companies have appointed GE alumni as CEOs since 1995 including 3M, Albertsons, Boeing, Chrysler, Conseco, Fannie Mae, Fiat, Home Depot, Honeywell, Intuit, Nortel, Pfizer, and Siemens. However, while no one questions the rigor of a management education at GE, it is no guarantee of success for the hiring company. In fact, the results are decidedly mixed, as the examples in Table 14.1 show.

One of the most visible examples of GE alumni leadership has been Bob Nardelli. Nardelli was one of the two losers, along with Jim McNerney (3M and Boeing) in the race to succeed management legend, at least in his own mind, Jack Welch. Jeffrey Immelt won the race, so Nardelli jumped ship and joined Home Depot to great fanfare in December 2000. He quickly set out the ambitious goal of growing revenues at the $58 billion retailer to $100 million by 2005. He failed. Revenues only reached $81.5 million; not bad, but a failure by his former boss's standards. Yet by many measures his tenure at Home Depot could be considered a success. Revenues grew 41 percent and earnings more than doubled to $5.8 billion while withstanding a significant economic downturn during 2000–2001. Yet by January 2007 he had resigned. His failure was no doubt cushioned by an exit package valued at more than $200 million. Ironically, it was not the financial results

Table 14.1 Winners Versus Losers

Winners	Losers
Larry Bossidy—AlliedSignal and Honeywell	Paolo Fresco—Fiat
Jim McNerney—3M and Boeing	Gary Wendt—Conseco
Steve Bennett—Intuit	Lawrence Johnston—Albertsons
Stanley Gault—Goodyear	Mike Zafirovski—Nortel
Kirk Hachigian—Cooper Industries	Bob Nardelli—Home Depot and Chrysler

that did him in. Nardelli's major missteps were to alienate two key constituencies at Home Depot—shareholders and employees. Despite the growth achieved by Home Depot under Nardelli, shareholders were not rewarded. The share price declined 8 percent during his tenure while that of competitor Lowe's grew 180 percent. Nardelli, meanwhile, was well rewarded even before his lucrative exit package with total compensation averaging $11 million a year from 2000 through 2005. The final straw came at the 2006 annual meeting; no members of the board apart from Nardelli attended and he refused to answer any questions during the meeting. Shareholders decried his arrogance, and the writing was on the wall.

Often overlooked in the analysis of Nardelli's tenure was the impact he had on a defining characteristic of Home Depot under its founders, Bernie Marcus and Arthur Blank— the company's culture. Home Depot did not have employees, it had associates; the corporate office was not a headquarters but a Store Support Center. Everything was geared to enabling the associate on the shop floor to meet the customer's needs. Home Depot prided itself on the skills and knowledge of its associates to work with customers to solve their problems or make their projects a success. Under Nardelli's GE-inspired make-the-numbers style of management, standardization, simplification, and efficiency became the mantra. Longtime associates found poorly trained, part-time hires replacing valued colleagues; managers disappeared from the shop floor to work on their spreadsheets; local management autonomy was replaced with centralized management—management communism started to take root. Home Depot's feisty competitor, Lowe's, sought to capitalize on Home Depot's mistakes by offering improved levels of service and more customer friendly stores. So while Nardelli delivered decent numbers, his downfall shows that despite what some macho managers may think, numbers are not everything.

Retaining Talent—Not Always a Good Thing

A few years ago I was talking with the CEO of a well-known consumer products company. He was boasting of the firm's track record in keeping its most talented employees: "We have not lost one of our top tier managers in years," he proudly reported. On the surface this seems like an achievement of which he should rightly be proud, but think about the implications for a moment. Is 100 percent retention of your best employees really such a good thing? After all, if none of them ever leave, there can only be two possible explanations: Either you are paying them too much, or they are not as good as you think they are! If you really do have the best talent, competitors or peers will know about it; after all, your performance will show it. Any organization seeking to succeed covets the best people; if you have them, others will seek them out and try and lure them away. Not all will be immune. Some turnover of top talent is therefore not only inevitable but also desirable.

> **Mythbuster Wisdom: Are People Really Your Most Valuable Asset?**
> No CEO worth his or her salt will ever admit that employees are not the company's most important resource, although in some cases you have to wonder. Are BP's employees more valuable than its oil reserves? What about DeBeers' gold mines, or Coca-Cola's recipe?

Everyone recognizes a star, but all too often it is the number 2 that makes the difference. Would The Beatles have been The Beatles without George and Ringo? After all, in Hamburg, Pete Best was on drums and Stu Sutcliffe tried to play bass. How many NBA titles would Michael Jordan have won without Scottie Pippen? How funny would Oliver Hardy have been without Stan Laurel? One of the hallmarks of a great organization is that the loss of a star does not result in a fall-off in performance. How would your organization cope with the loss of the top 5 percent of your sales force? Or, in the not-for-profit world, the departure of your two biggest fundraisers? The hallmark of a talented organization is not just the preponderance of stars, but also the strength of the team backing up those stars. Seamless transitions of leadership demonstrate that past leaders invested considerable time in developing the leaders of tomorrow.

The Illusion of Competence

Anyone can make money in a great market, but are they really competent managers? Exxon grew to be the largest company in the world by both sales and profits in 2005. Wal-Mart reclaimed the sales title in 2006 and 2007 before Exxon again assumed the top spot in 2008. But was Exxon well managed or just lucky? Figure 14.1 shows the 10-year trend in Exxon's share price compared to the price of a barrel of oil over the same period. I have no doubt that there are many exceptionally talented managers at Exxon, but few managers can consistently buck the long-term economic cycles that govern so much of performance. The almost perfect correlation between oil prices and Exxon's operating income at least proves that management did not screw things up.

Public recognition of success and artful self-promotion can create an almost mythical air around companies or individuals. At various times, companies such as Apple, Coca-Cola, Dell, Enron, General Electric, Goldman Sachs, Tesco, Toyota, and individuals such as Richard Branson, Warren Buffett, Bill Gates, Steve Jobs, Donald Trump, and Jack Welch have donned the mantle of being nearly invincible—for some it was too much to bear. I term this the illusion of competence by which a company's or individual's performance is built up to such a degree that no one lets the facts get in the way of a good story. I first identified this

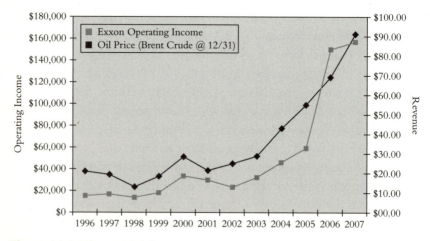

Figure 14.1   Exxon Mobil

Exxon Operating Income compared to Brent Crude Prices 1996–2007

trend among the average consumer as the Internet began to revolution-ize everything from share dealing to car buying.

I define the illusion of competence as the "aura of misplaced advice of questionable quality." It manifests itself when people gain so much new knowledge that they mistakenly believe that they are now experts. The Internet has given this phenomenon a powerful stimulus. Large amounts of information can be accessed easily. Examples include people who buy something on eBay for more than they would have paid at the local store and boast about the great deal they got; or how about those people who plunged into managing their own investments, gave up their real jobs to become day traders, and boasted of having got into Yahoo at $106 or Ariba at $75 in January 2000 and then doubled down by entering the Las Vegas real estate market in late 2005. Simply because customers can access millions of pages of free information and compare and contrast thousands of different products from the comfort of their armchairs does not guarantee that they will be transformed from suckers to seers. A vari-ation of this illusion exists with both organizations and managers. After all, organizations that dominate their industry and managers who reach the peak of their profession must be good, mustn't they? After all, they have toiled for many years to make it to the top. Yet for many, the step to the top of the rankings or the corner office is, as British pop/ska band Madness sang in 1979, "One Step Beyond."

CFO Magazine named Andrew Fastow CFO of the Year in 1999, almost exactly two years before he was fired and Enron started to implode. Fastow was found to be the architect of one of the biggest frauds in corporate history. Al Dunlap was Chainsaw Al to Jack Welch's Neutron Jack as he graced the covers of all the leading business maga-zines only months before his destruction of Sunbeam came to light. Dick Fuld, former CEO of Lehman Brothers, was named CEO of the Year by *Institutional Investor* magazine in 2006. Bernard Madoff, perpe-trator of the biggest Ponzi scheme in history, lured almost $30 billion to his funds by offering remarkably consistent annual returns averaging 11 percent with very little volatility and never having suffered a loss in 18 years, during which time the average hedge fund gained only 1 percent more, but with returns that fluctuated sharply from year to year. Madoff's website fostered the illusion of integrity and honesty: "The owner's name is on the door. Clients know that Bernard Madoff has a personal interest in maintaining the unblemished record of value, fair-dealing, and high ethical standards that has always been the firm's hallmark."[3] He was held in such high-standing that he served as Vice-Chairman of the National Association of Securities Dealers. In 2005 Bear Stearns was named *Fortune*'s Most Admired Securities Firm; just over two years later, the firm collapsed and had to be rescued by the government and J.P. Morgan.

The mortgage market is a perfect example of the triumph of greed over sanity. Supposedly intelligent bankers pushed the market to such extremes in their search for profits (or was it commissions?) that in Bakersfield, California, a Mexican strawberry picker with an income of $14,000 and no English was given everything he needed to buy a $720,000 house.[4]

Executives at Lehman Brothers were so confident that during the first eight months of 2008, the company bought back $741 million of its own stock at an average price of $49.60. On September 15, the company filed for bankruptcy. On February 1, 2008, Microsoft announced an offer for Yahoo valued at $31 per share; Yahoo's stock price on the day before the offer was announced was $19.86. Yahoo rejected the deal, and in April Microsoft raised its offer to $33 with Yahoo's price now hovering in the $26–28 range. Yahoo held out for $37, and Microsoft walked away; Yahoo's share price on December 1, 2008: $10.74. Other examples of illusionary competence include bankers who booked record profits (and took record bonuses) on mortgage-related securities; FEMA circa-2004 just before Hurricane Katrina; airport security before 9/11; UK weather forecasters who in 1987 advised it would just be "very windy" just before the worst storm in 284 years hit the south coast of England; and the Cleveland Browns during every pre-season since 1964.

Fool Me Once, Shame on You; Fool Me Twice, Shame on Me

In 1994, John Meriwether, the former vice chairman and head of bond trading at Salomon Brothers, founded Long-Term Capital Management (LTCM). LTCM was a hedge fund that sought profits by pursuing a highly leveraged arbitrage strategy. In simple terms, this meant that they borrowed enormous sums of money and placed bets on how the price of two similar securities would move in the future. Meriwether assembled an all-star team, including Nobel Prize–winning academics such as Myron Scholes and Robert C. Merton, who shared the 1997 Nobel Prize in Economics, and hotshot traders to create a business that sought to combine the mega-brains from academia with the street-smarts of born traders. For the first few years it worked, and LTCM delivered returns in excess of 40 percent; however, the strategy of exploiting small price discrepancies required an awful lot of capital. You need to place very big bets in order to make a lot of money from very small price differences. As a consequence, by the beginning of 1998, the fund had equity of $5 billion but had borrowed over $125 billion, which sort of redefined the term leverage. However, by then the firm had exhausted all the "good bets," it could find, so it embarked upon an even riskier strategy. Then, in August 1998, Russia defaulted on its government bonds, sending world markets into a panic. LTCM's bets started to turn sour and the company lost $4.6 billion in less than four months. The Federal Reserve Bank of New York organized a bailout, and LTCM's positions were slowly liquidated, with the fund closing down in early 2000.

The failure of LTCM became a poster child for the risks of hedge-fund investing, but proved little deterrent to investors as they sought ever-higher returns. By late 2007 the hedge-fund industry had amassed assets in excess of $2.5 trillion. Nor did the principles of LTCM suffer unduly. Myron Scholes returned to academia at Harvard and Robert Merton went on to become Chief Science Officer (now there's a great title for an economist) at Trinsum Group, a financial advisory firm.

LTCM architect John Meriwether reemerged just a year after LTCM's collapse armed with $250 million of new money as the head of JWM Partners. JWM intended to pursue many of the same strategies used by LTCM but with less leverage—i.e., less borrowed money. By 2007 JWM had grown to $3 billion in assets, but had Meriwether really learned anything? It seemed not. By March 2008, JWM was borrowing $15 for every dollar of equity, although at the same time Meriwether was reassuring investors in a letter, commenting, "We have sharply reduced the risk and balance sheet of the portfolio." So how did Meriwether's reduced-risk approach perform? By September 2008, the funds had lost 26 percent of their value, and as the credit crisis accelerated, the funds were down 42 percent by the end of November 2008.[5] In July 2009, Meriwether shut down JWM. It was reported that he might start a new trading partnership, which makes me wonder about the sanity of those who may fund him.[6]

The MBA Myth

Over the last thirty years, the Master of Business Administration or MBA degree has become a de facto entry requirement for many professions from investment banking to management consulting. Every year thousands of freshly minted graduates armed with their MBAs emerge, ready to storm the world of business. Confident and in debt, these business school products are ready to make their mark on the world. Armed with their five forces, discounted cash flows, and core competencies they seek out six-figure starting salaries and rapid progress up the corporate ladder. But is it worth all the effort? Are MBAs any better than the rest?

In the interests of full disclosure, I do not have an MBA. Starting my career in England back in the early 1980s, I didn't need one. However, I have hired and fired plenty of MBAs. In fact, for much of the last fifteen years I have been in the position where if I reviewed my own resume, I would have to reject myself due to the lack of an MBA. Today, no high-flyer can expect to progress without the letters MBA after his or her name.

In the United States alone there are more than 400 schools offering MBAs. In 2008, the total cost of an MBA education at a top fifty school in *BusinessWeek* magazine's annual ranking ranged from $145,000 at the University of Western Ontario to $320,000 at the University of Pennsylvania's Wharton School.[7] For that investment, a graduate can expect a post-graduation, annual salary increase of $25,000 to $50,000, which translates into a payback period of anywhere from three to twelve years. Of course, if you are an MBA graduate yourself, you will instantly understand that because all these data points represent averages, there are many proud holders of MBAs who fare worse than the average.

MBAs are getting more popular; the numbers of people taking the Graduate Management Admission Test rose by 25 percent between 2005 and 2008. Growth rates outside the United States are almost four times that reflecting both greater understanding of the value of an academic business education and increased global competition for the best jobs.

But it is not all smooth sailing in the MBA world. In 2005, Warren Bennis and James O'Toole wrote a provocative piece in the *Harvard Business Review* entitled, "How Business Schools Lost Their Way." They opened their argument thus: ". . . MBA programs face intense criticism for failing to impart useful skills, failing to prepare leaders, failing to instill norms of ethical behavior—and even failing to lead graduates to good corporate jobs." It appeared that financial engineering had won out over doing the right thing. In March 2009, a *Wall Street Journal* article was headlined, "Faculty Emphasize the Value of Skepticism."[8] The article described how many business schools were rethinking the content of their MBA programs in light of the global economic crisis and placing increased emphasis on encouraging healthy skepticism of sophisticated but often opaque financial products. Some commentators laid part of the blame for the crisis at the door of the business schools, "seeing an arrogance in the schools' culture"[9] and too much focus "on short term gains and shareholders returns."[10] This probably means that new courses on ethics, cynicism, and why big bonuses are bad will appear shortly.

The essence of the criticism is that business schools focus too narrowly on the technical specialties of their faculties rather than the moral, social, personal, and, above all, practical skills essential to being an effective manager. So if you want to gain a deep understanding of how to apply multiple statistical tests to a portfolio of alternative investment opportunities, then an MBA is for you. If you want to learn how to identify, develop, motivate, and reward globally aware managers, forget it.

Notwithstanding the criticisms, an MBA is increasingly becoming a globally accepted management qualification, but it is not essential. Bill Gates, Warren Buffett (he does have a Masters in Economics), Steve

Jobs, Michael Dell, and the Google boys don't have MBAs. But Phil Knight (Nike), Fred Smith (FedEx), Steve Ballmer (Microsoft), Charles Schwab, and Michael Bloomberg do, but then so do Bernie Ebbers (Worldcom), Ken Lay, Jeff Skilling, and Andrew Fastow (all Enron), and Dennis Kozlowski (Tyco). So take your pick.

As with most qualifications, possession of an MBA does not guarantee anything—it simply shows aptitude and application. So by all means screen applicants for their educational background, but in the real world there is no substitute for practical experience. Perhaps we should consider alternative types of MBA. For instance, as a kid growing up in England in the 1970s, MBAs were a rarity. In fact, I thought MBA stood for "**M**ust've **B**een to **A**merica." Today MBA should probably stand for **M**ust've **B**een to **A**sia. No doubt one day we will see it stand for **M**ust've **B**een to **A**frica.

The bottom line is, as Mark Twain once commented, "I never let schooling interfere with my education." As with all education, it is not what you learn that matters but how you apply it.

What Makes a Successful Leader?

The short answer appears to be luck. Being in the right place at the right time seems to be the best indicator of executive success. Jack Welch handed over the reins of a storied 20-year career as Chairman and CEO of General Electric on September 10, 2001. Was he lucky or skillful? There are thousands of books about great leaders (Attila the Hun—anyone?) and about what it takes to be a great leader, but it is a very fine line between success and failure. CEOs can move from praise to ridicule in very short order. In April 2009, *Portfolio* magazine (which announced its own failure less than a week later) produced lists of the twenty best and twenty worst CEOs of all time. Surprisingly, Attila the Hun, Jesus Christ, and Sun Tzu did not make it, despite their strong credentials. The top five "greats" were: Henry Ford, J.P. Morgan, Sam Walton, Alfred P. Sloan, and Lou Gerstner. Further down the list were the usual suspects: Gates, Jobs, Buffett. The top five worst CEOs, which surely must be an oxymoron, were Dick Fuld of Lehman Brothers; Angelo Mozilo (Countrywide); Ken Lay (Enron);

James Cayne (Bear Stearns), and Bernie Ebbers (Worldcom).[11] My suspicion is that if the magazine had compiled such a list just a few years earlier it would not have been a surprise to see these five on the list of greats along with fellow failure Carly Fiorina.

Interestingly, four companies managed to place CEO's on both lists! General Motors (Alfred Sloan and Roger Smith), Apple (Steve Jobs and John Sculley), IBM (John Akers and Lou Gerstner) and Carnegie Steel (Andrew Carnegie and Henry Frick). The last three were direct successors of each other, making for a stark comparison. History has not been kind to the losers.

Whether you ascribe to the Attila the Hun, Winston Churchill, or Jack Welch school of leadership there are a few qualities about which there should be no debate. During my 25 years in business I have had the opportunity to observe, work for, and work with many different types of leader, and there is one characteristic that all the best ones shared—they ask great questions. Great questions are not complex questions; in fact, the best seem blindingly obvious. Unfortunately, a relatively small proportion of people in leadership positions have the courage, confidence, or even the basic common sense to ask the right questions. Why is this? Is it fear of looking stupid?

That may be part of the answer, but there is a more deep-rooted problem. From our first day in kindergarten our performance is fundamentally based upon answering, not asking them. The "smart" kids are the ones who always raise their hands when the teacher asks a question. Our whole merit system is based upon getting the answer "right." As we move into the business world, contribution syndrome infects our every pore. We must be seen to be contributing in every meeting or on every project. For some, this manifests itself in a complete inability to sit quietly and listen. It seems to be part of their DNA to feel that if they are not talking, then they are not working. (Full disclosure: I have been riddled with this disease from a very young age.)

However, as you move up the corporate ladder, a subtle change starts to take place. The best stop talking. They sit quietly, taking in the contributions of everyone else, and limiting their own contribution to asking a few pertinent questions that lead the discussion in a constructive manner. The future leaders are beginning to emerge from their cocoon. Only a few make the change. Through their

Mythbuster Wisdom: Who Asked These Questions?

- At numerous venture capital-backed dot.coms in late-1999: "Can we really make money selling stuff for less than Wal-Mart even after including the shipping costs?"
- In the Oval Office in early 2002: "What if Saddam does not have weapons of mass destruction?"
- In the GM Board Room in late 2004 as the company bet on pickups and SUVs to drive a profit turnaround: "What if gas goes to $4 a gallon? How many $35,000 trucks that do 8 miles to the gallon are we going to sell in Toledo?"
- In the executive suite of mortgage lenders during 2006: "How can someone who (we think) earns $2,500 month make a $2,000 mortgage payment and live?" "How will we get our money back if a house is now worth $100,000 less than the outstanding mortgage balance and the borrower stops making payments?"

questioning, leaders can synthesize all available intelligence, deduce the range of viable alternatives, assess the risk and reward of each, and lead the group to an effective decision. Remember, listening beats talking, and simple questions beat great answers. Leaders are not afraid to ask the simple questions (see Chapter 15).

One final note on the myths of management: We create them. No one forces us into blind acceptance. It is up to all of us to stay vigilant. Just as we start to sweep away one set of myths, another set will arise in their place. The key is to keep asking dumb but great questions. This demonstrates a level of humility that is essential for effective leadership. Too many leaders, upon reaching the top of the career, assume that their knowledge has now expanded to such a degree that they know all the answers. Asking questions is beneath them; you must do what they tell you without question. Andrew Grove, former CEO of Intel, described the challenge thus: "History shows that most companies do not deal with transformation. One reason has to do with senior managers. They usually 'don't get it.' They have a difficult time accepting that the future will be vastly different from the present because they rose to power in the old business environment."[12] If nothing else, events of the last few years must surely convince us that there is a new definition of business as usual—that is there is no such thing anymore. Good luck busting the myths.

So What?

- Focus on retaining talent, but if no one leaves, start worrying.
- It's not what you learn, but how you apply it.
- Analytics are no substitute for instinct.
- Graduating with an MBA is the beginning not the end.
- Any prediction based upon past performance is suspect.
- Even the smartest people make some really dumb decisions.
- If it sounds too good to be true, it is.

Notes

1. Booz & Co., "CEOs Hold Steady in a Storm," Booz.com, May 12, 2009.
2. Suzanne Varnica, "WPP Chief Tempers Hopes for AD Upturn," *Wall Street Journal*, September 22, 2009.
3. Website of Bernard L. Madoff Investment Securities.
4. Michael Lewis, "The End," Portfolio.com, December 2008.
5. "As Markets Swing, Meriwether Hears Echoes of His Own Collapse: LTCM Lost Billions a Decade Ago; Now, a Second Fall?" *Wall Street Journal*, September 20, 2008.
6. "Meriwether Shuts Firm, Sans Drama This Time," *Wall Street Journal*, July 9, 2009.
7. "Business School Rankings: Ranking Return on Investment," *BusinessWeek*, September 10, 2008.
8. Beth Gardner, "B-Schools Rethink Curricula amid Crisis," *Wall Street Journal Europe*, March 27, 2009.
9. Ibid.
10. Ibid.
11. Kevin Maney and Liz Gunnison, "The Best (and Worst) CEOs Ever," *Portfolio*, April 22, 2009.
12. Andrew S. Grove, "What Detroit Can Learn from Silicon Valley," *Wall Street Journal*, July 13, 2009.

Chapter 15

Ask The Dumb Questions

Consultants, fast track managers, and other aspiring management superstars all suffer from the same disease. It is called contribution syndrome. No matter what the situation, they feel compelled to contribute. It is essential that they show how smart they are and how much they know at every possible opportunity. Get more than three of them in the same room and it becomes impossible to get a word in edgeways as they compete to share their immense wisdom and insight. And then a funny thing happens. They make it to the top, they reach for the brass ring, and suddenly the rules change. Instead of giving answers, their value is now measured by the questions they ask—some make the change; others don't.

Fiction: May 2007

Rich Martin, Cruciant's VP of Marketing and Product Development, is reviewing the status of all new products under development. He is particularly interested in Project Trojan Horse. Trojan Horse forms a key part of Cruciant's strategy for entering new markets. The concept is pretty simple. Cruciant takes existing products that are already proven in its core markets and, in partnership with an established local company, launches them in new markets, leveraging the branding and distribution network of the local company. This provides Cruciant with a very low-cost and fast means of establishing the product in the market. Cruciant does not need to establish recognition for its brand in the market nor does it have to invest in building a sales and distribution network from scratch, both of which are time consuming and expensive. The early test results are encouraging; partners in Malaysia and Indonesia have seen great interest in Cruciant's products when rebranded under the partner's name and sold alongside the partner's own products. Rich wants to take the results of the study to the executive committee and secure approval for a rapid rollout to fifteen other countries. As Rich comments, "This looks like a certain winner. We can beat Global Local to market by months; they are spending boatloads of money on branding and sponsorship but only have distribution coverage for one-tenth of each market. We can be selling product while they are still putting up billboards."

Rich is clearly enthused. As the discussion continues, one of the members of the Trojan Horse team, Miranda, highlights a couple of possible risks. "We must not forget that there is some risk with this strategy. We are placing our success in the hands of our partners and our ability to control exactly what they do will be somewhat limited as a result. We will also have to address what we do when we want to broaden our presence in these markets and establish our own brand. That could cause some confusion in the marketplace." Rich listens carefully and responds, "Great points, Miranda. We need to make sure the contracts we draw up with the partners are watertight. Get legal to review them one more time. With regard to taking the Cruciant brand into these markets, I think it will be lot easier when we already have successful products in the market. I expect our partners will love having some of our marketing dollars thrown at their markets."

Rich takes Project Trojan Horse to the management committee and largely based upon his own enthusiasm it is approved quickly—he makes no mention of Miranda's concerns.

Six Months Later . . .

Rich is euphoric as he tells the executive committee, "The initial returns are in and Trojan Horse is a "home run." Sales are 12 percent ahead of plan and Global Local still hasn't moved out of test marketing."

Another Six Months On . . .

Cruciant's Indonesian partner has been caught up in a major scandal involving bribes to local politicians in order to secure approvals for new stores. The company's CEO has been arrested and *The Economist* is reporting that the funds used to pay the bribes came from royalties paid by Cruciant. In Malaysia, Cruciant has been in dispute with its partner over pricing. The partner has been discounting Cruciant's products by as much as 40 percent in order keep growing market share. The original partnership agreement based the royalty the partner would earn on sales revenue, not units, and there were no stipulations as to the minimum price that the partner must charge. Not only are many of the products being sold at a loss but also some enterprising people are buying Cruciant's products at deeply discounted prices in Malaysia, shipping the products over to Europe and North America and reselling them at prices up to 20 percent below the listed price. Rich is fuming. He demands to know why these risks were not identified before the rollout. The team sits in silence. None of them is willing to point out that Rich's tremendous enthusiasm for the project cut short any substantive discussion of what could go wrong. Miranda is conflicted. She knew the risks and tried to point them out but Rich dismissed them. Should she have been more forceful? But then again, Rich is a VP and she is only an analyst. She resolves that if she ever makes it to VP, she will always listen to the analyst who guards against overenthusiasm.

Facts: Keep It Simple

Beware complexity. Bernard Madoff, perpetrator of the biggest fraud in investing history, delivered consistent returns even in the most volatile of times through an apparently sophisticated stock and option trading strategy; Enron spewed out enormous profits from a complex web of trading operations; and Long-Term Capital Management's sophisticated mathematical models developed by Nobel Prize winners virtually guaranteed profits. The key learning appears to be, "If you don't understand it, don't invest in it."

However, it appears that in today's world, complexity has become synonymous with sophistication. The more expensive the car, the more complicated the controls. A high-end Mercedes has almost as many lights, dials, buttons, and knobs as a Boeing 737. Microsoft's Excel spreadsheet program has functionality that 95 percent of its users don't need and can't find.

One of the most important design challenges today is to develop user interfaces that make it easy to use all this complexity. Some work very well such as Apple's interface for the iPod and iPhone; others such as BMW's universal iDrive knob on the 2002–2007 versions of its 7 Series were less successful at harnessing complexity.

The cult of complexity had made its way into the management suite, and it is rarely productive. Strategies, designs, and operating models glory in complexity yet miss the fundamental truth that complexity equals risk. Unfortunately, complexity does not just extend to the strategies for making money but also to mechanisms used for managing risk. It is not that managers ignore risk—quite the contrary. Most businesses have numerous risk management mechanisms: Potential customers are credit scored; accounts receivable balances are aged and analyzed; foreign exchange exposures are hedged; insurance is purchased; emergency procedures are developed and tested for a diverse range of possible events from terrorist attacks to the failure of the telephone system. Risk management is everywhere. Unfortunately, the processes are so fragmented and complicated that it is almost impossible to gain a good understanding of the overall risk to which an organization is exposed. From the rapid demise of Enron in 2001 (stock price in October 2000: $90; November 2001: bankrupt) to the hidden risks of subprime mortgages that exploded into public view during late 2007 and 2008 it is clear that risk is a misunderstood and mismanaged concept for most businesses.

In March 2009, Joe Price, CFO of Bank of America, admitted that most financial services industry executives had failed to foresee the economic meltdown because they relied on backward-looking models. He commented, "I think we all, including myself, during a lot of this expansion period [used] historical norms, including the worst stress periods that we had seen in the last couple of decades during our lifetimes, as a benchmark to what could happen."[1]

The failure of these historic benchmarks came as a shock. Price went on to say that the events of 2008 "by multitudes blow through those stress events." Joe Price is one of the most astute financial executives I have worked with, so his comments bring home the reality that traditional management models may no longer be valid.

The irony is that despite all the sophisticated risk analysis, statistical modeling, stress testing, and other number crunching, the biggest problem is the failure of anyone to systematically ask the dumb questions. How often do you hear anyone ask the simple question, "What if you are wrong?" when a strategy, plan, or budget is presented? Or how about the simple, "Does this make sense?" when someone outlines a new business concept such as selling dog food over the Internet and shipping it via UPS.

Of course, the most potent question anyone can ever ask is the simple three-letter inquiry, "Why?" Normally, this is uttered in response to a parental, "No." In the world of commerce it is best used in serial repetition. Ask the "why" question at least five times in response to earnest arguments for a particular scheme or plan. The quality of responses will quickly determine how well thought out the plan really is.

In addition to such penetrating questions as why, why, why, why and why, an effective manager always takes the contrarian view. After all, how often do the sponsors of a particular scheme express doubts as to its soundness? They have spent weeks carefully crafting the plan, they are fully committed to its success, and they are willing to stake their reputation on it. It is highly unlikely that they are going to admit to any concern whatsoever.

The best time for skepticism is before a penny has been spent. Ask the obvious contrarian question, "What if you are wrong?" Testing the validity of the assumptions in any proposal is common sense. Who at Countrywide asked the question, "What if we cannot rely on ever-rising home values to repay mortgages when all these subprime borrowers default?"

The obvious follow-up question to "What if you are wrong?" is "How will you find out?" It is common sense to define the leading indicators of impending doom. Defining the right metrics early and then assiduously monitoring them can buy the most vital commodity of all—time. Time to react to changes that make a particular project or investment no longer attractive, before good money and resources are thrown after bad. Coke abandoned new Coke after 90 days; Toshiba gave up on HD-DVD after all the major film companies backed Blu-ray; Tropicana dropped a January 2009 packaging redesign after less than a month and brought back the old packaging after a customer backlash. All three failed, but they mitigated the impact of failure by acting quickly.

The biggest danger for any management team is complacency. When times are good, it is easy to be lulled into a false sense of security. Salaries and bonuses move up, stock prices appreciate, and successful leaders grace the covers of *Fortune* and *Forbes*. This is the time of greatest weakness, and someone needs to stand up and ask the question, "Can we really keep this up?" Motorola dominated the mobile phone market, Pan Am and TWA ruled the skies, Yahoo was Google before Google, Sears was Wal-Mart before Wal-Mart, Marks & Spencer led the UK High Street, Sony dominated the portable music player market. All lost their leadership positions in very short order. Remember, keep it simple and ask the dumb questions.

Isolating Management Stupidity

Next time your boss calls you into her office for one of those little chats, be prepared to seize the initiative. After the uncomfortable small talk, the discussion usually turns serious and the boss typically opens with, "Well, it is that time of year again. We need to review your goals and objectives for next year." Typically, this ushers in a rather formulaic discussion of how well you performed against some range of nebulous goals using a set of competencies (radical stuff like teamwork, interpersonal skills, and problem solving) that a very expensive consulting firm has defined as being essential for corporate growth. The objective of the discussion is for your manager to check the box in the personnel management system that relates to performance reviews and goal setting, while your objective is to claim credit for as much of the corporation, department, or team's success as possible while establishing that any near-misses in meeting the agreed-upon goals were purely the result of adverse circumstances over which you had no control—e.g., global warming, the subprime mortgage crisis, or the IT department. The outcome is a negotiated compromise that ensures you max-out on your personal goals for the 20 percent of your annual objective and a commitment to strive to make major strides forward next year.

Next time you are faced with one of these meetings, try taking a different approach. When your manager asks you describe what you think your goals should be for next year, simply reply:

"My only objective is to isolate your stupidity."

The facial reaction alone should be worth the price of admission, so make sure to capture it on your mobile phone's built-in camera. As your boss struggles to decipher the import of this seemingly profound statement, offer her a lifebelt in the form of: "Let me explain what I mean" and proceed:

"Over the last few years we have embarked upon numerous projects. We have re-engineered, benchmarked, applied best practices, leveraged technology, zero-based, right-sized, six sigma'd, process mapped, and self-directed, yet we always have an excuse when we make a bad decision. It is always: We did not have the right information; the process was broken; the systems did not work properly; corporate said no; or our people weren't properly trained. Imagine for a minute we eliminated all these excuses. We do have the right information, the processes work seamlessly, the systems all function correctly, corporate does not interfere, and our people are all well trained. Sounds pretty cool, doesn't it? Well, if this truly was the case, then the only excuse left for a bad decision would be the stupidity of the decision maker, wouldn't it? So there you have it. My goal for next year is to eliminate all the excuses we use for making bad decisions so that the only one left is your stupidity and since we both know you are not stupid (keep tongue firmly in cheek while uttering these words), just think of how outstanding our performance is going to be." Sounds like fun, doesn't it?

The dangers of management stupidity were recognized long ago. In 1956, Lionel Urwick wrote in the *Harvard Business Review,* "There is nothing which rots morale more quickly and more completely than . . . the feeling that those in authority do not know their own minds." Unfortunately, while all the other excuses remain, mediocrity in management will persist.

Follow the Herd

Why do smart people get sucked in? In June 2001, venture capitalist Lise Boyer commented on the fallout from the dot.com collapse. "I can't figure out who behaved irrationally. Investors watched their neighbors make piles of money, and they just followed suit."[2] So following the lemmings as they charge over the cliff is not irrational behavior? Linus Torvalds, creator of the Linux operating system, was asked to comment on the causes of the dot.com crash, and he responded, "It's too easy just to blame greed."[3] "He is a smart guy and he may be right, but make no mistake—greed and envy are incredibly powerful motivators. How else do you explain how so many really smart people were taken in by Bernie Madoff and Alan Stanford? It certainly explains why I piled into a few select high technology stocks in late 1999 and was able to claim some nice tax write-offs over the next few years.

Of course, it was just a few short years after the dot.com bubble burst that flipping condominiums in Miami or Vegas became the surefire way of making millions. For the future, expect similar frenzies to emerge for care of the elderly as Baby Boomers age but don't die and alternative energy as the planet strives to create a negative carbon footprint. All such booms (and busts) follow the same basic pattern, as the parable of the leaky valve illustrates.

The Parable of the Leaky Valve

Arthur Rudolph, the rocket scientist who managed the development of both the V-2 rocket that terrorized London toward the end of World War Two and the Saturn V rocket that took man to the moon, described risk management thus: "You want a valve that doesn't leak, and you try everything possible to develop one. But the real world provides you with a leaky valve. You have to determine how much leaking you can tolerate."[4] As Rudolph described, leaky valves have been a perennial problem, but fear not because in a garage somewhere in Southern California, two twenty-something Stanford-educated engineers have begun demonstrating a truly leak-free valve to friends. News begins to travel through the Valley and a couple of venture capitalists see the enormous potential. Hype begins to build as the utopian vision of a leak-free world finally becomes possible. The two engineers become multi-billionaires as the IPO for SoDry Inc explodes onto the stock market. Suddenly the race is on as commentators confidently announce that the leak-free valve has been invented. Other companies pile into the valve market, offering everything from creative valve design services to an environmentally friendly valve-recycling program. This creates valve market frenzy; the stock prices of any company even vaguely connected to the industry soar. Companies in many different industries tout their company's valve credentials; advertising campaigns scream about the virtues of a leak-free society. Everyone loads up on leak-free valves and installs them everywhere. As a consequence of rapidly rising demand, valve producers ramp up production and new suppliers enter the market. In the race to meet demand, quality suffers and a few minor leaks are reported. These are dismissed as temporary blips of no long-term consequence and stock prices soar ever upward. Eventually, so much pressure builds up in the system that a few critical valves give way, inducing panic. Investors lose confidence and the whole valve ecosystem enters as tailspin, dragging down all other segments of the economy. Inquiries are held and valve speculators are prosecuted. A few unscrupulous operators are found to have been selling regular, old leaky valves as genuine, no-leak valves and are paraded through the courts. Government passes stern new rules for valve producers and demands transparency and accountability in the marketplace. Slowly the economy recovers, and central bankers assure everyone that this type of frenzy can never happen again as new safeguards have been enacted to ensure sufficient liquidity and controls in the market. Meanwhile, rumors build that two research scientists working in the Amazon jungle have isolated a cure for the common cold from the sap of a rare tropical plant.

So What?

- Leadership is more about the questions you ask than the answers you give.
- Don't be afraid to ask the simple questions.
- Complexity is incompatible with transparency.
- The more complex the management process, the greater the risk of failure of that process.
- If you don't understand it, don't trust it, invest in it, buy it, or sell it.
- The ultimate measure of the effectiveness of any decision-making process is that management stupidity is the only possible explanation for bad decision making.

Notes

1. David M. Katz, "How the Crisis Fooled BofA CFO Joe Price," CFO.com, March 10, 2009.
2. Lise Buyer, "The Big Question" *Red Herring*, June 14, 2001.
3. Ibid.
4. Obituary of Arthur Rudolph, *New York Times,* January 3, 1996.

Chapter 16

The Business of Spin

A cursory review of CEO speeches, annual reports, corporate press releases, and other corporate propaganda reveals a recurring pattern of overstating successes, blaming failures on others, offering confident exhortations that the future is bright, reminders of how great the company's employees are, and how strong the company's partnerships are with both suppliers and customers. It is impossible for any business leader (or politician for that matter) to admit to any weakness or failure until the damage has been done; even then they usually explain that it is not really their fault. In early 2007 AIG's then-CEO Martin Sullivan commented that he had, "gained an entirely new appreciation for AIG's strength and resilience,"[1] and assured investors that the company, "continued to improve our financial control environment, providing greater transparency in our financial disclosures and remaining on the forefront of good corporate governance."[2] I am sure that was heartening for shareholders to hear just over a year before the company's failure was only averted by a government bailout. In reality, truth in business has been largely subverted by public relations.

Politicians have been renowned exponents of "spin" for years; now it has moved from the Oval Office to the corner office. Spin, which I define as "the ability to represent absolutely any situation no matter how dire in such a way that it appears in a favorable light," is an essential tool in the arsenal of corporate leaders. From the simple substitution of the word "opportunity" for "problem" through the well-rehearsed litany of extraordinary, unprecedented, and exceptional events to explain any misstep, the language of corporate communications is designed, as one commentator put it, to "create favorable starting points with stakeholders on which the company depends."[3] Today, CEOs have media coaches and endeavor to always stay on message. That's why it is so refreshing when an executive or company has the courage to admit to a screw-up because it is so rare. For example, in December 2008, Facebook CEO Mark Zuckerberg had the courage to admit, "I'm not proud of the way we've handled this situation, and I know we can do better." He was commenting on the botched launch of a new feature in the fast-growing social networking site that had caused a massive backlash from the user community.

Zuckerberg's honesty is still the exception; obfuscation is the norm. Everyone knows that when an executive is leaving an organization to "pursue new opportunities" or to "spend more time with his or her family" that he or she has really been fired. CEOs blame once in a lifetime events or unprecedented market gyrations for unexpected losses, and product recalls or delayed launches are blamed upon coordination or communication problems with suppliers, a phrase Boeing used frequently as the launch of the 787 Dreamliner was regularly delayed.

The irony is that we as investors, customers, or employees are supposed to believe this twaddle. There can only be two possible explanations, (1) business executives believe we are stupid, or (2) they are. Cruciant has no qualms about its high public profile—the company is riding high; it is firmly in the "there's no such thing as bad publicity" camp.

Fiction: Steve Borden's Office—January 2008

Amy, Cruciant's Head of Public Relations, walked into Steve Borden's office for their 9 AM meeting. She was smiling broadly and was clearly the bearer of good news: "Steve, I have just got off the phone with

Forbes. They want to do a cover feature on you and Cruciant. They see us as one of the most innovative companies out there and particularly like our focus on emerging markets. They want a reporter to shadow you for a couple of days and then develop an in-depth feature on how you are leading us through the process. I thought we could organize a program that includes a tour of the R&D operation followed by a couple of meetings with the development teams. This could be great for the company's profile and also provide some nice recognition to our people."

"Sounds great," Steve replies, "maybe we can link it with my trip to Europe and the speech I'm giving at the World Economic Forum in Davos. I bet the journalist would enjoy riding on the G-V."

After the cover story comes out, Cruciant's stock price jumps by 12 percent and Steve is invited onto CNBC's Squawk Box morning show as a guest host, joining the likes of Jack Welch and Warren Buffett. During his appearance, the show's regular host, Joe Kernan, comments, "Cruciant is really redefining the way American companies can successfully enter emerging markets. Steve and his team are well on their way to creating a global brand on a par with Coca-Cola, IBM, and General Electric." Steve couldn't help but smile. The clip was soon on the Cruciant website and links to the video were emailed to all Cruciant's major investors, suppliers, and other business partners. Later in the show, Steve was one of six talking heads offering their view on the future of the economy. Everyone had a different point of view, but the overall consensus was that the engine of economic growth would continue to drive healthy profits for the world's best companies despite some localized concerns in the U.S. housing market. As the program ended, Steve accepted congratulations from the regulars and hopped in a limo with Amy to head back to the office. He was elated, but something was nagging at him. There had been six very smart, very successful, and very rich commentators prognosticating on the markets, and no two had the same opinion. If folks this talented cannot agree, what chance did Cruciant have of getting its plans and forecasts right? He quickly dismissed the thought. He had a great team with a clear vision and a compelling strategy. In fact, it was so compelling that the company would succeed even if there was a recession in United States because so much of its growth was going to come from rapidly growing emerging markets that would not be impacted by a few mortgage foreclosures in California and Las Vegas.

A few weeks later, Steve joins the President on a trade mission to Southeast Asia; he is named one of the top 100 global executives by *Business Week*; is invited to deliver a guest lecture at Harvard Business School; and mentioned as a possible future CEO of both Procter & Gamble and IBM. In July 2008 he receives a discreet phone call from a well-known former CEO of one of America's premier companies asking him if would like to join the Augusta National Golf Club. Now he knows that he has arrived. The condo in Scottsdale is sold, and an expansive ranch just outside Jackson Hole is purchased. In early September, The Stephen and Karin Borden Foundation announces a donation of $70 million for a new business school at his alma mater. Two weeks later, Lehman Brothers files for bankruptcy, and not long after, Cruciant's growth strategy lies in tatters. Of course, it is not the company's fault as is made clear during the quarterly earnings calls throughout 2008.

First Quarter Earnings Call—Stock Price of $48—April 2008

Steve and Henry are in a conference room with Charlotte Myers-Rich, the Head of Investor Relations.

Charlotte: "Welcome to Cruciant's first quarter earnings call. Speaking today will be Steve Borden, Chairman and Chief Executive Officer, and Henry Pritchett, Chief Financial Officer. Steve?"

Steve: "Thanks, Charlotte. I am delighted to report that earnings rose by 13 percent on a year-over-year basis, while sales rose 9 percent. Both are ahead of our long-term guidance of 10 and 5 percent respectively (Note to aspiring CEOs: Always give Wall Street targets below your own internal targets.) The first quarter further demonstrated the validity of our strategy coupled with superb execution across all regions. Even though we are in the early stages of rolling out our innovative new products in emerging markets, we are seeing tremendous acceptance in the marketplace and customers are clearly excited about our offerings. Product development plans are on track, and we expect to see the benefits of these investments starting in Q2 and ramping up throughout the balance of the year. In summary, our unique value proposition is translating into results and with our excellent team firing on all cylinders, I fully expect that you will see growth in line or just a little ahead of expectations in the next quarter. I will now let Henry take you through the detailed financial results."

Second Quarter Earnings Call—Stock Price of $35—Late July 2008

Steve: "Good morning. We had another strong quarter from an internal point of view. However, the unexpected political turmoil in one of our key markets did have an impact. Earnings rose 9 percent and sales were up 4 percent. I consider this to be an outstanding performance in light of the unprecedented events occurring in the marketplace. While our stock price has been negatively impacted, we believe this is an overreaction. Our strategy remains sound and we are executing incredibly well. We remain fully committed to making this year's numbers and expect the last quarter to be no more than a temporary blip. When conditions normalize, we fully expect to regain momentum. At this time we see no reason to change tactics."

Third Quarter Earnings Call—Stock Price of $23—Late October 2008

Steve: "Good morning. For the third quarter, sales grew by 2 percent and our earnings slipped by 3 percent. This performance clearly falls far short of our original guidance but is broadly in line with the revised guidance we gave last month. As you all know, the credit crisis in North America is now spreading to all global markets. We are seeing softness in the U.S., and the effects are now being felt in other regions. Weakening exchange rates are also having a negative effect on our results. Overseas markets, particularly in Asia, remain strong, and we do not foresee any weakening in demand from what remains our key growth market. In light of the unprecedented dislocations in the U.S., we have decided to slow down our investments in new products and conserve our cash to ensure we maintain full liquidity. Our credit lines remain open, and we are taking the normal prudent actions such as freezing all new hiring, cutting back on nonessential travel, and trimming the marketing budget. Our raw material inventory levels have spiked upward as demand has slowed. Part of this was due to a lack of visibility into our supply chain as we dealt with the different purchasing systems we inherited from our acquisitions over the last two years. Our operations team is looking at solutions as we speak.

Compared to many others we are in a very strong position and I see our execution advantage as being an opportunity to gain ground on our less sound competitors. I remain confident in our ability to execute."

Fourth Quarter Earnings Call—Stock Price of $3.65 —January 2009

New Chairman and CEO Chuck Williams Leads the Call
Chuck: "Good day to all of you. I am delighted to join you on this, my first call as Chairman and CEO. I just wish we had more good news to share. First of all, I want to pay tribute to my predecessor, Steve Borden. Steve contributed so much to the growth of this great company. Last year was brutal for the world economy, and we at Cruciant suffered along with everyone else. For the year, sales were down 1 percent, and we posted a small aggregate profit of one cent a share before charges. Almost all of the declines were logged in the fourth quarter as a result of write-downs on inventory and an almost complete collapse in demand across the emerging markets. I will let Henry go through the detailed results in a moment, but I want to take a few minutes to outline my game plan. In the thirty days I have been on board, I have visited all our major customers, met with managers and employees across the world, and reviewed all aspects of our strategy. It is clear to me that this great company needs to regain its focus—delivering great products at a competitive price to customers who value them. With that as my guiding light, I am announcing today that we will be shutting down our Asian and part of our European operations. We are going to focus on four core markets, the United States, Canada, the UK, and Germany, which together account for 80 percent of our sales and more than 100 percent of our profits. By refocusing on markets we know well with products that are fully developed, we can target our marketing, product development, and sales

efforts to drive up profitability—fast. We are also going to use this re-trenchment as an opportunity to invest in the systems we need to manage an integrated global business instead of a loosely connected series of partially integrated acquisitions. The benefits in terms of increased visibility and transparency should become apparent to all over the next year. I fully expect that Cruciant will rapidly regain its rightful position as one of the great American companies delivering solid and predictable results for many years to come. I will now hand over to Henry who will take you through the detailed financial results in what will be his last earnings call before taking early retirement after many years of outstanding service. Henry . . ."

Facts: The Business of Spin

Less than 48 hours before Bear Stearns sought emergency funding from the Federal Reserve, the company's CEO, Alan Schwartz, commented, "Our liquidity and balance sheet are strong." During the furor over lead contamination in toys made in China, the Chinese commerce minister sought to ease concerns by saying that: "Over 99 percent of China's export products are good and safe." This sounds pretty reassuring until you realize that that would mean that 10,000 out of every one million toys made in China contained excessive levels of lead. Business and political leaders have mastered the art of talking a lot and saying very little. Yet despite considerable evidence to the contrary, our natural instinct is to have some faith in apparently authoritative sources of information. When, in February 2008, then–AIG Chief Executive Martin Sullivan commented, "AIG has the ability to absorb the current volatility while committing the resources to grow and take advantage of opportunities," we were inclined to believe him. A few weeks later Sullivan was out and new Chairman and Chief Executive Robert Willumsted came on board. Results continued to get worse, but Willumsted was still confident enough to comment in August 2008 that the company's poor second quarter results "do not reflect the earnings power and potential of AIG's businesses." Five weeks later the U.S. government spent $85 billion (later rising to more than $170 billion) to take control of the company. These are not isolated incidents. The credibility of business leaders is at stake, and after reviewing numerous pronouncements of supposed fact or at least informed opinion and then looking at subsequent events, I can only conclude that stupidity and deceit appear in equal measure.

Even supposedly trusted sources get it wrong. In January 2007, David Lereah, chief economist of the National Association of Realtors, commented on the level of house prices, "It appears we have established a bottom." One of the early signs of the building financial crisis came in August 2007 when a fund run by Goldman Sachs required a capital infusion of $3 billion from its parent. Goldman, being the ultimate "Master of Universe" institution obviously would not admit to any real problem despite the fund's 30 percent decline in value in just one week. Goldman's CFO stated categorically that "This is not a rescue." A Goldman spokesman went on to say that the capital infusion would give the funds managers "more flexibility to take advantage of the opportunities we believe exist in current market conditions." Well, that's all right then, isn't it?

Over at Yahoo, former CEO Jerry Yang described a 10 percent staff cut announced in October 2008 as a move to enable the company "to become more fit." Later the same month, American Express described a 7,000-person reduction in staffing as part of "a re-engineering program." At eBay, the firing of 10 percent of the workforce was an employee "simplification." You can call it what you like, but eliminating thousands of jobs used to be called a mass layoff.

The front cover of Bear Stearns 2006 Annual Report touted the firm's track record as "Eighty-three years of profitability." James Cayne, Bear's CEO, went on to describe the firm's position in his letter to shareholders thus: "Our balance sheet is now over $350 billion and the strong credit quality of Bear Stearns continues to be recognized by bondholders as well as rating agencies. In 2006 Standard & Poor's upgraded Bear Stearns to A+ with a stable outlook—a rating that we believe reflects the dedication to risk evaluation and management that has given us the ability to expand carefully and conservatively. The strict risk discipline imposed on our trading desks is reinforced by the strong sense of ownership that permeates the culture of the corporation."

Cayne went on to comment, "Now is an exciting time in the development of Bear Stearns." He was right about that. A little over a year after the report was published, Bear Stearns "dedication to risk evaluation and management" and its "ability to expand carefully and conservatively" could be questioned, while the "strong sense of ownership" left many employees with shares in a worthless entity.

Guess which company trumpeted its skills in its 2007 annual report this way: "In this challenging environment, our clients looked to us more than ever for new and different solutions and to be their trusted partner. Our client-focused strategy, which we have consistently followed since becoming a public company in 1994, was the key to our success. We remain committed to creating shareholder value through our focus on the four pillars of our strategy: driving diversified growth; delivering the whole Firm to our clients; managing risk, capital, and expenses; and preserving and strengthening our culture. We benefited from our senior level focus on risk management and, more importantly, from a culture of risk management at every level of the Firm."[4]

Answer: Lehman Brothers.

It's not just financial institutions that get it spectacularly wrong. "Steve & Barry's Rule the Mall"[5] ran the headline in a *BusinessWeek* article in 2006. The clothing retailer, founded in 1985, became a retail sensation in 2005 when it more than doubled its store count to 132 by offering fashions at prices that undercut both Wal-Mart and Target. Through a combination of aggressive sourcing, virtually no advertising, and big incentives from mall owners desperate to fill empty space, Steve & Barry's was able to grow rapidly. The company exploited weakness in the mall market. As traditional chains vacated space, Steve & Barry's stepped in and opened supermarket-sized stores, taking up 3.5 million square feet in 2005 alone. Mall owners were only too happy to throw rich inducements at the company, sometimes offering build-out fees of up to $80 per square foot compared with a more normal $20–30 per square foot. One real estate executive commented that: "They are the most talked-about retailer in the mall industry. They're on everyone's list [of preferred tenants]."[6] One of the founders (Barry) stated that he wanted to maintain a 10-year compounded sales growth rate of 70 percent and have 568 stores by 2008.[7]

The company continued its rapid growth. By 2008 the company had 276 stores, only half of "Barry's" prediction but still double the number of two years earlier, and had signed licensing deals with tennis star Venus Williams, actresses Amanda Bynes and Sarah Jessica Parker, surfer Laird Hamilton, and basketball players Stephon Marbury and Ben Wallace. However, the credit crunch caused a shortage of cash as new funding dried up and mall owners delayed making payments to the chain for store refurbishments. In July 2008, Steve & Barry's filed for bankruptcy protection, but the saga was not quite over. In August 2008, Bay Harbour Management, a New York–based private equity firm, bought the company out of bankruptcy for $168 million. Bay Harbour managing principal Douglas Teitelbaum said at the time that, "this company offers better value than I've seen anywhere."[8]

Teitelbaum's perception of value must have been a little off as only three months later Steve & Barry's filed for bankruptcy a second time. This time there was no reprieve, and Bay Harbour was able to book a $168 million loss in less than three months, which just goes to prove the exceptional returns offered by private equity.

In April 2001, Jeff Skilling, CEO of Enron, announced quarterly results that showed a 281 percent rise in revenues and an 18 percent increase in earnings, both largely fictitious numbers as would soon become apparent. Skilling showed no signs of concern, "First quarter results were great. We are very optimistic about our new businesses and are confident that our record of growth is sustainable for many years to come."[9] Four months later, Skilling resigned, using one of the stock phrases for executives on the way out. He was leaving for "personal reasons." While executives at Enron tried to keep the leaky ship afloat, Chairman Ken Lay announced in October that third quarter earnings were up 35 percent. The company also reported that it was taking a non-recurring restructuring charge of $1.2 billion but offered few details. It turned out that the charge was just the tip of iceberg that would sink Enron just a few weeks later.

The art of spin is perhaps most prevalent when CEOs tout the value of large acquisitions. Phrases like unparalleled synergy, extending our franchise, unique growth opportunities, and one plus one equals three trot off their tongues as shareholders brace themselves for the almost inevitable disappointment.

In May 1991, AT&T's CEO Robert Allen led his company in the takeover of NCR. The price was almost $7.5 billion, more than double the value of NCR before AT&T launched its hostile bid. Upon announcing the deal, Allen waxed eloquent on its value. The acquisition would "create an enduring American institution with the technological, financial and marketing strength to succeed against foreign competition in the emerging global information market." Allen went further: "I am confident that together AT&T and NCR will achieve a level of growth and success that we could not achieve separately. Ours will be a future of promises fulfilled."

Apparently, in this instance enduring meant four years. In May 1995, AT&T announced the spin-off of NCR at a market capitalization of $3.4 billion or about 45 percent of what it paid. This equates to losing $2.8 million of shareholder value for every day that AT&T owned NCR.

Unbelievably, just three years later, new AT&T CEO Michael Armstrong embarked upon another strategic acquisition binge as he sought to move the company into the cable business. In 1998 AT&T acquired America's second largest cable business, TCI, for $59 billion and then in 2000 added Media One for a cool $44 billion to the mix, thereby becoming the largest cable company in the United States. Just eighteen months later AT&T sold its cable business to Comcast for $52 billion—$51 billion less than they paid for it. In 2004 AT&T sold its cell phone business to Cingular, and then in 2005 SBC acquired what was left of AT&T for $16 billion and Ma Bell was no more. Of course, the name got a reprieve as SBC took on the AT&T name. Amazingly, despite successive management teams having spent billions of dollars on acquisitions and having taken in rather less when divesting those same acquisitions, they had not managed to completely destroy the value of the AT&T brand.

Mythbuster Wisdom: Bankruptcy—The New Management Secret

The global recession of 2008–2009 raised the art of executive spin to a new level. As falling sales and asset values combined with high debt levels sent many companies into bankruptcy court, we were suddenly informed that bankruptcy was not actually a bad thing, unless of course you were a creditor.

Apparently, a quick trip through bankruptcy court was the corporate equivalent of a spa retreat. All those nasty toxins could be erased from the system, and you would emerge revitalized and rejuvenated. Donald Stebbins, the Chief Executive of Visteon, a $9.5-billion automotive parts company that was once part of Ford, stated on the day the company filed for bankruptcy in May 2009 that the course of action was the best way, "to maximize the long term value of the company."[10] For two-thirds of the U.S. automotive industry the combination of bankruptcy and partial nationalization was the corporate equivalent of Viagra. Chrysler spent a mere 42 days in bankruptcy, allowing it to shed lots of unwanted debts, contracts, and other obligations in order for it emerge as an attractive partner for Fiat. General Motors beat Chrysler's record by two days and emerged apparently revitalized. CEO Fritz Henderson promised that the new GM would be faster and more responsive to customers. Apparently six weeks in bankruptcy had achieved what thirty years of market decline could not. Only time will tell.

Masonite, a maker of doors, used its passage through bankruptcy to clean up its balance sheet so it could make some acquisitions. Chief Executive Fred Lynch emphasized the positives when he said, "Whenever you can de-lever the way we have through Chapter 11, it clearly puts you in a position to be on the offensive. Our new investors have all expressed interest in growth organically and through acquisitions."[11]

Clearly, bankruptcy is now one of the most effective management tools available. No doubt future business strategies will plot a course through bankruptcy court en route to market leadership based upon these unique insights.

Executives even manage to rationalize their dubious performance after they have left. After retiring from Kodak in 1999 amid rumors of the "did he fall, or was he pushed" variety, former CEO George Fisher was asked to comment on his prediction made five years earlier that Kodak's digital photography operations would be profitable by 1997 but had actually racked up losses of over $100 million. Fisher's response: "You call it losses, I call it investment."[12] Ken Lay, Chairman of Enron, sought to defend his actions by commenting, "I can't take responsibility for criminal conduct of somebody inside the company." So in Lay's mind the buck stopped way short of the Chairman's office. When that strategy didn't work, he moved on to the I wasn't smart enough defense when he said, "Am I a fool? I don't think I'm a fool. But I think I sure was fooled."

What Planet Were They On?

By any measure, 2008 was a bloodbath for the automotive industry in general and for General Motors in particular. Sales dropped by 11 percent compared to 2007, the company lost its title as the world's largest automaker to Toyota after a 70-year reign, and then its Chief Executive had to go cap-in-hand to the U.S. government and beg for a bailout. Not much good news to report really. Well, you'd be surprised. Those masters of spin beside the Detroit River managed to craft the following for the company's January 2009 press release:

"GM Announces 2008 Global Sales of 8.35 Million Vehicles

- GM Asia Pacific sales volume grows 3%; Chevrolet sales in China grows 16% to nearly 200,000 vehicles; 1.09M vehicles sold in China sets record with 6% volume growth
- Third consecutive year of more than 2 million vehicles sold in Europe; Chevrolet sales breakthrough 500,000 mark with record share; Opel sets sales record in Central and Eastern Europe with volume up 13%
- GM beats the industry with more than 1.27 million total vehicle sales in Latin America, Africa and Middle East Region led by top-selling Chevrolet Corsa, Celta, and Aveo
- GM continues emerging markets leadership with 2008 market share growth in 14 of 26 markets"[13]

Apparently a pretty impressive performance from a company firing on all cylinders, don't you think? But perhaps the ultimate example is the story of Citigroup.

Spin Cycle: Citigroup 2006–2009

In December 2006, with Citi's share price above $54, then–Chairman and CEO Chuck Prince clearly stated the firm's objective:

"Our goal is to be a more client-driven organization that is more accessible, innovative, and able to strike quickly at the many unique global growth opportunities."[14]

Presumably, this meant investing billions in the securitized mortgage market, virtually guaranteeing enormous profits. A month later, during the company's quarterly earnings call, Prince emphasized that the firm was focused on "generating sustainable growth in U.S. consumer, growing international consumer, corporate and investment banking and wealth management businesses more quickly" while "remaining highly disciplined in credit management."[15] Investors must have been heartened to know that the bank was not slackening its credit discipline or taking excessive risk as it pursued profits.

By July 2007 the share price had slipped just a little to $50, but there was no cause for concern. When second quarter results were announced, it was all good news—record earnings per share (up 18 percent) and record revenues (up 20 percent). Chuck was delighted: "We have very clear priorities to drive growth and we are executing on all of them."[16]

On October 1 (share price: $45) Citi pre-announced its third quarter results. Something was not quite right as Chuck confessed that:

"Our expected third quarter results are a clear disappointment. The decline in income was driven primarily by weak performance in fixed income credit market activities, write-downs in leveraged loan commitments, and increases in consumer credit costs."[17]

However, he was not too downhearted:

"While we cannot predict market conditions or other unforeseeable events that may affect our businesses, we expect to return to a normal earnings environment in the fourth quarter."

So while Chuck cannot predict the future, he knows it is going to be all good.

Two weeks later the stock price has edged down to $42.36 and the company announces a 60 percent decline in earnings. Chuck is upset:

> "This was a disappointing quarter, even in the context of the dislocations in the subprime mortgage and credit markets."[18]

So the results sucked but it was a dislocation in the subprime mortgage and credit markets and not anything to do with the bank buying securities backed by mortgages offered to people who could not afford the payments that caused the problem. Well, that's all right then. Chuck went on to reassure us: "Importantly, many of our businesses performed well this quarter." Well I am sure that's some consolation to shareholders as earnings declined 60 percent.

By November 5 the stock is down 27 percent to $31.05. Less than three weeks later the headline on CNBC is "Prince Out at Citigroup; Writeoff Figures Climb."[19] Finally, Chuck comes clean as Citigroup announces that the write-downs may total $11 billion:

> "I am responsible for the conduct of our businesses. The size of these charges makes stepping down the only honorable course for me to take as chief executive officer. This is what I advised the board."[20]

On a conference call the day of Prince's resignation, November 5, 2007, rock star Wall Street banking analyst Meredith Whitney, who many praised for predicting Citi's problems, probed Citi CFO Gary Crittenden on the firm's ability to maintain its dividend. Crittenden responded: "We're fully committed to maintaining the dividend at its current level. I'm pretty confident in our ability to manage the balance sheet."[21]

On January 15, 2008 (stock price: $24.45) Citigroup announced that it was cutting its dividend by 40 percent! It also reported a loss for the previous quarter of $9.83 billion. New CEO Vikram Pandit stated the obvious:

> "Our financial results this quarter are clearly unacceptable."[22]

Whatever happened to the return to the normal earnings environment of three months ago? However, there is no need to get too disheartened as Pandit reassures investors that:

> "We are taking actions to enhance our risk management processes and to improve expense productivity. We [Citigroup] have a unique franchise that is well positioned in growing markets with tremendous capabilities to serve clients around the world. We intend to build on our advantages to deliver superior results for our clients, investors, and employees."

In one paragraph Pandit hits all the essentials of positive spin. In the 2007 annual report, published early in 2008, Pandit continued to look forward:

> "But 2008 is a new year, and I hope that after reading this letter you will share my excitement about our businesses. In my first few months as CEO, we have taken decisive action on a number of issues. Our actions will leverage Citi's footprint and many fundamental strengths, and enhance the company's ability to generate sustainable, long-term growth in earnings."

In April (stock price: $25.11), the bank reports a loss of $5.1 billion but Pandit asks us to remember that the losses are not really his or the bank's fault:

> "Our financial results reflect the continuation of the unprecedented market and credit environment and its impact on our historical risk positions."[23]

There we have it: the first use of "unprecedented"; can "extraordinary" be far behind? The reference to historical risk positions makes clear that the problems were all Chuck's doing.

By July (stock price: $16.19) things are looking up:

> "We continue to demonstrate strength in our core franchise. We cut our second quarter losses in half compared to the first quarter."[24]

Well, that must make shareholders feel a whole lot better about the $2.2 billion loss for the quarter.

In October 2008 (stock price: $12.14), Citi announces a loss of $2.8 billion for the third quarter, with revenues declining 23 percent and expenses going up 2 percent, but things aren't all bad—the bank still has great people:

> "I am very proud of my Citi colleagues for staying focused on our priorities and for their relentless commitment to serving our clients during these turbulent times."[25]

On January 16, 2009, the stock price falls below that of a venti latte to $3.46—down 94 percent in two years. Of course, by now the whole global financial system is on the verge of collapse and the fourth quarter was very bleak, but Pandit is not downhearted:

> "Our results continued to be depressed by an unprecedented dislocation in capital markets and a weak economy. However, a number of our core customer franchises continued to perform well as Citi's customers remain active and engaged with us."[26]

There we have it, the second use of "unprecedented." It's not really our fault that we lost $8.29 billion in 90 days, and remember, our customers still love us; they just aren't paying us!

Oh, and by the way, we still have great people, albeit not as many of them as a few months ago:

> "I want to recognize the hundreds of thousands of Citi colleagues who have kept their focus on our clients and our business throughout what has been an enormously disruptive and distracting period in our industry. Despite unprecedented turbulence in the global financial markets, they have conducted themselves with the highest professionalism and integrity. Because of their work and dedication, I have no doubt we will emerge from the current environment stronger, smarter, and better positioned to realize the full earnings power of this great franchise."

On March 9, 2009 Citigroup's share price sank to an all-time low of $0.97, a decline of 98.2 percent from January 2007. Finally, in April

2009 (stock price: $3.65), the fog lifted as the company reported a profit of $1.6 billion. Pandit was quick to praise the overall strategy:

"Our results this quarter reflect the strength of Citi's franchise and we are pleased with our performance."[27]

The turnaround was on track, so he felt confident to re-emphasize the strategy:

"We will continue to reduce our legacy risk, aggressively manage expenses and improve efficiency."

Note the subtle use of the word "legacy"—meaning it was still the other guy's fault. So the current regime has successfully explained away billions of dollars of losses and the almost total destruction of shareholder value as being caused by:

1. Market dislocations
2. Unprecedented credit environment
3. Unforeseeable events
4. Legacy risk (i.e., it was Chuck Prince's fault)

Finally, Pandit just wants to remind you that people are the company's most important asset:

"As a final note, I want to personally thank all Citi employees around the world who are the foundation of Citi's success."

Well, they are certainly worth more than all those toxic assets on the bank's balance sheet. Although the earnings release goes on to note that there are now 65,000 fewer stars than two years earlier with 13,000 hitting the street in the last ninety days alone. It must make you proud to be a Citigroup shareholder—after all that is all you have left, the shares are worth virtually nothing and the dividend has evaporated.

Southwest Airlines: Succeeding Despite the Market

The fourth quarter of 2001 was not a good time to be an airline. Actually, it appears that there have been few good times for airlines in the last thirty years. Between 1980 and 2007 the airline industry

> ## Mythbuster Wisdom: A Primer on Spin
> There are some basic words and phrases that CEOs should try and use at every opportunity. Key words include: integration, leverage, synergy, disciplined, empowered, talented, agile, optimized, partner, authentic, innovative, focused, customer, and quality. Essential phrases include people are our most valuable asset, intense focus on the customer, we are an innovation company, exploit first mover advantage, achieve above average growth, execute flawlessly, unique value proposition, good corporate citizen, environmental sustainability, sustainable competitive advantage, and deliver superior returns to our shareholders.

has failed to make any money at all. Total losses exceed total profits by $7.8 billion despite annual revenues growing from $33 billion in 1980 to over $172 billion in 2007. Only one airline, Southwest, has succeeded in sustaining outstanding performance through all the turbulence. Southwest is rightly lauded for its consistent profitability over many years, yet in that fourth quarter of 2001, Southwest turned in a performance that was staggering given the context of the times.

In the fourth quarter of 2001, Southwest delivered 542,050 seat-miles per employee, compared to 369,790 at American and 373,400 at United. By this measure, the productivity of Southwest employees was more than 45 percent better than at American and United. Southwest achieved these results despite both American and United operating much longer flights with bigger aircraft. More remarkably, Southwest managed to achieve these results without laying off a single employee or cancelling a single flight other than during the three days following 9/11 when the FAA shut down the whole industry. By the end of 2001, Southwest's market capitalization exceeded that of the rest of the industry combined. Southwest CEO James Parker commented that the company was "able to pay substantial profit sharing" for 2001 despite the enormous impact of 9/11. Southwest's results for the fourth quarter of 2001 showed a 59 percent decline in net income, but the company still made a profit of more than $63 million.

As an aside, since moving to the United States in 1991, I have boarded over 2,500 flights and have flown on Southwest Airlines precisely three times. I suspect I am not really their target market.

Tall Poppy Syndrome

Perhaps it is due to their origins as convicts shipped out from Great Britain, but Australians have a healthy disdain of wealth, power, and pretension. As soon as someone gets a little big for his or her boots that person is a prime target for biting but often humorous criticism. As an Englishman, or "Pom," I automatically qualify as a tall poppy. So what does this have to do with management myths? Well, tall poppies are prevalent in the world of business. Status is everything, and as managers progress, the perks of position can quickly move from rewards to entitlements. That is where the rot sets in.

Pom or Pommy, *slang*, Australian term used to describe someone from Great Britain, derivation unclear but two possible sources are:

1. Derived from the "pom-pom" on top the soldiers' hats on the ships that transported prisoners to the colonies.
2. Shortened version of pomegranate, which was Australian rhyming slang for immigrant.

Entitlement clouds judgment. Why else would the Detroit automotive CEO's ride on separate private jets to Washington in November 2008 to beg for billions of dollars of government aid? Being able to separate personal status or habit from corporate welfare or just plain old common sense is an essential but often lost skill. Again, politics and business have much in common as the expenses scandal that rocked British politics in 2009 showed. Every time such a dilemma presents itself simply ask yourself some simple questions:

"Does it cost less than the value I am really going to create today?"

"Do I really need it?"

"How would this look if reported in tomorrow's newspaper?"

"What would granny think?"

Entitlement disease or just plain greed has become even more apparent over the last twenty years as intense media coverage of business has seen the emergence of the rock star CEO. The explosion of interest in business has served to make many business leaders into fully fledged celebrities. Perhaps the first rock star CEO was Lee Iacocca, who led Chrysler through its dramatic bailout in the early 1980s. Following close behind were Jack Welch of General Electric and Robert Goizueta of Coca-Cola. Since then the conveyor belt has offered up a motley crew of leaders who at one time or another shone brightly in the leadership universe. Some were founders who went on to successfully grow their businesses into powerhouses; others were hired hands.

Table 16.1   Hot Hits in the Executive Suite

Founders	Managers
Bill Gates (Microsoft)	Meg Whitman (eBay)
Steve Jobs (Apple)	Carly Fiorina (Hewlett-Packard)
Sam Walton (Wal-Mart)	Percy Barnevik (ABB)
Larry Ellison (Oracle)	Sandy Weill (Citigroup)
Michael Dell (Dell)	Sir John Harvey-Jones (ICI)
Howard Schultz (Starbucks)	Ken Lay (Enron)
Phil Knight (Nike)	Al Dunlap (Sunbeam)
Richard Branson (Virgin)	Eric Schmidt (Google)
Akio Morita (Sony)	Alfred P. Sloan (GM)
Ingvar Kamprad (IKEA)	Thomas Watson Sr. (IBM)

Again, a manager's past success is not necessarily a good predictor of future success. George Fisher was a star at Motorola but flamed out at Kodak; Michael Armstrong spent 31 years at IBM, was a vaunted CEO of Hughes Corporation, but failed at AT&T. Steve Jobs succeeded, failed, and then succeeded again at Apple; on the side he was a clear hit with Pixar but what about NeXt? Bob Nardelli just missed out on the top job at GE after leading the company's Power Systems group. He moved on to become CEO of both Home Depot and Chrysler where his performance failed to match the hype. His fellow loser in the race to succeed Jack Welch at GE was James McNerney. McNerney went onto a successful tenure at 3M before taking the top job at Boeing where he has encountered some turbulence. Carly Fiorina arrived as CEO of Hewlett Packard in 1999 as an accomplished but rather anonymous marketing executive. Not for long. Her marketing skills were soon to the fore as she made brand "Carly" the hottest thing in business. High-profile interviews, speeches at the World Economic Summit in Davos, features in all the top magazines burnished the brand. Then in 2002 came the crowning glory—Carly was victorious in a hard-fought takeover battle for Compaq. Now the hard work began, and by 2005 it was clear that one plus one barely added up to one, never mind three when it came to the HP/Compaq combination. By February 2005, Fiorina was out. The public explanation was a spin-worthy "disagreements on company strategy." Another rock star had burned out. Ironically, Fiorina's replacement, the much lower key Mark Hurd, changed little in Hewlett-Packard's strategy and yet achieved a significant turnaround in performance, including regaining the number one spot in global market share for PCs.

The ability of a star CEO to truly impact a business is perhaps best summed up by Warren Buffett (who else?), who commented, "When a management with a reputation for brilliance tackles a business with a reputation for bad economics, it is usually the reputation of the business that remains intact."[28]

Mythbuster Wisdom: Beware Public Adulation

- In 1999, *CFO* Magazine named Enron CFO Andrew Fastow as CFO of the Year.
- *Fortune* named Enron America's Most Innovative Company six years running.

Nice Work If You Can Get It

The line between privilege and entitlement has become increasingly blurred in recent years as business leaders see luxurious offices, personal use of private jets, lavish parties, and designer second homes as essential accoutrements for maintaining their position as ambassadors for their companies. After a few years in the executive hot house, it becomes all too easy to justify almost anything as essential to the performance of the job. Dennis Kozlowski, former CEO of Tyco, reached such an exalted position that his company provided tens of millions of dollars of company money for his personal use. Apparently, he was entitled to a $16.8 million apartment on Fifth Avenue in New York together with a further $3 million for renovations and $11 million for furnishings; a $7 million apartment on Park Avenue for his former wife; and more prosaically, a $15,000 umbrella stand, a $2,900 set of coat hangers, and a $445 pincushion.[29] All were apparently essential to his being able to function as Tyco's leader.

John Thain, soon after becoming CEO of Merrill Lynch in November 2007, spent $1.2 million refurbishing his office (surely this meant gold-plating it?). Only after the expenditure came to light did he offer to reimburse the costs. Thain went even further in December 2008 when he pushed for a $10 million bonus for himself after orchestrating Merrill's rescue by Bank of America. His argument was that it could have been much worse if Bank of America hadn't stepped in. Four weeks later it was much worse, as Merrill revealed losses for the fourth quarter of $15.8 billion. Days later, Thain was fired by Bank of America.

You don't have to be a CEO to deserve a little personal service. Ford executive vice president, Mark Fields, one of the company's highest flying executives, had written into his employment contract that he could commute to his home in Florida using one of the company's private jets at a cost of $50,000 a week. This became public in November 2006 while Ford was eliminating tens of thousands of jobs, and a few weeks later Fields had a sudden change of heart and announced that he could slum it with the riff-raff and fly commercial albeit in first class.

Mythbuster Wisdom: How Entitled Are You?
The Hierarchy of Ego
Are you concerned about your status? Feel that you are not getting enough respect? Check out where you rank on the Beaufort scale of corporate ego . . .

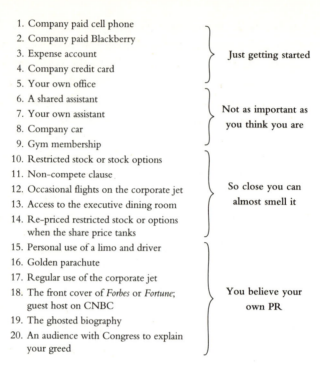

1. Company paid cell phone
2. Company paid Blackberry
3. Expense account
4. Company credit card
5. Your own office
   } Just getting started
6. A shared assistant
7. Your own assistant
8. Company car
9. Gym membership
   } Not as important as you think you are
10. Restricted stock or stock options
11. Non-compete clause
12. Occasional flights on the corporate jet
13. Access to the executive dining room
14. Re-priced restricted stock or options when the share price tanks
    } So close you can almost smell it
15. Personal use of a limo and driver
16. Golden parachute
17. Regular use of the corporate jet
18. The front cover of *Forbes* or *Fortune*; guest host on CNBC
19. The ghosted biography
20. An audience with Congress to explain your greed
    } You believe your own PR

Figure 16.1   The Hierarchy of Entitlement

Beyond Spin: Sometimes It Is All Smoke and Mirrors

There's a big difference between getting it spectacularly wrong (Bear Stearns, Steve & Barry's, Circuit City) and cheating, although investors often end up feeling the same way—much poorer. Ironically, one of the best features of periodic recessions is that it helps flush a lot of the dodgy people and businesses out of the system as the demise of Bernie Madoff and Allen Stanford illustrates. Bad strategies, poor execution, and fraud are much more easily covered up when markets are booming; however, as soon as growth slows, the gap between those who can and those who have been faking it becomes clear.

There seem to be five distinct types of scam that explain most of the big scandals: the Bad Boss, the Dodgy Executive, the Rogue Trader, the Institutional Cancer, and the Market Plague.

Bad Bosses come in two main forms. First are business leaders who believe that the company is their personal piggy bank—its main purpose is to maintain the lifestyle of the owner or executive and provide ample funds for any purpose without the need for credit checks or lending limits. Allan Stanford, Dennis Kowlowski, the Rigas family at Adelphia, and Robert Maxwell (see the next section) are good examples of this breed. The second group may not necessarily feather their own nests with ill-gotten gains, but they get so locked into a level of performance that when things turn against them, they resort to creative accounting to maintain their reputations. Bernard Madoff and Worldcom's Bernie Ebbers fit the bill here. As for Dodgy Executives they don't run the company, but they use their position to take full advantage of their power in an illegal manner. Andrew Fastow at Enron is the poster child for this group.

Rogue Traders become consumed by risk. They are given too much freedom and are allowed to take on excessive risk or misuse company funds and assets. Nick Lesson at Barings, Brian Hunter at Amaranth, and Jerome Kerviel at Societé Generale come to mind. Some Rogue Traders benefit personally from their actions; others simply damage or even destroy their employer's business.

The Institutional Cancer exists when a culture of bad behavior pervades all or part of an organization leading to malfeasance—the bribery scandals at Siemens and ABB along with some dodgy accounting at Computer Associates and Satyam Computer Services in India are good examples. Finally, there is the Market Plague, which occurs when a market is so riddled with bad behavior that no single culprit can be identified—all are guilty. The behavior of many mortgage brokers during the housing bubble, investment bankers that overhyped dot.com stocks and research analysts who were incapable of ever issuing a sell recommendation illustrate this breed.

With most of these scams there are clear warning signs visible well in advance that are largely ignored. After the event, the typical reaction is to castigate anyone who missed the warning signs. Politicians conduct "show-trails," sorry hearings, to demonstrate how shocked they are at such bad behavior and enact new legislation to ensure that such things will never happen again. This is done to reassure the electorate that they were not asleep at the wheel. Naturally, the new regulations don't work, but they do stimulate growth within the legal, accounting, and government sectors.

Spot the Crook

The 1980s were a fertile time for ambitious entrepreneurs in the United Kingdom. Prime Minister Margaret Thatcher's economic reforms created a very favorable environment for business, and capital flowed easily as the UK reestablished itself as a global financial center. Three of the most successful businessmen of the period were Asil Nadir, Robert Maxwell, and Richard Branson—colorful characters all. Unfortunately, only one of them was honest.

Asil Nadir was a Turkish Cypriot who acquired a majority stake in a small textile company called Polly Peck in 1980. Over the next decade, Nadir rapidly grew the business through a series of acquisitions that expanded the core textile business and took Polly Peck into new areas including packaging, fruit, and electronics. In 1989, Polly Peck acquired a majority stake in a struggling Japanese electronics business, Sansui. This was one of the first foreign acquisitions of a Japanese company. Around the same time Nadir also bought the Del Monte fresh fruit business from RJR Nabisco. Shortly thereafter, Polly Peck, with a market capitalization of more than £1.7 billion ($2.5 billion), was added to the *Financial Times* 100 index of Britain's largest companies. Then in September 1990, the UK government's Serious Fraud Office raided the offices of the Nadir's holding company, triggering a collapse in Polly Peck's share price. Five days later the company was toast. Investigations revealed a total lack of financial controls. During 1988 and 1989, Nadir had transferred more than £200 million ($300 million) from Polly Peck to accounts in Cyprus. Later an official report described his actions. "Mr. Nadir was able to initiate transfers of funds out of [Polly Peck's] London bank accounts without question or challenge. Further, he was able to conceal his actions until such time as the cumulative cash outflow became so great that the group was unable to meet its obligations to its bankers."[30]

Nadir was charged with sixty-six counts of fraud, all of which he denied. In a postscript worthy of the Keystone Cops, Nadir escaped to Northern Cyprus, which has no extradition treaty with the UK, while the detectives who were supposed to be watching him were taking a break to save on the cost of overtime!

Robert Maxwell was a larger-than-life figure in Britain throughout the 1970s and 1980s. He was born into a very poor Jewish family in pre-World War II Czechoslovakia; his birthplace is now part of the Ukraine. He came to Britain in 1940 as a 17-year-old. He joined the British Army and fought all the way from the Normandy Beaches to Berlin, rising to the rank of Captain and being awarded the Military Cross. He made his fortune in publishing after acquiring Pergamon Press in 1951 and building it up into a major publishing house. From 1964 to 1970 he served as a Labour Member of Parliament. In the 1970s he built up his empire by acquiring the tabloid *Daily Mirror* and *Sunday Mirror* newspapers and becoming a vocal competitor of Rupert Murdoch's *Sun* and *News of the World* in Britain's vicious tabloid wars. He also saved the Oxford United football team from bankruptcy while also trying to buy Manchester United. By the late 1980s suspicions were emerging about Maxwell's empire, and he was even being hounded by investigative reporters from his rival's newspapers. In order to prop up his empire, he sold a number of businesses and borrowed large sums from his company's pension schemes; he also found time to buy the New York *Daily News.* Then in November 1991, Maxwell apparently fell overboard while on his yacht in the Atlantic Ocean and drowned. After his death, the perilous state of his business empire came to light, and Maxwell's companies filed for bankruptcy in 1992. Rumors also swirled that he was being investigated for possible war crimes in Germany in 1945 and that he was a Mossad agent for many years. One story even suggested that the Mossad assassinated him after he attempted to blackmail them.

Richard Branson was actually the first one of the three to run foul of the law, but he learned his lesson. In 1971 he settled charges with the UK authorities that he imported records into the country without paying the required taxes. Since then his career has been both exciting and successful. He has launched numerous businesses under the Virgin brand, some of which were failures—Virgin Weddings, Virgin Cola, and Virgin Vodka. Others, such as Virgin Atlantic and Virgin Mobile (which he sold for $1 billion in 2006), have been successful.

With hindsight the disparity in performance between the honest and the dishonest is obvious but at the time we tend to ascribe exceptional performance to excellence rather than lying and cheating. Enron was widely lauded for its innovations, and Madoff was seen as a source of safe and stable investment returns in volatile markets.

During the mid-1990s I spent almost two years consulting with one of America's largest telecommunication companies. At the time the battleground was not mobile phones, but long distance phone service. The three big players were AT&T, MCI Worldcom, and Sprint. The battle was intense as each company fought for market share with ever more aggressive marketing and a fusillade of promotions. I think I received close to $1,000 in checks from the three players as an incentive to switch my long distance provider.

AT&T was the dominant player, a legacy of its former monopoly position, but Worldcom was the most aggressive player, and the results were impressive. At the time, executives at my client found it hard to believe the numbers that Worldcom kept putting up quarter after quarter. There was much anguished discussion as to how Worldcom could be producing the profit numbers it posted given the basic economics of the business at the time. Worldcom stock kept rising, and executives were handsomely rewarded. Of course, just a few years later it transpired that Worldcom's results were not real and former Chairman and CEO Bernie Ebbers was sentenced to twenty-five years in jail in 2005, but that was of little consolation to competitors who had been forced to participate in an unfair fight for years.

A lot of the pressure to make the numbers is caused by the impact of the quarterly earnings grind—the need to continuously meet or exceed the expectations of investors and analysts in order to maintain, never mind increase, the stock price. The market can be a fickle critic. Great results can be met with near apathy while the slightest misstep can trigger a massive fall in a company's market value. CEOs and CFOs seek to manage expectations through regular communication with investors; the most visible vehicle is the quarterly earnings estimate. The temptation to bend the rules to make the numbers can be intense. A *Financial Times'* editorial in 2006 characterized the effect of delivering quarterly earnings estimates this way. "The investment community has, in effect, been asking companies to lie to them four times a year."[31] The paper went on to report that this "leads to the unintended consequences of destroying long-term value, decreasing market efficiency, reducing investment returns, and impeding efforts to strengthen corporate governance."

It is only a short step to crossing over the line of legitimacy, and many companies have been found out. Slush funds, bribes, and other inducements are all fair game when the quarter is on the line. Getting caught can be expensive. Siemens, the large German technology company, paid $1.3 billion in fines in 2008 to settle charges that it paid bribes to secure contracts as far afield as Venezuela and Israel. Of course, spin also impacts the way such settlements are communicated. Siemens was able to avoid acknowledging that it actually paid any bribes, but $1.3 billion seems like a lot of guilt to me.

Spin is not going away any time soon, so we need a few tools to separate the hype from the reality. I highly recommend cynicism and skepticism.

So What?

- Reputations take years to earn but minutes to destroy.
- Reputational risk can be more significant than all other business risks combined.
- The financial impact of reputational damage is usually far greater than the direct financial losses in terms of losses, fines, and other expenses.
- Star power is no substitute for results.
- The higher the profile, the greater the scrutiny.
- Past success is no guarantee of future success.
- Making the numbers is not the only objective.
- Honesty, candor, and humility still have a place in business (I hope).

Notes

1. AIG Annual Report 2006.
2. Ibid.
3. Lehman Brothers Annual Report 2007.
4. Cees van Riel, *Essentials of Corporate Communication*, (Abingdon UK: Routledge, 2007). (Routledge 2007).
5. "Steve & Barry's Rules the Mall," *BusinessWeek,* April 10, 2006.
6. Ibid.

7. Ibid.

8. "Jeffrey McCracken and Peter Lattman Apparel Chain Faces Closure Three Months After Rescue," *Wall Street Journal,* November 18, 2008.

9. Kurt Eichenwald, *Conspiracy of Fools* (New York: Broadway Books, 2005), p. 443.

10. "Auto Supplier Visteon Files for Chapter 11 in U.S.," *Wall Street Journal,* May 29, 2009.

11. "Barbarians in Court," *Wall Street Journal,* June 18, 2009.

12. Claudia H. Deutsch, "Chief Says Kodak Is Pointed in the Right Direction," *New York Times,* December 25, 1999.

13. General Motors Corporation, Sales and Production Release, January 21, 2009.

14. Citigroup 2006 Annual Report, Chairman's Letter.

15. Citigroup, Fourth Quarter 2006 Earnings Release, January 19, 2007.

16. Citigroup, Second Quarter 2007 Earnings Release, July 20, 2007.

17. Citigroup, Third Quarter 2007 Pre-announcement, October 1, 2007.

18. Citigroup, Third Quarter 2007 Earnings Release, October 15, 2007.

19. Charlie Gasparino, "Prince Out at Citigroup; Writeoff Figures Climb," CNBC.com November 5, 2007.

20. Ibid.

21. Ibid.

22. Citigroup, Fourth Quarter 2007 Earnings Release, January 15, 2008.

23. Citigroup, First Quarter 2008 Earnings Release, April 17, 2008.

24. Citigroup, Second Quarter 2008 Earnings Release, July 18, 2008.

25. Citigroup, Third Quarter 2008 Earnings Release, October 16, 2008.

26. Citigroup, Fourth Quarter 2008 Earnings Release, January 16, 2009.

27. Citigroup, First Quarter 2009 Earnings Release, April 17, 2009.

28. Carol J. Loomis, "Why Carly's Big Bet Is Failing," *Fortune,* February 7, 2005.

29. Andrew Ross Sorkin, "Tyco Details Lavish Lives of Executives," *New York Times,* September 18, 2002.

30. Jason Nisse, Pelin Turgut, and David Randall, "Fugitive Nadir Paid £200m of Firm's Cash into Secret Accounts in Cyprus," *The Independent,* September 7, 2003.

31. "Misguided Guidance," *Financial Times,* July 25, 2006.

Epilogue

Cruciant—From Good To Great? January 2010

"Today private equity powerhouse Filet, Hackem, and Gutem announced that former Cruciant CEO Steve Borden is joining the firm to oversee FHG's portfolio investment in innovative technologies. FHG founder Arnie Gutem commented, "Steve is an exceptional executive who combines strategic vision with proven leadership skills. Adding Steve to the firm positions FHG to take a more aggressive approach toward expanding our presence in the innovative technology space. We expect good value to emerge in the sector and with our unmatched capital-raising ability and Steve's management skills, we think we can capitalize on select opportunities as they rise."

Two Years Later . . .

After early success with the back to basics strategy following the ouster of Steve Borden, Cruciant runs into trouble. The severe cuts made in R&D have starved the sales teams of new product. A number of Cruciant's competitors take advantage and are able to gain several points of market share. Borden's replacement as CEO, Chuck Williams, keeps emphasizing the results of the turnaround he initiated, but after three quarters of below-market returns, Cruciant's share price has fallen by 47 percent. In one particularly tense analyst call, Williams berates the analyst community for its lack of patience. He emphasizes that the cuts he had made had been essential to return Cruciant to a sound financial position and that the company now has over $2 billion in cash sitting on its balance sheet. The analysts simply ask what Cruciant is going to do with all that cash and why it is not using some of it to bring new products to market and stem the market share losses the company is experiencing. At the end of the call, in an embarrassing moment for the company, Williams, thinking his microphone is turned off, comments, "Bloody analysts, six months out of business school, never run more than an egg and spoon race in their life, and their opinion tanks my stock price 40 percent."

As the markets open the next morning, Cruciant's stock price plummets another 19 percent and rumors begin to circulate that Williams is out and that Cruciant is "in play." Later in the day, CNBC pundit Jim Cramer all but guarantees a buyout: "At its current price and with $2 billion in cash, it is a steal. The arb's are going to love this one."

Early the next morning, Bloomberg reports that private equity firm FHG has launched a $35 billion takeover of Cruciant at $17.50 a share, a 50 percent premium to the previous day's close. Cruciant and Williams quickly respond that the offer seriously undervalues Cruciant but also commit to do what is best for Cruciant's shareholders. That evening Williams spends an hour or so in his study at home calculating the value of his likely payout if the deal goes through. There are the 500,000 shares he was granted upon hiring, plus the two 500,000 share option grants with strike prices of $12 and $15 a share, and of course the change of control provision in his employment agreement triggers a lump sum payout of $3 million, plus a three-year consulting contract at $500,000 per, plus an office, secretary, driver, and use of the company jet thrown in. If he can get FHG to lift its offer to $20 a share, he stands to walk away with $21 million. Not bad for two years' work.

Over the next three weeks, FHG and Cruciant engage in a very public war over the right price for the business. One of Cruciant's competitors, InTech, launches a rival bid at $18 a share, but the markets prefer FHG's all-cash offer. Late on a Sunday afternoon, Arnie Gutem calls Chuck Williams at home and says, "If we raise our offer to $20 a share, can you get your board to agree to a friendly deal?" Chuck flashed the thumbs up to his wife who is sitting in the room, but keeps his voice controlled, "Well, Arnie, that certainly changes things a little. I am not sure it will be enough, but I will set up a conference call with the board this evening and put your offer to them."

At 8:30 AM on Monday morning, Reuters reports that Cruciant's board has accepted a revised offer of $20 a share from FHG and that the deal is expected to close by the end of the second quarter. Of the total price, FHG and its investors are putting up just 5 percent of their own money, while the balance is being funded by loans totaling $8 billion from a consortium of banks. FHG announces that Cruciant's cash flow will be more than sufficient to service the debt load.

July 1, 2011

Steve Borden hops out of his chauffeur-driven Mercedes and strides purposefully through the large glass doors of Cruciant's Manhattan headquarters. Two hours later he conducts an all-hands videoconference at which he promises "to finish the job we started all those years ago" and "restore Cruciant to its rightful position as the market leader in innovative technologies." He ends by commenting, "It's great to be back."

As he finishes his remarks, the Cruciant Gulfstream jet is touching down in Jackson Hole, Wyoming. Chuck Williams and his wife descend the steps to be met by Christine Zemanski, Jackson Hole's premier realtor. They get into her Range Rover and head off to look at a fifty-acre estate in the region that is priced at $13.2 million.

Eighteen Months Later . . .

Borden has wasted no time in taking action. He sold off Cruciant's German and Canadian operations, using some of the proceeds to re-enter the Asian market. Sales took off as the newly developing economies in China, India, and SE Asia lapped up Cruciant's products.

Borden also moved all of Cruciant's manufacturing to SE Asia, realizing massive cost reductions. IT and finance operations were outsourced, again reducing costs. After just eighteen months back in charge, Borden has lifted sales by 9 percent and earnings by 15 percent. More important, cash flow is improving nicely. Arnie Gutem announces that FHG is delighted with its investment in Cruciant and will be paying its investors an $800 million dividend, giving them a 40 percent return on their investment in just eighteen months. The dividend will be funded by a new loan supported by Cruciant's improved cash generation. Cruciant's debt load now totals $11 billion.

In Cruciant's headquarters, Steve Borden jots a few numbers on a piece of paper. He took the Cruciant job at an annual of salary of just $250,000, one-sixth of what he had made in his previous stint as CEO. However, FHG gave him a 5 percent equity stake in the company, provided he hit the cash and earnings targets over the first six quarters. He has done that, so his share of the $800 million dividend amounts to $40 million, and because Cruciant is now a private company, no one will ever know.

INDEX